Negotiating Ethnicity

Negotiating Ethnicity

SECOND-GENERATION SOUTH ASIAN AMERICANS TRAVERSE A TRANSNATIONAL WORLD

BANDANA PURKAYASTHA

RUTGERS UNIVERSITY PRESS
New Brunswick, New Jersey, and London

Library of Congress Cataloging-in-Publication Data

Purkayastha, Bandana, 1956–
  Negotiating ethnicity : second-generation South Asian Americans traverse a transnational world / Bandana Purkayastha.
    p.   cm.
  Includes bibliographical references and index.
  ISBN 0-8135-3581-6 (hardcover : alk. paper) — ISBN 0-8135-3582-4 (pbk. : alk. paper)
  1. South Asian Americans—Cultural assimilation.   2. South Asian Americans—Ethnic identity.   I. Title.
  E184.S69P87   2005
  305.891'4073—dc22

                                                                    2004016428

A British Cataloging-in-Publication record for this book is available
from the British Library

Manufactured in the United States of America

For Aheli,
and all the participants in this study who shared their lives with me.

Contents

Preface and Acknowledgments

The arrival of large numbers of non-European immigrants since 1965 has prompted many scholars to examine how these immigrants and their children are adapting to the United States. This body of work shows that many of the "new" immigrants arrived with very high levels of education, often with far more education than whites. Instead of settling in ethnic enclaves in cities and then working their way up toward middle-class lives in the suburbs, these highly educated immigrants found white-collar occupations and settled directly in the suburbs; their children grew up in these surroundings. Others, who arrived with less education, began with lower-tier jobs and lived in enclaves in cities. A smaller group arrived with substantial sums of money that they invested in the United States, and these investments transformed sections of cities and suburbs, especially on the Pacific coast. Many of these "immigrants" did not always live in the United States, but their children often went to schools here. Through the 1990s, as scholars tried to document all these patterns of immigrant adaptation in the U.S., they began to propose ways of moving beyond the older assimilation model.

Some research on the "new" second generation—a label that some scholars use for the children of the post-1965 immigrants—suggests that instead of thinking about second generation individuals who assimilate into "the mainstream," we need to consider which segment of American society absorbs them and what happens as a result of such integration (Portes 1995a, 1995b; Zhou 1997). This model of segmented assimilation has been especially interesting to me. As a first generation, post-1965 immigrant, I had long been intrigued by specific questions about the adjustment of other highly educated contemporary immigrants to the United States. It was difficult for me to reconcile the experiences of people like myself who had settled in middle-class suburbs, with the tenets of the assimilation framework that assumed we would acquire linguistic proficiency and work our way up the economic ladder over generations. As I rebuilt my career and started my graduate studies in sociology in the early 1990s, I discovered some scholarly work on Indian immigrants like myself; yet these studies focused on our education, occupations, suburban residences, and extolled how well we had integrated into the United

States (for example, Saran 1985). Yet, my involvement in community activism among this same population made me aware of a variety of "invisible" struggles of women and men with devalued credentials, underemployment, pay inequities, and a range of other legal and social barriers that did not seem to appear at all in the scholarly literature on immigration and adjustment. When I tried to look through the literature on marginalization I found that it focused primarily on the experiences of poor blacks and Hispanics; often class position and racial marginalization were used synonymously leading to the impression that becoming middle class would solve all "race" issues. But in the 1990s, some scholarly work began to focus explicitly on patterns of simultaneous exclusion and inclusion that characterize middle-class minorities (for example, Feagin and Sikes 1994; Tuan 1998). The emerging literature provided more nuanced ways of understanding economic integration *and* social marginality, and it began to focus on the within-group differences in experiences of marginalization (Anthias 2001b; Modood et al. 1997). As I became more and more interested in the experiences of the second generation, which was growing into adulthood in the 1990s, it seemed to me that we should also focus on the post-immigrant generation specifically. Looking at "Indian Americans," a category which includes descendents of pre-1965 immigrants, the post-1965 immigrants and their children, and a growing number of people who are in the United States on temporary work permits, does not, among other things, allow us to examine generational differences or differences of experience by class. Yet, given the increasing bifurcation of the United States economy and the changes in immigration and citizenship laws from the mid-1990s, such focused studies seem to be warranted.

The segmented assimilation model addressed many of these issues that I had grappled with as a lay person, and subsequently, as a late entrant into the world of American sociology. This model proposed that the new second generation was following diverse paths and integrating into unequal segments of American society. Some replicated the "time-honored pattern of growing acculturation and parallel integration into the majority middle-class; a second [path] leads straight in the opposite direction, to permanent poverty and assimilation into the underclass; a third [path] links economic mobility with preservation of the immigrant community's solidarity" (Portes 1995b, 251). This model implied that residential locations shape the specific ways in which groups encounter opportunities and constraints. It also opened up the question about outcomes of adaptation: not all groups would benefit from acculturating with their segment of America. Indeed, these scholars pointed out that cultivating ties with the ethnic community instead of acculturation is often beneficial to the second generation. So the scholarly work on this perspective got me interested in systematically investigating the experiences of the children of highly educated, post-1965 middle-class immigrants.

I specifically wanted to know about the second generation that had grown up in middle-class suburbs. I was well aware that these second generation individuals were often among the few minorities in their schools and neighborhoods, unlike their ethnic peers who might live in enclaves or more diverse areas. I had heard some stories about racial discrimination but I did not know whether this was widespread. I wanted to know whether the children of middle-class immigrants were able to follow the first path of becoming middle-class American, or did they follow the third path and continue to rely on their ethnic community? What structural circumstances affected them? Studies on educational achievement showed that long-term residence in the United States is not a sufficient predictor of how children of immigrants fare, as the assimilation model had predicted. These studies showed that children of highly educated immigrants consistently outperformed the third or fourth generation descendents of European migrants (Zhou 1997). But what happens in other aspects of their lives? Do they become simply American? Do they become ethnic American like their white peers, where there are no conflicts between being ethnic and being American? Or do they remain ethnic, because they are marked as different from their white peers?

As I thought further about the project, several other issues emerged and I had to go beyond the segmented assimilation model. First, I had to grapple centrally with the question of racialization. It seemed to me that the difference between the first and third paths would depend on how these groups were considered by outsiders: they might be middle class and see themselves as American, but would others see them in this way? How are they constructed in relation to the laws and policies of this country? Do they enjoy all the rights that their fellow citizens enjoy? As I conducted some preliminary interviews, it became very apparent that many participants felt they were singled out in their schools because of their phenotype and religion. So I had to consider racialization as a critical grid for understanding ethnicity in this study. Second, as I considered what kind of networks such groups retain within the community, it made me look closely at the context within which "community" or "family" is defined. For many of the middle-class immigrants and their children their networks are geographically dispersed; often a range of transnational networks seemed to influence how they imagined their lives. Thus, it seemed important to consider, not just how such adaptations take place in response to structural relations within the United States, but how the groups' experiences within a transnational context might influence their modes of adaptation (in the United States) as well. Third, as I looked at the emerging transnational literature (for example, Levitt 2001; Portes 1997; Vertovec 2001) that focuses primarily on the first generation immigrants, I encountered another problem. Most of this literature describes how immigrants move between countries retaining ties with their homes and host countries. But first generation immigrants, who move between "host" and "home" countries and create a transnational space that transcends the boundaries of the specific countries, are able to do so because they are embedded in specific sets of structural and cultural relationships in these countries. The second generation is not necessarily positioned in the same way. Where is home for them symbolically, and, more importantly, what kind of social structural relationships do they encounter when they move between countries? Are they welcomed in their parents' countries of origin? Do they encounter barriers because of their religion or gender or class? This is a question that has to be asked apart from inquiring about the nature of their extended family ties. For many groups, their transnational movements may be facilitated by their ability to speak "the" language of their parents' home countries. But there are other groups, like the Indians, who come from countries with multiple languages and very distinctive cultures. How does the second generation experience such diversities? What opportunities or constraints do they encounter? It became increasingly clear to me that if we are to consider transnational influences on ethnicity—which we undoubtedly need to, given the intensification of global influences on groups—we need to consider the structures in other places as well. In other words, we need to move beyond considering structures at the node (the country of influence) and acknowledging a transnational context that we treat as a neutral background that is easily traversed by all sorts of people. Instead we need to consider the histories, current emerging political, social, economic, and cultural conditions in other places, as we design more nuanced models of ethnicity, because these *sets* of structural relations influence people in very different ways.

Overall, this book reflects some of the recent ideas on studying second generation groups in the United States, and addresses some of the gaps in the literature. I follow the general suggestion of the segmented assimilation model to consider second generation groups in relation to the context in which they grow up in the United States and limit this study to the children of immigrants who grew up among mostly middle-class, white Americans. This group is different from the children of South Asian immigrants who arrived after the mid-1980s. Unlike the parents of the second generation in this study who are apt to be highly educated and most often moved directly to suburban America, the arrival of the later group of South Asian immigrants has been governed by a very different set of immigration laws and citizenship criteria. The immigrants who arrived after the mid-1980s are more likely to have lower levels of education and show greater concentration in blue-collar jobs. While the subjects of this study grew up in mostly white suburbs, the children of the later migrants are more likely to have grown up in areas where there are larger numbers of racial minorities (including more South Asian Americans). Instead of taking it for granted that all of these second generation South Asian Americans are the same because they share a cultural background, I assume their experiences differ based on the social relationships in which they are embedded. Thus I focus on the children of the 1965–1985 group of migrants alone. Further work is required to document the lives of the second generation individuals whose parents arrived in the late 1980s and 1990s. I hope this study will act as a step toward more nuanced within-group comparisons.

I draw upon the experiences of forty-eight participants of Indian, Pakistani, Bangladeshi, and Nepalese origin whose parents arrived between 1965 and the middle of the 1980s, in order to limit this study to the children of highly educated immigrants. I show how the children of these immigrants try to construct their ethnic lives in ways that address the challenges they face in the United States as well as in other countries. Focusing on the subset that grew up in middle-class suburbs allows me to examine the social landscape of this segment of the United States. I am able to disentangle issues of race and class and examine, for instance, whether these middle-class non-white Americans are affected by racialization. There is a widespread notion that being part of middle-class America makes the children of the post-1965 immigrants just like the middle-class descendents of twentieth-century European immigrants. While there are some similarities, the experiences of the South Asian Americans reflect complex inclusions *and* exclusions that constitute the contemporary social landscape of the United States.

I HAVE RECEIVED a great deal of support during the course of this project, although I name just a few people and units. I would like to thank the University of Connecticut Research Foundation for the grant that helped me get started with this project. I also acknowledge the help provided by the Asian American Studies Institute and the Urban and Community Studies program at the University of Connecticut. These units provided student assistance during crucial periods of this research, and my colleagues were a constant source of support and encouragement. Special thanks to Chantal Krcmar and Melanie Peele, who were my graduate assistants, and enthusiastically shared the task of gathering some of the data for this project. Anne Theriault, now at Puerto Rican and Latino Studies, UCONN, volunteered to take on some of the transcription in the midst of her extremely busy schedule during the early part of the project; I am deeply grateful to Anne for helping me get over the "teething troubles" with transcriptions. My sincerest thanks to Shanthi Rao, friend and "cousin-in-law," along with Dipa Roy, Bidya Ranjeet, Monika Doshi, Azizunessa Fasihuddin, and Anjana Narayan who actively helped me network with different communities. Sabihah Dodi, Amrita Purkayastha, Annapurna Sinha, and Sabiha Vahidy enthusiastically helped me gather a range of photographs; some of these pictures appear in this book. I also thank David Meyers who, as the Social Sciences Editor at Rutgers University Press, encouraged me to write this book while I was simply thinking about articles. Kristi Long, Senior Editor, has been a constant source of support.

Special thanks to friends and colleagues Mark Abrahamson, Mary Bernstein, Roger Buckley, Noel Cazenave, Fe De Los Santos, Davita Glasberg, Thomas Lewis, Marita McComiskey, Nancy Naples, Kenneth Neubeck, Kathryn Ratcliff, Angela Rola, Louise Simmons, Ronald Taylor, and Gaye Tuchman for their friendship, unstinted help, and support through the years. I am especially grateful to Kathryn Ratcliff for reading some of the earliest versions of the manuscript and for her thoughtful feedback. Karen Chow and Wei Li provided crucial help during the editing stage of this book, and Anita Duneer helped out selflessly to complete the manuscript during a year fraught with family medical emergencies. And, as always, sincerest thanks to my mentors and friends Myra Marx Ferree, Mark Abrahamson, Margaret Abraham, Nazli Kibria, Jyoti Puri, and Marlese Durr for helping me to navigate the corridors of academia.

My husband Indra, and daughter Aheli, have lived with this manuscript for a long time; they have put their lives on hold and given up numerous pleasant activities because I was working on this project. This project was completed primarily because of their steady, cheerful, and unstinting help. My extended family—the Roy Choudhurys, the Gangulys, and the Purkayasthas—in India, France, Nigeria, and the United States continue to act as my cheerleading team, and who, along with friends Lipika Gangopadhyay, Riten Bhattacharya, Jean Miles, Rhoda Obermeier, and Diana McMeeking, embody the kinds of support such geographically dispersed networks can offer.

And, most of all, my gratitude to all the unnamed participants in this study, who shared their experiences with me. Despite their busy schedules, they often provided me with new snippets of information about what was going on in their worlds. I hope this book adequately reflects some of their successes and concerns.

Negotiating Ethnicity

Chapter 1

Introduction

IN 1965, FOLLOWING THE Civil Rights movement, the United States rescinded several long-standing rules restricting the permanent migration of non-whites to this country. Since the ban on Asian migration that had been in place from 1917 was also lifted, larger numbers of "new" migrants from several Asian countries came to the United States. However, these immigrants had to meet new requirements in order to migrate: they either had to possess the high skills in demand in the United States or they had to be family members of these highly qualified migrants.[1] A significant proportion of the migrants from the Indian subcontinent, who arrived during the next two decades, embodied the selection criteria of these laws. Scholars documented how such "new" immigrant groups, who were proficient in English, found and acquired white-collar jobs, such as medicine, scientific research, engineering and information technologies, settled in middle-class suburbs and appeared to fulfill the American Dream (for example, Jensen 1988; Saran 1985). Their language proficiency, high human capital, non-ethnic residential location, and earnings from mainstream jobs appeared to confirm the openness of United States society toward all groups, irrespective of their racial status, who worked hard to achieve middle-class status. Certainly the mainstream media described them in these terms, valorized them for their "achievements," and, along with other Asian Americans, labeled them the "model minorities."

However, hidden by these accolades, a different story unfolded. Many of these highly educated "strangers from a different shore," as Takaki (1994) has called them, experienced racial discrimination in various arenas of life. By the 1980s, several community sub-groups successfully lobbied the Census Bureau to move them from the white racial category to Asian American so that they could challenge their discrimination as racial minorities.[2] According to recent work on this group, structural integration *and* ethno-racial marginalization, economic affluence *and* social marginality have been facets of these immigrants' experiences (for example, Prashad 2000a; Shankar and Srikanth 1998). Given these contradictions, it is important to enquire how the children of these middle-class non-white immigrants, many of whom are now in college or starting their own occupational careers, are faring in the United States.

This question is particularly important because long established scholarly work *and* widely held social beliefs predict that as immigrants become more middle class, learn English, and begin to live, work, and go to school with the mainstream population, ethnic identities become less salient. Yet little research, with the recent exception of Kibria (2002) and Tuan (1998), has been done specifically on the children of highly qualified, non-white immigrants to find out whether this proposition holds true across all groups. Surveys on the new second generation (the children of the post-1965 immigrants) indicate that the children of high-status professionals who appear to be integrated into the mainstream, are most likely to choose ethnic labels that acknowledge their parents' national origin (Rumbaut 1995). The responses of the participants in this study indicate a similar trend. These second generation South Asians (henceforth South Asian Americans) used a variety of hyphenated labels such as Bengali or Bangladeshi American, Indo- or Indian American, Nepalese American, Pakistani American, American of Pakistani origin, or American of Indian origin to identify themselves. In this book, I explore why they chose hyphenated labels and what their explanations and experiences about growing up as middle-class non-whites in the United States tell us about the dimensions—character, contradictions, and dynamics—of contemporary ethnicity.

Scholarly work on ethnicity in the United States offers a series of competing explanations for such preferences: perspectives of symbolic ethnicity, segmented assimilation, and racialized ethnicity. First, some scholars, like Gans (1979) or Waters (1990) might argue that the South Asian Americans' choice of ethnic labels is related to the ways in which they symbolically acknowledge their cultural heritages. Their choice of hyphenated labels reflects the declining significance of race-based barriers in the United States, especially for these young adults who are structurally assimilated in terms of residential location, education, and jobs. They use hyphenated labels because they are able to celebrate their cultural heritage when and where they choose to do so in multicultural America. Second, other scholars like Portes (1995a) and Zhou (1997) contend that assimilation is a segmented process and point out that children of immigrants adjust to different (and unequal) strata of American society. As a result, many second generation groups continue to rely on their ethnic community networks for resources to get ahead and become part of middle-class America. Their associations with(in) their ethnic community are reflected in these labels. A third explanation, racialized ethnicity, would link these answers to racial barriers that continue to constrain the ethnic options of such groups. Like other Asian Americans, the South Asian Americans might choose hyphenated labels to illustrate the "glass ceilings" they experience in mainstream America that act as barriers to full integration; that is, they are racialized "in conjunction with and despite their involvement and participation in [the mainstream]" (Kibria 2002, 12). These explanations indicate very different reasons—either the absence or the continuing salience of racialization—that might prompt South Asian Americans to choose hyphenated labels. One of my primary objectives is to analyze the social structural relations that shape the experiences of South Asian Americans in the United States.

While much of the work on ethnicity has assumed that nation-states act as "containers" of the lives and horizons of ethnic groups, scholars have begun to examine the influences of contemporary global forces on groups who reside in post-industrial societies such as the United States. Some scholars, like Appadurai (1996), have argued that global-level processes intensify the circulation of ideas, images, technologies, money, and people, and, consequently, weaken the extent to which nation-states can determine the lives of ethnic groups. The growing literature on transnational "villagers" also supports the idea that immigrants are no longer locked into the structural relations in their host countries; they can build lives in more than one country, moving back and forth to maximize the opportunities in their lives (for example, Glick-Schiller et al. 1992; Levitt 2001; Portes 1997; Vertovec 2001). Focusing on geographically dispersed networks, Wellman (1999) and his colleagues have argued that people are increasingly tied with networks across vast geographical areas through cheaper phone calls, e-mails, chat groups, and visits "home," so that the horizons of their lives often extend beyond single nation-states. Such dispersed communities can act as supportive resources for groups, providing friendship, care, comfort, and material resources, much along the lines that old ethnic enclaves provided support in little social worlds in urban areas in the United States. Indicating a different way of being connected to a globalized world, scholars like Halter (2000) and Lury (1996) point out that people are able to "shop for identity": material cultural items are increasingly produced in several countries and distributed globally through segmented marketing. Middle-class groups in post-industrial societies, such as the South Asian Americans, are able to construct ethnic or other identity-based lifestyles through their consumption patterns. Their use of hyphenated labels might simply reflect a trend that is common among most middle-class people in post-industrial societies: shared consumption patterns serve as expressions of group membership. Scholars like Cohen (1998) have pointed out that many organized groups are actively engaged in creating collective identities at a global and transnational level based on places of origin, religion, sexual preference, race, gender, and a host of other identity markers. These groups try to attract people from many nation-states and provide them with opportunities to explore and adopt new—more globalized—identities. Thus, the general theme that runs through the globalization and transnationalism literature suggests that South Asian Americans might choose hyphenated labels to indicate the ways in which they are not just American, but that their lives are woven into a context that extends far beyond the boundaries of the United States. This leads to my second, related objective in this book: to examine *how* such global-level processes influence South Asian American ethnicity.

As I examine the complex social processes behind hyphenated labels and analyze what it means to be the children of non-white immigrants in contemporary middle-class America I pay attention to the context and the social processes as well as the role of agency at the individual and collective level. I weave some of the insights outlined above to focus on these three overlapping themes. First, on the issue of context, I examine the interplay between what happens in the United States *and* what happens elsewhere. Although some scholars focus on the United States alone and others have argued that globalization obliterates the significance of nation-states, I follow a middle path. I assume the social processes in these different levels intersect. I argue that the node of the lives of these South Asian Americans is centered on the United States, so that their South Asianness and Americanness is shaped by what happens in this nation-state. At the same time, the horizons of their lives extend far beyond the geographical boundaries of the United States. A range of connections—their involvement in transnational friends and family networks, their ability to consume a range of "ethnic" items from around the globe, as well as the networks they develop through organized groups—act as additional influences on the meanings, content, and boundaries of their hyphenated identities.[3] Second, I examine the social structural relations in the United States to analyze to what extent (if at all) racialization affects this group of South Asian Americans. Whether they have to contend with externally imposed boundaries or whether their assertion of ethnicity is a free choice delineates their position in relation to their white peers in contemporary middle-class America. My interviews with forty-eight participants of Indian, Pakistani, Bangladeshi, and Nepalese origin suggest that racialization remains a central feature of their lives. In fact, this focus on a group that is otherwise well integrated into middle-class America emphasizes the continuing salience of racialization for groups of non-European origin. How they are racialized through their participation in middle-class society and how they attempt to negotiate some of these external boundaries imposed upon them leads them to influence the development of specific networks. That is, they begin to develop networks with others in similar structural positions in the United States, as well as maintaining the networks described by the globalization scholars. Third, as I focus on their efforts to negotiate external boundaries, I also show that the hyphenated labels contain embedded nationality, gender, religious, and other boundaries. For instance, even as they use ethno-national labels, there are significant conflicts and disagreements over the meanings and boundaries of such ethno-national identities. The data in this book also show that their persistent use of ethno-national labels masks the emerging effort to develop a more pan-ethnic South Asian American layer in response to how outsiders "lump" Indian, Pakistani, Bangladeshi, and Nepalese Americans together based on their phenotypic similarity. However, conflicts and dis-agreements mark the content, meanings, and boundaries of this South Asian American layer as well.

Overall, this book shows that South Asian Americans negotiate multi-layered ethnicity to balance their position as racialized middle-class Americans along with their complex social location within a larger transnational arena. The title of this book, *Negotiating Ethnicity,* reflects this theme: ethnicity as a dynamic outcome of complex social relations that operate at multiple levels within a globalized world.

PERSPECTIVES ON ETHNICITY

This section provides further details about some of the theoretical per-spectives I mentioned in the preceding section. I consider the symbolic eth-nicity, segmented assimilation, and racialized ethnicity models and discuss *why,* according to these perspectives, ethnic group members choose hyphenated labels. The particular emphasis—whether it reflects individual choice or group networks—illustrates the nature of the social relationships within which they are embedded. For each of these perspectives, I also show how the global influences might intersect with some of the social structures within nation-states. This discussion is followed by a brief explanation on ethnicity, culture, transnational spaces, and the second generation.

Ethnic Groups in a Contemporary World

ASSIMILATION AND SYMBOLIC ETHNICITY. Several scholars expect that the new waves of post-1965, non-European migrants will follow the assimilation path of eastern and southern European migrants (for example, Alba and Logan 1993; Alba and Nee 1997). Part of this expectation is based on the pro-file of the larger population of second generation groups, many of whom have to acquire linguistic skills, education, and mainstream occupations to become upwardly mobile. However, the case of the South Asian Americans used in this study helps us to disentangle questions about social mobility from questions about assimilation and integration. The group of South Asian Americans that are the focus of this study meet all the criteria of integration with middle-class white peers in terms of linguistic proficiency, education, occupations, and residences. So the crucial question is why they use hyphen-ated labels, instead of saying they are American. I mentioned in the previous section that racialization plays a central role in the lives of South Asian Amer-icans and influences their answer. Nonetheless, I begin by considering the insights of a variant of the assimilation model, symbolic ethnicity, because it offers ways of comparing experiences of white and non-white middle-class groups.

The symbolic ethnicity model is grounded in ideas about the pluralistic nature of contemporary American society and "new" ways of "doing ethnicity." Drawing on ideas of scholars like Cohen (1977) and Greeley (1971), who have suggested that ethnic identification may not completely decline with prolonged integration into the mainstream, this model points to ways in which changes in the context may facilitate the inclusion of diverse groups into the American mainstream. The more open and multicultural a society becomes, the greater the freedom for groups to celebrate their cultural heritages. As the United States has become more open to multiple cultures in the second half of the twentieth century, scholars like Gans (1979) and Waters (1990) argue that it has allowed "white-ethnics"—groups such as the Irish or Italians who were once considered non-white—to practice a new kind of ethnicity.

There are two aspects of this model that are important for understanding the complex pattern of inclusion and exclusion that South Asian Americans experience in multicultural America. The symbolic ethnicity model describes the lack of need for networks and how white-ethnic groups are free to choose a variety of cultural "tools"—particular types of cultural practices that are picked because they best fit the context—to construct this kind of ethnicity. According to this view, as the social costs of being an ethnic group member have declined, white-ethnic groups have no need to maintain "deep ties" and supportive networks based on religious, linguistic, and other characteristics, which require time commitments and sacrificing some individual preferences in the interest of "the community." When white-ethnics feel the need to practice some aspects of their cultures they are free to choose which aspects of their culture they want to emphasize. Since outsiders are not defining them as ethnic and different, they can choose when, where, and how they want to do so. An individual might decide that she would like to acknowledge her Irishness and invite friends (of different persuasions) for a St. Patrick's Day dinner. She could just label this dinner to acknowledge St. Patrick's Day, pick one or two items that are "Irish" and enjoy the dinner among a circle of friends. Instead of depending on shared community practices to learn about ethnic cultures, there is an "increased dependence on the mass media, ethnic stereotypes, and popular culture to tell people how to be Irish or Italian or Polish" (Waters 1990, 166). Items that can be easily consumed—certain kinds of music, clothes worn for ethnic parades, or particular foods available easily in supermarkets or via the internet—are some of the tools that can be used to assert ethnicness.

While the symbolic ethnicity model focused on the United States, it fits well with some globalization literature that emphasizes the role of markets in facilitating the consumption of items as symbolic ways of doing ethnicity. If we were to examine how increasing globalization affects practices of symbolic ethnicity, we could point to the increasing availability of "ethnic products" for consumption in societies that impose no costs on these specific ways of asserting ethnicity. Individuals and groups are likely to find it easier to use similar items of material culture irrespective of where they are located in the world. The economic shift from manufacturing to the production, marketing, and control of knowledge and image-based products in post-industrial societies has generated new trends in selling cultural products, such as, Tai Chi, yoga, kilts, or shamrocks that are identified with specific cultures (Zukin 1995). These products are sold because of their association with "cultures," but companies produce and market these products in ways that help *them* retain the benefits of "expertise" and mass production, creating and sustaining segmented identity markets (Halter 2000; Lury 1996). Groups can simply consume certain sets of products to emphasize their ethnicness and become part of a global village of shared consumption practices. These economic institutions create certain kinds of "ethnic" or lifestyle desires by promoting preferences for particular clothes, music, foods, and other cultural products. Segmented identity markets, as defined by companies, can influence whether individuals are drawn to these types of lifestyles, and whether they identify their choices as "doing ethnicity."

Set within the middle-class segment of post-industrial, multicultural America, the South Asian Americans in this study are certainly influenced by these forms of doing ethnicity. They too are able to access a range of products that they might use to add ethnic accents to their lives. Like their white-ethnic peers, they might want to gather with friends, much like the St. Patrick's Day dinners, for Hindu or Muslim festivals such as Diwali or Ramadan, to celebrate their cultural heritage. But, as I illustrate in later chapters, while South Asian Americans use some of the same "tools" described by Waters (1990) in her study of white-ethnics, the underlying social relationships ensure that they are not as free to exercise their ethnic options like their white-ethnic peers. Their cultural tools are often ascribed negative meanings by outsiders, so that being ethnic negatively affects their ability to be American. Indeed, this study shows that South Asian Americans expect to reconcile their ethnic and American identities much like their white peers. But, like the Chinese and Korean Americans described by Kibria (2002), the defining feature of their ethnicity is that they are *unable* to exercise such options within the United States. Their lack of freedom to exercise their ethnic options makes their ethnic practices different from all those who practice symbolic ethnicity.

SEGMENTED ASSIMILATION. In contrast to symbolic ethnicity, the segmented assimilation model proposed by Portes (1995a), Zhou (1997), and their colleagues begins by emphasizing different segments of American society that influence different "ethnic outcomes." According to these scholars some groups are able to assimilate into middle-class America, although they caution that declining economic opportunities as well as phenotypic differences make this an unlikely path for most of the "new" second generation (Portes and Zhou 1993). The second path, which refers to downward mobility and assimilation with poor Americans in inner cities, need not concern us in this study, since the focus here is on a group that was selected for its location in middle-class suburbs. But the third path provides further insights into other possible relationships between ethnic groups and patterns of integration. Groups that reside among more working class or poor communities, attempt to maintain ethnic networks in order to be upwardly mobile in America. For example, Punjabi (Indian) second generation youth, who do not adopt the ways of their native, working-class, white neighbors appear to be upwardly mobile because they draw upon their ethnic community networks (and their ethic of hard work and struggle) rather than the values and resources of their neighbors (Gibson 1988). Similarly, Vietnamese adolescents in New Orleans who grow up amidst the "watchful and ever vigilant eyes" of the ethnic community, and do not assimilate with their black and Hispanic peers, are on an upwardly mobile path of Americanization (Zhou and Bankston 1998). While these children of immigrants within tight-knit communities are subject to the social control of the ethnic group, their membership in ethnic networks allows them to mobilize valuable social resources that ease their adaptation into America.

Where would South Asian Americans in this study fit into the segmented assimilation model? They grew up in middle-class, mostly white suburbs, and are either poised for, or already settled in, upper-tier jobs. Are they part of middle-class white America? The crucial issue is to investigate *why* such groups maintain ethnic group networks. One explanation is that as children of immigrants in white-collar occupations they benefit from the knowledge, information, and support of their ethnic networks (Portes and Sensenbrennar 1993). So like their peers who are situated amidst more working-class neighbors, the groups in middle-class suburbs might maintain their ethnic networks for rational reasons of maintaining upward mobility.

In its discussion of the second and third modes of adaptation this body of literature focuses on geographically proximate ethnic networks. However, as Kistivo (2001) has pointed out, it is possible to extend the idea of ethnic networks beyond the boundaries of nation-states, and consider how groups assimilate to segments of the United States by using resources from their transnational ethnic networks. Thus transnationalism and assimilation may not be contradictory processes. Just as the growth in technology and communications facilitates the availability of "cultural products," that facilitate the practice of symbolic ethnicity, such transnational networks make it easier for groups—especially the middle-class groups and their families in multiple countries who can access such technologies—to maintain ties with people who are scattered all over the globe. Their ability to maintain meaningful connections with globally dispersed family and friends' networks replicates a type of virtual ethnic enclave. The ongoing ties then become a source of a variety of social resources and support (Rex 1995; Wellman 1999). One of the key conditions of the assimilation model was that increasing social and geographical distance—which meant moving away from ethnic enclaves and setting up social and other networks with the mainstream—would lead to the dilution of ethnic ties. The growth of more efficient ways to connect to people in other places—by using e-mail lists and web-boards to supplement phone calls—means that contemporary groups can overcome some of the limitations set by geographical distance on earlier immigrants.

But even as we extend the context of ethnic ties to a transnational arena, we are left with the question about how racialization might contribute to the need to maintain such ties. While segmented assimilation suggests that responses to phenotypes might be a factor preventing some second generation groups from becoming part of middle-class America, this model does not ultimately investigate the effect of such racialization on groups such as the South Asian Americans in this study.

RACIALIZED ETHNICITY. A third set of literature, which focuses centrally on racialization, provides further directions on investigating the lives of contemporary non-white groups. These scholars assert that irrespective of their class position, their inability to define themselves as individuals, a freedom enjoyed by whites, upholds the main boundary between racialized ethnics and whites (for example, Bonilla-Silva 1996; Espiritu 1997; Glenn 1999; Kibria 2000; Omi and Winant 1994; Wu 2002). Recognizing the independent effect of racialization processes in the construction of ethnicity, Waters has cautioned that "the ways in which ethnicity is flexible and symbolic and voluntary for white middle-class Americans are the very ways in which it is not so for non-white and Hispanic Americans" (1990, 156). Thus a hyphenated label, such as South Asian American, is likely to indicate that these Americans cannot be American in the same way as their white peers.

This literature provides some insights into the experiences of other middle-class groups. Based on their empirical work on second and later generations of Asian Americans of East Asian origin, Kibria (2002) and Tuan (1998) have shown that these groups may adopt the ways of middle-class whites, participate in mainstream organizations and institutions, and become racialized through this participation. Since there are fewer "achievement differences" among these Asian American groups and whites—criteria that are often used in the construction of boundaries between blacks and whites—the boundaries between whites and Asian Americans are constructed with reference to these supposedly deep-seated cultural characteristics of Asian Americans that make them foreign or less American. So practicing symbolic ethnicity is not an option for these groups because their cultures are the "tools" that define racial boundaries. As Anthias (1992), Kibria (2000), and others have argued on the basis of research on the United States and the United Kingdom, not all cultural symbols are equivalent; for example, saris or *sherwanis* (tight trousers and loose knee-length shirt worn by men in northern and western India and Pakistan) are not equivalent to German drindle-skirts or *lederhosen*. And, in contrast to the segmented assimilation model that emphasizes individuals maintain active networks in order to garner valuable social resources from the ethnic group, the racialized ethnicity perspective shows that the degree of connection with the ethnic community may vary considerably. Thus, the racialized ethnicity perspective indicates that it is not sufficient to look at whether or not groups maintain ethnic networks, or whether they practice culture occasionally, but it is necessary to ask *what* kind of networks groups maintain and *why* they do so. It is also important to find out what kind of cultural practices groups emphasize and the role such practices play in constructing their ethnicity. These are questions I pursue in this book on South Asian Americans.

While this literature focuses primarily on the boundaries that marginalize groups, it also indicates that racialized groups actively challenge, negotiate, and attempt to shape the forces that marginalize them. In contemporary United States, they appear to adopt two main, and often contradictory, strategies for challenging their racial marginalization. First, many groups try to avoid being completely incorporated into the United States racial social system. Some Caribbean, Latin American, and Asian American groups reconstruct and assiduously maintain ethno-national identities, often as a way of resisting being integrated into the stigmatized minority racial categories of the United States (Fernandez-Kelley and Schauffler 1996; Foner 2001; Levitt 2001; Waters 1995). Olzak (1992) has pointed out that "objectively assimilated" members of minority groups realize the caste-like barriers between themselves and the mainstream. Such members then mobilize ethnicity to challenge these boundaries, a development she designates as reactive ethnicity. They recreate and mobilize aspects of their ethno-national identities to mark themselves as distinctively different from the other racial groups in the United States. A key question for analysis is whether such a process is underway among the South Asian Americans.

Second, many groups exhibit a process of racial ethno-genesis, where multiple racialized cultures develop a common denominator *in the United States,* which then serves as a means of challenging racialization. They mobilize aspects of their ethnicity to form new, larger pan-ethnic collectivities. This "new culture" does not replace prior cultural forms, but adds a layer of cultural commonality among groups that did not see unity between them before. These emerging groups often fit more easily with the racial categories defined by the government: defining the basis for resource disbursement, drawing electoral district boundaries, and distributing other crucial resources. Pan-ethnic movements, whether of Native Americans, Latinos, or Asian Americans, illustrate the political mobilization of ethnic commonalities among groups to create larger racialized pan-ethnic identities that challenge, more effectively, the racial marginalization experienced by groups (Espiritu 1992; Nagel 1996; Padilla 1985). Understanding this process of racial ethnogenesis is an important part of my study. I investigate which kinds of pan-ethnic solidarities appear among the South Asian Americans. As I will show later, some participants in this study are attempting to become Asian Americans, and some are building more pan-ethnic solidarities such as "South Asian" to address the multiple boundaries they encounter.[4]

Overall, the racialized ethnicity model focuses primarily on what happens within the United States. However, I would argue that there are several ways in which it can be extended to include the insights of the globalization scholars. First, their emphasis on how groups maintain ethno-national identities provides a way of looking at the influence of transnational family networks in developing such identities. The many ways in which immigrant groups and their children maintain family ties across nations, which I described with the segmented assimilation model, can also be a reaction to the racialized boundaries that people face preventing them from maintaining families in one place. The earlier work on split households among minority populations provides ample testimony to this phenomenon (for example, Dill 1994; Espiritu 1997). But the literature on transnational links also shows that the non-white immigrants maintain a variety of links between their countries of origin and the new country of settlement (for example, Chen 1992; Eckstein and Barberia 2002; Fong 1994; Kurien 2002; Levitt 2001; Wong 2000). For instance, Levitt, who studied the Dominicans in the Boston metropolitan area, showed that far from transferring their loyalties to the United States alone, Dominicans are transnational villagers, they "are keeping their feet in both worlds. They use political, religious, civic arenas to forge social relations, earn their livelihoods, and exercise their rights across borders" (Levitt 2001, 3). The construction of such transnational communities involves setting up organizations and structures that facilitate ongoing movement and participation across national borders. In other words, when groups are unable to construct their lives in ways of their choosing in their host countries, they often create alternative transnational structures to mitigate the effects of racialization.

Second, some of the insights of racialization scholars are reflected in developments taking place in many countries simultaneously. Scholars such as Vertovec (2001) point out that as countries form larger security and political consortiums, older ideas and structures for organizing ethnic groups within nation-states are being replaced by more globally applicable ethnic identities that need to be "managed" within these larger political arenas. For instance, Muslims are a new globally racialized category, irrespective of national and cultural difference, and are subject to an increasing series of rules across regional blocks (Kishwar 1998; Rex 1995). At the same time, the notion of human rights—based on the idea of universal personhood rather than rights accorded to individual citizens by nation-states—is bringing new pressures on nation-states to ensure equal access to a variety of rights to marginalized groups (for example, Cohen 1998; Falk 2000; Sen 1999; Soysal 1998). The resurgence of such demands has caused many Euro-American states to pro-pose and develop multicultural policies as "a kind of corrective to assimilation approaches and policies surrounding the incorporation of immigrants" (Ver-tovec 2001, 3). However, to what extent states should support multicultural-ism, whether people should be allowed to practice cultures privately—within their homes and occasionally in public spaces as long as they meet all the existing laws regarding what is appropriate—and whether states should for-mally recognize some cultural group rights is highly contested (Grillo 1998; Okin 1999; Rex 1995; Sheth 1999). Such multiculturalism freezes boundaries between groups by considering cultures to be innate within people even as it opens up spaces for groups to assert their distinctiveness (Vertovec 2001).

These political changes contribute to the pattern of inclusion and exclu-sion that mark the lives of South Asian Americans. Some of these new policies affect them (as well as their family members) as they travel in different parts of the world. The conflicts over multiculturalism influence exactly what they are able to assert in public as their ethnicity. And, as some aspects of ethnic iden-tities, for instance, specific religions, become marked in multiple countries, such categorizations can begin to introduce chasms within the ethnic groups as people try to disassociate themselves from the most stigmatized aspects of their ethno-national ethnic identity.

OVERALL, I FOLLOW the racialized ethnicity model to frame the experiences of the South Asian Americans. While they may "objectively" appear to be middle-class Americans, and many of their cultural practices may be similar to the practices of their white-ethnic peers, when we examine the nature of their networks and why they maintain such networks, we become more aware of the social structural processes that continue to maintain boundaries between them and their white peers in spite of their position in middle-class America. Their own efforts to negotiate their ethnicity, whether they build ethno-national identities, or more pan-ethnic boundaries, or both (as the data for these participants show) are closely related to the social structural relationships in which they are embedded. Their specific experiences, which I describe throughout the book, provide a more detailed picture of the shape and form of contemporary ethnicity in a globalized world.

Racialized Ethnicity, Culture, and Transnational Networks

The previous section described some of the social structural relations implicit in earlier models. In this section, I focus on two additional issues. I clarify how I see culture/s shaping ethnicity and argue that groups use culture as a tool and a building block to build and sustain collectivities within *situated contexts* (for example, Andersen 1983; Anthias 2001b; Barth 1969; Conzen et al. 1992; Espiritu 1992; Nagel 1994; Olzak 1992). I also discuss how post-immigrant generations appear to be positioned within transnational spaces.

My conception of cultures-in-context provides a way of clarifying two underlying assumptions of this study. First, this concept moves away from the essentialist notions of cultures. While some of the globalization literature tends to emphasize attachment to points of origin or cultural similarities as the main factors influencing the development of diasporic groups (see Anthias 1998 for a critique), I move away from such ideas about ethnic groups with deeply rooted cultural tendencies. Research on blacks and Asians in Britain shows that instead of replicating essential identities the descendents of immigrants sift and pick cultural tools to negotiate their positions within *their* structural circumstances (for example, Gilroy 1993; Hall 1990). As Anthias has argued, later generation groups often engage in building bridges with other groups in similar structural locations, creating transethnic identities, so the culture of ethnic groups keeps changing. "The new British Muslim identity is not confined to an ethnic group . . . it is an amalgam, neither purely religious nor specifically ethnic [but] an identity [that expresses] a culture of resistance" (Anthias 2001a, 625–626). The work on racialized ethnicity, described in the previous section, also reinforces the idea of groups picking cultural tools to reformulate new kinds of ethno-national and pan-ethnic groups in response to specific structural circumstances. The global and the local come together as transnational cultural resources act as "assets" for building ethnicities that allow groups to transcend some of the deleterious effects of racial boundaries.

Second, the notion of groups using cultural tools depending on their particular context also implies that "the culture" is rarely practiced by all the members in the same way. Instead, differences of social positions *within* the group—of gender, class, religious background, national origin, citizenship, and other such socially constructed differences—are likely to shape what is chosen and practiced. As Das Gupta (1997) argues, the new "Indian" ethnic identity for second generation females in the United States has to be understood, not simply with reference to their positions as non-white females within the United States, but by the pressures to be "Indian" and "American" in specific ways. Instead of being able to pursue lives reflecting benign differences, as the pluralist "multicultural" model would suggest, these women have to constantly contend with the overarching demands for conformity that are placed on non-white immigrants to prove they are "American," as well as dealing with the demands made by the hegemonic ethnic group to uphold an upper-caste, upper-class orthodox form of Hindu Indianness. Thus, the link between culture and ethnicity is as complex within groups as it is between groups.

Another major focus of this study is to look at the nature of transnational influences: how, and to what extent these are relevant for understanding ethnicity of the second generation. Most of the research emphasis has been on the networks and institutions that first generation migrants build (Levitt 2001; Portes 1997). This literature recognizes some of the structural constraints within the United States, but less attention has been paid to the constraints and opportunities these migrants may encounter in other national contexts. While immigrants and their children may be forming a variety of networks and other ties across nations, what they actually build is governed by *sets* of nation-based rules. Whether they were born in a country, and their degree of familiarity and political status in a country influence how easily they can build these networks. Scholars such as Levitt have argued that children of transnational migrants "will continue to be active in their countries of origin from their firm base in the United States" (Levitt 2001, 5). However, because of the different structural positions of the two generations in these different countries, they might differ in terms of their attachments, embeddedness, and emphases. In other words, the transnational context is not a neutral background; national laws and policies (and those of supra-regional geopolitical blocks) shape the types of activities and networks of such groups, which in turn influence the types of cultural expressions that mark such groups as "ethnic."

How then should we think about transnational influences among the post-immigrant generations? I would suggest that we think of this influence in terms of nodes and fields: the node is located in the country of primary residence (United States) and the field is composed of several layers that range over the globe, encapsulating multiple structural circumstances. As Foner (2001) has suggested, the second generation need not keep equal institutional ties in both worlds; instead they might build a range of more informal, personal networks of friends and family which can also act as conduits for such transnational ties. We can envision ethnicity as expressing a state of balance between constraints and opportunities arising out of multiple nations. Typically, the structures at the node will be more relevant to the everyday lives of the second generation.

Such ethnicity is dynamic and multilayered, fragmented yet coherent, with embedded boundaries that reflect the complex sociopolitical context in which it takes shape. Global flows, multilayered identities, and cross-border networks construct the horizons of contemporary groups such as the South Asian Americans.

SOUTH ASIAN AMERICANS
IN THE UNITED STATES
The Participants in This Study

The South Asian Americans in this study are the children of the middle-class, non-white South Asians of Indian, Pakistani, Bangladeshi, and Nepalese origin, who arrived in the U.S. between 1965 and 1985.[5] Since each of the countries contains multiple linguistic groups (and very distinctive regional cultures), the South Asian Americans represent an amalgam of cultures. In addition, the cultural diversity is enhanced by their religions; this group includes Hindus, Muslims, Sikhs, Christians, and Jains. The participants in this study were either born in the United States or they arrived before they were twelve years old, so that their crucial teenage years were spent in this country. And, because of the profile of their parents, they grew up in middle-class households amidst mostly white peers and neighbors.

I used multiple starting points and a snowball sample to track this relatively elusive group in order to conduct in-depth interviews with them. (The details of the methodology and the participants are provided in the Appendix.) The forty-eight participants in this study were either in college or in white-collar occupations. I asked the South Asian Americans to identity themselves by offering them a choice of labels ranging from American to a variety of hyphenated labels; I also gave them the option to choose any other label that was relevant to them. Except for three individuals who identified themselves in terms of their parents' country of origin, all the other participants in this study chose hyphenated labels. The voices of this second generation are centrally featured in this study. In addition, I used ethnographic data, archival information, and focus group discussions for further insights into the nature of ethnicity among middle-class, non-white groups in the United States at the turn of the twenty-first century.

This study is limited to the children of South Asian immigrants who arrived between 1965 and the mid-1980s.[6] One reason for focusing on this group alone is my theoretical interest in the experiences of the children of highly skilled, non-white immigrants who are structurally integrated in terms of their residences, education, and jobs. Since the selection criteria of the immigration laws have been critical in shaping the "average profile" of immigrants, which in turn positions them in different ways vis-à-vis the middle class in the United States, I restrict this study to the children of immigrants who arrived within this period. The preference categories within the immigration laws between 1965 and the middle of the 1980s ensured that the levels of education and occupational concentration in professional and managerial jobs among the South Asian immigrant parents have been significantly higher than that of native whites in the 1970s and 1980s (Barringer et al. 1995). The national-level data on these migrants, with Indians making up close to 80 percent of the group, continues to document their "high-achieving" profile in the 1990s and 2000 (U.S. Census Bureau 2000). However, since the mid-1980s, in response to new laws, especially the diversity visas and family reunification criteria, class-based disparities within and across these groups in specific locales are increasing rapidly.[7] Furthermore, a series of new immigration and naturalization laws since the mid-1980s has altered the proportion of highly skilled members who have the political right to stay for longer periods in the United States. A growing number of people, especially from India, who arrived in the 1990s to work in the United States came on temporary visas that did not allow them the political rights to settle in this country. Adding the children of the latter groups would confound the focus of this study.

The mid-1980s cutoff is theoretically meaningful for another reason. As the previous section emphasized, a key issue for understanding the ethnicity of the participants in this study is to find out if racialization has been significant in their lives. Here too, the 1980s represents a time of change. The official racial status of this group changed from white to Asian American after several first generation groups lobbied for this change (Khandelwal 2002). While the pre-1980s South Asian migrants moved from white to Asian American, most of their children have grown up, officially, as "Asian American." (And the latter groups have officially been Asian Americans since their arrival.) This change of racial status complicates the racial position of the South Asian Americans since few people, including many first and second generation South Asians, consider them(selves) to be racially Asian American (Kibria 1998). Unlike blacks, whose "ethnic-ness is mostly subsumed under their status as blacks" (Omi and Winant 1994; Waters 1995), the racial ambiguity of the South Asian Americans, that is, their lack of fit with the existing racial categories of white, black, and Asian American make them an interesting group for exploring how race and ethnicity intersect.

The Choice of an Appropriate Label

Since this study focuses on the children of immigrants from India, Pakistan, Bangladesh, and Nepal, the choice of an appropriate label becomes a complicated issue. The label of "South Asian Americans" does not indicate a unitary group with an already established, deeply entrenched ethnic identity. The South Asian American label reflects some emerging social relations. They are frequently lumped together by outsiders as Indians or as Indians or Pakistanis, so this external attribution serves as one reason for using the South

Asian American label. In addition, several second generation groups label themselves by the Hindi/Urdu term "desi," which indicates a South Asian origin. Social service agencies are also beginning to use the term South Asian American to label this group. However, my choice of this label is also based on other historically grounded factors that are important for understanding the experiences of this and other similar groups. Ethnic boundaries emerge, as the previous section indicated, in response to structural circumstances, and looking at South Asian Americans who trace their roots to these four countries allows me to look at emerging similarities and divergences among this group that is characterized by significant cultural heterogeneity. In the next sections, I present the prior history of voluntary and enforced migration that continues to shape the nature of South Asian American ethnicity. Then I discuss some of the other implications of this label.

South Asian Migration

Although the South Asian Americans in this study were born in or have lived most of their lives in the United States, their parents' migration histories are important for understanding some sociopolitical facets of their ethnicity and their structural position in the United States.

A key factor in the lives of South Asian Americans is that Bangladeshis, Indians, Pakistanis, and Nepalese are, for the most part, relatively new immigrants to the social landscape of the United States. This recent history masks an earlier phase of racial restrictions on the migration of these groups. Chandrasekhar (1982), among others, has documented that by 1905 five thousand Indian men had arrived in the United States. The Indians of this time were British colonial subjects, mainly composed of people from what are now India, Pakistan, and Bangladesh, and were, almost without exception, male. At the time, female migration was severely restricted through an overlapping series of statutes. The migrants were, despite their designation as "Hindoos," overwhelmingly Sikh in their religious affiliation. The nativists' fears about a "tide of turbans" led to the passage of a series of laws to prevent further migration of these unacceptable migrants (Ancheta 1998; Gonzalez 1996; Kitano and Daniels 1995). Combining the ill feelings toward Japanese Americans, Korean Americans, and Chinese Americans (whose migration had been banned in the late nineteenth century) an immigration ban on all Asians, regardless of their origin, was instituted in 1917. In addition, responding to local sentiments against these settlers, Asian heritage groups living in the United States were deprived of citizenship and all associated rights through a series of laws that were passed through the 1920s (Ancheta 1998). In the United States, the various restrictions led to very imbalanced sex ratios, with around 109 females to over 5,000 Indian males according to Kitano and Daniels (1995). Thus the population of Indians simply dwindled away or forged new, but statistically insignificant, ethnic communities such as the Punjabi Mexicans described by Leonard (1992).

Consequently, when the South Asians started migrating to the United States after 1965, they appeared to be a new group. The number of South Asian immigrants grew from 36,100 between 1960 and 1970, to over 1.5 million in 2000 (Statistical Abstract 2002, Table 7).[8] According to the new laws, this immigrant generation was allowed full access to citizenship rights and nuclear family reunification privileges. Thus, unlike the children of earlier Indian migrants who were forced to live in split households in different countries, all South Asian Americans in this study grew up in the United States in nuclear two-parent families.

The timing of the arrival of the first generation immigrants has significantly affected the structural location of the second generation. The migration and settlement of the first cohort is directly related to the Civil Rights Movement, which culminated in the scrutiny of a broad array of race-based laws, and led, among other changes, to the lifting of the ban on Asian migration. The highly educated South Asian immigrants arrived in the United States just as the overt race-based occupational and residential barriers within the nation were being lowered. This period was also one of economic restructuring, which led to the arrival of these highly skilled migrants. Thus, based on their education and training *in other countries,* these migrants were able to move into white-collar occupations and buy homes in the suburbs during a time when native racial minorities were still contending with a series of structural impediments, especially regarding education and housing, that prevented them and their children from "achieving" similar patterns of integration. Consequently, the children of these South Asian migrants who were born in and/or spent most of their lives in suburbs were often among a very small number of racial minorities in these locations. Their structural position as middle-class *non-whites* in suburban America is very important for understanding their ethnic experiences.

Although the migration literature is often framed in terms of sending and receiving countries, with the corresponding implication that people like the Indians are likely to migrate from India, the reality is more complex. In order to understand the influences on South Asian Americans, we also have to consider the history of migration of South Asians as colonial subjects of the British. Until 1947, people from contemporary India, Pakistan, and Bangladesh were all Indian subjects of the British. The restrictions against Indians in the United States occurred in conjunction with British efforts to control the migration of their colonial subjects as indentured laborers to different parts of the British colonial empire (Chandrasekhar 1982). British Indians were sent to different parts of Asia, Africa, and the Caribbean to supplement local labor. Thus the South Asian Americans often have family spread over several countries.[9]

But the history of migration of the South Asians to the United States must also be grounded within an earlier history of exile and migration. These episodes of political conflict and forced migration that many of the immigrant generation experienced before they arrived as economic immigrants to the United States continue to shape how the first generation views people from the other South Asian nations.[10] When the immigration prohibition on Asians was lifted in 1965, India and Pakistan (the latter still included Bangladesh) had been independent countries for nearly two decades. As British rule ended in 1947, the political boundaries of these countries were drawn on the idea that these nation-states would reflect the concentration of Hindu and Muslim majorities. A massive refugee movement attended the establishment of these new political boundaries as large numbers of Hindus, Sikhs, and Muslims tried to reach one country or another. Also, by 1971, after a long period of agitation by Bangladeshis to establish their linguistic and cultural autonomy, Pakistan was split into two countries, Bangladesh and Pakistan. Like the formation of India and Pakistan, bitter conflicts and traumatic events accompanied the formation of this new state as well. As I illustrate later in this book, these histories of partitions, the ensuing bitterness of relocation, and the subsequent political conflicts continue to influence how many families define their ethnic boundaries today. These boundaries affect the ways in which the South Asian Americans are able to construct their lives.

With their newly acquired independence, both India and Pakistan established new educational systems. By 1965, countries such as India were producing highly trained scientists, doctors, and engineers, the kind of highly skilled labor that was in high demand in the United States. While the earlier channel of migration of these highly skilled individuals mostly targeted the United Kingdom, growing racial violence and new stringent immigration controls in the United Kingdom made the newly available opportunities in the United States more attractive.[11]

Thus, apart from those who came from South Asia, several South Asian groups also migrated to the United States from the United Kingdom. The anti-Asian sentiments in Britain were paralleled by anti-Asian sentiments in East Africa. From the early 1960s, the increasing sentiment of "Africanization" led to the expulsion of "Asians" (that is, South Asians who had migrated in the nineteenth and early twentieth centuries) from Kenya, Uganda, and Tanzania (Joseph 1999). Many of these refugees moved to England. Later, many of these refugees were sponsored by the American branches of their families to migrate to the United States. As a result of these episodes of political upheaval and exile, many South Asian Americans have family members—aunts, uncles, and cousins—dispersed over several countries of the world. Although specific

South Asian countries may remain important reference points for constructing ethnicity, this history of many recent migrations also makes it difficult to
neatly associate people with single countries of origin.

Choosing Labels

I initially conceptualized this group as a socio-geographical amalgam to
include second generation individuals who trace their roots to the four South
Asian countries because I was aware that many college students referred to
themselves as South Asian American. This "regional" label also seemed justified
because people in the mainstream often saw them as one group. But this label
became more methodologically meaningful as I began to encounter problems
with clearly classifying people according to single countries of origin. As I mentioned in the previous section, many of the participants trace their origins to
more than one country, and relatives and extended families are spread over several South Asian countries as well. Given this complex recent history, some of
these families symbolically identify with one or another homeland, complicat-
ing the understanding of ethnic experiences in terms of single nations of origin
as sources of influence on their ethnicity in the United States. Thus, the South
Asian American label represents an attempt to capture the social-structural context of their ethnicity, which transcends boundaries of particular nation-states. It
indicates the need to move away from the versions of ethnicity which are based
on single points of origin, and look at what happens *between* the South Asian
countries, and between the United States and other countries. Conceptualizing
ethnicity as an effect of multiple sets of social-structural conditions encapsulates
these multiple histories and structural relationships. In addition, the South Asian
American label, which many of the second generation use, aims to construct
bridges across the four groups. At the same time, however, there are fissures
among Indians of different cultural backgrounds, as well as friction between
nation-based groups. Thus the South Asian American label seems to be more
appropriate than nation-based labels. In other words, the political and cultural
dimensions of the emerging South Asian American ethnicity, as it is defined by
some South Asian Americans, is contested and challenged by many participants
who prefer to formulate their sub-national or cross-national cultural referents.
This book presents the dynamics of emerging similarities and ongoing tensions
and fragmentations among South Asian Americans to illustrate the construction
of ethnicity in the contemporary world.

ORGANIZATION OF THIS BOOK

The following chapters present the different dimensions of South Asian
American experiences; these dimensions cumulatively influence South Asian
American constructions of ethnicity. Each chapter draws on the experiences
of the South Asian American participants to show how global and local forces

intersect. Chapter 2 begins by describing why the South Asian Americans in this study chose hyphenated identity labels. This chapter illustrates that racialization, which begins in elementary school and continues throughout their lives, is central to their understanding of their ethnicity. While it becomes clear that they are subject to many overlapping forms of racialization, nonetheless, their experiences of marginalization do not wholly fit the patterns of other racial groups. South Asian Americans have to negotiate how they fit into the racialized structure of the United States. The chapter provides a preliminary discussion of how South Asian Americans negotiate these racial boundaries to deal with their multiple marginalities.

Chapters 3 and 4 examine family ties and "family cultures" in the United States. Chapter 3 describes the structure of South Asian American family networks and why South Asian Americans maintain such ties with extended family members. Their racialization within the United States appears to promote ethno-national identities, and South Asian Americans draw on symbolic and material resources from the larger family network to mitigate some of the influences. Maintaining such transnational family ties is contingent upon the South Asian Americans' ability to traverse multiple structural constraints. Their ambiguous social-structural position—that they are Indian in the United States, but are American in India—illustrates the complex links between local and transnational ethnic identities. Chapter 4 focuses more specifically on the nuclear family in the United States, and the local ethnic community, which, together, act as a source of ethnic norms. This chapter describes the intersecting race, gender, religion, and national boundaries, and how South Asian Americans negotiate these boundaries.

Chapter 5 explains patterns of ethnic consumption and traces the interplay between the economy and ethnicity. This chapter shows how South Asian Americans are brought together in collectivities because of their shared patterns of consumption. Using shared consumption patterns to build networks across nation-based identities allows South Asian Americans to negotiate some of the boundaries that emerge through families and ethnic communities and constrain their ethnic options. However, the emphasis on these building blocks also creates new within-group hierarchies.

Chapter 6 focuses on second generation organizations and how they develop collective identities. The organizations develop sets of representations and relations, and they do so by conforming to some externally imposed boundaries, challenging others and creating some new boundaries. This chapter illustrates how cultural tools are used to forge ethnic identities, which ones are chosen, and how these are used as building blocks of dynamic and fluid ties. This chapter also shows the links between South Asian American organizations and first generation dominated community interests, and it provides a glimpse of intra-group conflict. Overall, the multiple boundaries and restrictions the South Asian Americans experience within the mainstream, their families, and linguistic or religious (local and transnational) communities, are negotiated through these processes of creating *their* ethnic cultures.

The concluding chapter reflects on the nature of South Asianness and Asian Americanness. It explains the similarities and differences with the contemporary theory on racialized ethnicity and discusses the implications of transnational forms of racialized ethnicity.

POSTSCRIPT: AN ETHNIC ENCOUNTER

As I was completing this book, I was drawn into a discussion among three South Asian Americans about a popular movie. "Rubina" is of Pakistani origin, while "Arya," a Hindu and "Manjari," a Jain, are of different regional Indian origin. The discussion illustrates many of the themes of this book.

Rubina had stopped by to show me some pictures of an event she had organized. She started chatting with Arya as I looked through the album. The topic of their conversation was the recently released movie, *Bend It Like Beckham*. Both of them had seen the movie—Rubina in the United States and Arya in Switzerland. Clearly they both liked it. I had seen the movie after a colleague from India, whom I met at a conference in Australia, recommended I see it while I was in Sydney. I jokingly asked them "So why did you like that movie?" Arya said, "Because it is about someone my age and she is Indian," while Rubina replied, "We rarely get to see Indian movies in mainstream cinemas, it is great!" Then Rubina added, "My aunt really hated it though, she said it was so anti-Pakistani." I was intrigued because I had not picked up any anti-Pakistani messages in the movie. Rubina explained that her aunt was really talking about two scenes in the movie. In one scene, the leading character, Jasminder, tells her soccer teammates that her parents would not countenance her marrying either a white or a black person and definitely not a Muslim. In the second scene, Jasminder has been sent off the field for fighting with an opposing team member; she tells her coach that she reacted strongly because the other girl had called her a "Paki." Rubina went on to say that she, personally, loved the movie, and as far as she was concerned, just as Indian families discouraged their children from marrying Pakistanis, "Muslim" families (conflating religion and nationality) were equally guilty of discouraging their children from marrying "non-Muslims." Arya, who had discussed this movie with her cousins in England, remarked that perhaps Rubina's aunt did not know that "Paki" was a racial epithet in England that was used against all people from the subcontinent. Both seemed to take it for granted that hearing such racial slurs was a "normal" part of the lives of females like Jasminder.

Then they both went on to discuss other details of the movie. They both mentioned how the white friend's mother said "oh your name is so pretty" after she mangled the pronunciation, which seemed to fit with their own experience.

They mentioned the energetic Punjabi *bhangra* song and dance sequence in the movie, and Arya added that much to her surprise, she had heard the song on a mainstream radio program recently. They both laughed knowingly about how Jasminder's mother said they had family in California who could look out for her daughter once she went to college in the United States. This "family-in-every-corner-of-the-globe" syndrome seemed to be familiar with them.

Manjari, whom I had interviewed several months ago, joined in the conversation at this point. I told her we were discussing how one first generation South Asian individual had interpreted the two scenes as anti-Pakistani. Manjari, whose partner is of Pakistani origin, said that she too had interpreted the scene in that way. She thought that being mistaken for a person of Pakistani origin would elicit such a strong response when Indian families convey very strong messages to their children about shunning Pakistanis.

This vignette, in many ways, captures some of the major themes of this book. First, all three discussants referred to the family in the movie as "Indian." The movie features a Sikh family in London; the father had migrated to England from East Africa. It was clear that Jasminder had grown up in England. Her struggle to negotiate the right to play soccer on a regular team illustrated the intersecting family, community, and mainstream norms of gender and race prevalent in the United Kingdom. However, to the South Asian Americans discussing the movie in the United States, this was a story about "Indians."[12] Their use of this Indian *racialized master status*—conflating nationality, migration history, and ethno-religious background—is consistent with their own experiences of racialization in the United States. All three felt that in one way or another, the movie reflected their own experiences, irrespective of whether they were United States natives, and whether their parents came from India, Pakistan, or some other country. Just as they were not surprised by the use of a racial epithet, they seemed to take it for granted that an Indian nation-of-origin would continue to act as the racial master status.

Second, why the aunt and Manjari interpreted "Paki" as being anti-Pakistan reflects another aspect of their lives. The bitter, multi-decade long conflict between India and Pakistan is reflected in this conversation. It "made sense" for them to imagine that an Indian would react badly to being called Pakistani. For these three young Americans, these political conflicts in other parts of the world continue to work their way through family norms of a section of South Asians about who is acceptable, especially as a partner. Ironically, Arya's family had moved as refugees after the partition, but she expressed the least connection to this divide. The other two females felt that this symbolic boundary was vigorously kept alive by significant portions of what they perceived as "the" ethnic community.

Third, it was evident in their discussion that the practices of families and their understandings of what is ethnic vary significantly. Arya and Rubina's differing interpretations of Paki are based on their specific experiences. Rubina had just organized a South Asian American group to build bridges between second generation Indians, Pakistanis, and Bangladeshis. She saw the strictures against marrying outside one's group as a common theme in families, irrespective of religion, across all the three nation-based groups. Arya was not aware of such strictures on inter-marriages, so her interpretation was influenced by her discussions of the movie with her cousins in England, and her subsequent understanding of different racial terms used in the two countries. "Paki" to Arya meant a racial epithet (against all South Asians) rather than an association with a specific country much along the lines the n____ epithet is used against African Americans in the United States. While Arya's cousins had distanced themselves, because of class/cultural differences, from the "Southall Punjabis," Arya herself, being removed from those social specificities, felt no obligation to distance herself from the "pan-Indian" characters. However, she did mention that the Indian mother in the movie was very unlike the women in her own family and that she had joked about this stereotype with her mother, telling her that she (the mother) needed to learn how to make "alu-gobhi" (potatoes and cauliflower), knit, and watch Hindi movies at home before she tried to impose some of the same gender restrictions on her daughter. Manjari and Rubina did not think the mother was too stereotyped.

Fourth, for all three of them—one of Pakistani origin and two of Indian origin but from very different linguistic and religious backgrounds—being able to watch such "Indian" movies was one of the few ways in which they could share experiences. While outsiders saw them as being "the same" because they were "South Asian" or "Indian," the content of their cultural commonality had to be worked out. Movies in English, or with English subtitles, offered them an easy way to bond, as did the music. Here again deeper understanding on the basis of shared language or history is not the basis for their shared ethnicity. Arya, with no knowledge of Hindi or Punjabi, mistook the song on the radio, which is a re-mix of bhangra-rap for the song in the movie. The song in the movie was a more traditional piece for weddings. However, the specificity of the song did not seem to be important to any of them: the symbolic importance of "Indian" bhangra music on regular radio and the "Indian" movie in regular theaters was all that mattered. The availability of these material cultural items in shaping their racialized ethnic options is an important facet of their ethnicity.

Lastly, the four of us were discussing this "Indian" movie produced in England, by a British "Indian" director who migrated from Kenya, that we had seen in three different continents within a space of six months. We were a part of the global world woven together by technology, our own movements, media presentations, and a complex web of family and political configurations across multiple countries that shaped our understanding and horizons.

CHAPTER 2

Racial Boundaries and Ethnic Binds

Samina: Regardless of whether I was born here, I am always considered different. Even just growing up in Connecticut in my non-diverse town, I'd say I am American and people would go, "no but really where are you from?" Anywhere I go, even minorities don't consider me American. I don't know whether only a white American Christian person is considered American, but African Americans are considered American too. Nothing else is really acknowledged. Usually the first question of whoever I meet is "where are you from?" or if [all] they know [is] white, black, and Hispanic, it's like "are you from Puerto Rico?"

Prativa: Everyone considers the oriental region as Asia. So they'll say "no, no you are not Asian." So I just say "I am from a unique country—Nepal."

[Question: Can you explain your choice? Why did you not pick the first label—American?]
Anita: Because I have culture to me.

"ASIAN INDIAN AMERICAN," "American male of Bangladeshi origin," "Nepali American," "Pakistani American" . . . what do these hyphenated labels reveal about the ethnicity of South Asian Americans? Even though many scholars have taken the objective criteria of the integration of these groups—their residential location, linguistic proficiency, education, occupational concentration—to conclude that "assimilation" into the white middle class works in their favor, Samina, Prativa, and Anita's statements reveal a more complicated picture. Their responses highlight some of the core themes that the South Asian Americans in this study articulated to explain their choice of hyphenated labels. They are, like other Asian Americans and Latinos, seen as foreigners (Suro 1998; Takaki 1994). Because they are not generally considered to be part of their "race group," that is, Asian American, they often identify themselves with labels that reflect their parents' country of origin. In addition, they are perceived as having extracultural traits that set them apart from the white majority whose cultures remain normal and transparent (Frankenberg 1993; Glenn 1999). The pervasiveness of such experiences illustrates how South Asian Americans are marked by a variety of social boundaries.

These social boundaries, which mark their physical appearances and cultures as "different," constitute the fundamental dissimilarity between their ethnic options and that of white-ethnics who, despite class similarities, are no longer constrained by boundaries imposed by external forces. The South Asian Americans cannot practice symbolic ethnicity because these boundaries act as ethnic binds. This chapter shows that inter-group interaction, institutional arrangements, and ideologies that ascribe denigrating meanings to physical appearances and cultural practices, contribute to the construction and maintenance of such boundaries. Like other minority groups, they have to deal with the characteristics attributed to them by the dominant group as a condition of constructing and negotiating their ethnicity.

This chapter focuses on two main themes: the external ascriptions that the South Asian Americans mentioned most often as well as their descriptions of how they attempt to deal with such boundaries. I begin with their description of how they come to recognize their racialized status: their experiences of racialization in schools, and how their phenotypic and cultural characteristics are used to articulate differences between them and whites in other arenas. Then I discuss how they are constructed as non-American, especially during periods of political conflict. This is followed by a discussion on how they attempt to subvert and negotiate these external constraints. This chapter shows how the interaction of global and local forces shapes some of their ethnic binds.

ETHNIC AND RACIAL BOUNDARIES

In her recent work on later generations of Chinese and Korean Americans, Nazli Kibria (2002) argues that the racialized ethnicity among groups such as Asian Americans has to be understood in terms of their participation in middle-class America. This chapter shows that this is true of South Asians as well. Objectively, South Asian Americans are like middle-class white Americans; the participants in this study were either in college, building white-collar careers, or already working in a variety of upper-tier professions. Yet, it was also clear that their participation in mainstream institutions leads to their racialization: all of them described a series of incidents in educational settings and in other public places that made them aware of their "difference" from their white peers. They described both overt exclusions based on reactions to their physical appearance as well as more subtle forms of exclusions, such as denigration of "their" cultures, especially during the formative high school years. This process of marking them as different and inferior maintains the distinction between who is included within the white "mainstream" and who is not. This is the main difference between them and any white-ethnic group: the latter do not encounter high social costs of racialization. Unlike the South Asian Americans, white-ethnic groups can practice a voluntary, individualistic form of symbolic ethnicity. The South Asian American experiences of racialization also show their lack of fit with any existing racial category. Many of their experiences are similar to the experiences of middle-class blacks. Like other Asian Americans, they are often constructed as foreigners, but what is marked as their foreignness is different from what constitutes foreignness among other Asian Americans (Kibria 2000). Thus, they are placed in racially liminal positions.[1] They have to balance these contradictory aspects of their lives in order to negotiate their ethnicity. As they try to avoid being drawn into racially inferior positions as Americans, they also have to prove their Americanness.

Racial Labeling and Other Exclusions

This section illustrates three aspects of South Asian American experiences to show how they are shaped by the external reactions to their phenotypes. First, individuals' early encounters with racial labels during their elementary or junior high school years make them aware of "their race." Second, a number of other incidents through their school and early college years reinforce their non-white status. Third, the ideological construction of desirable masculinities and femininities, which uphold racialized and gendered phenotypic distinctions between them and their white peers, further contribute to the ongoing sense of their difference.

AWAKENING TO THEIR RACIAL STATUS. Most South Asian Americans mentioned a series of early encounters with racial labels that made them aware they were not Americans like their white peers. Given the middle-class backgrounds of their parents, they attended mostly white schools. Here, the meanings attached to their phenotypic characteristics set them apart from their peers.

A sampling of these experiences in school illustrates these boundaries. Soma, who attended a nationally ranked public school in Connecticut and graduated with outstanding credentials, and Deepa, who graduated as a valedictorian of her school in upstate New York, are both physicians. Both were born in the United States and have built the kind of white-collar, professional careers that are often valorized as "models" by the media. They both described early encounters that defined their racial status:

SOMA: I remember I was once walking down the corridor in elementary school and this really popular and cool kid, called me nigger. The other kids just laughed. I was devastated; I did not know how to protest. But incidents such as these have stayed with me for all these years.

DEEPA: I had a real identity problem [when I was young]. From the time I was in fifth grade, [through] junior high, the girls and boys used to refer to Rina [another South Asian American in the school] and myself as black monkeys.

While most of the South Asian American youth were labeled black, a few were labeled "Spanish" or Native American. The demographic of the school seemed to matter. Varsha, who was awarded a prestigious scholarship to attend a university in her state, had grown up in a suburb that was also home to middle-class, black families; thus she was not the only "non-white" student in school. Samina, in contrast, lived in an overwhelmingly white, affluent suburb.

VARSHA: But I think I am [not just] American because of my skin color. I mean it is a racial element, and just the way I look . . . because you know when people look at you they look at your physical appearance and they look at your skin color. . . . Like a lot of people, they thought I'm Spanish, something like that. So it's kind of different. . . . I'm like no, I'm not Spanish. And they're like, what are you? And I'm like Indian, you know. It's so awkward to even be classified like that.

SAMINA: I realized my physical appearance differed from the majority of those children around me around first or second grade. It seemed the white male children had a problem with me, but not the females, I don't remember the females being part of this. These males mistakenly thought Indian was Native American. So they would dance around me making a chanting noise. It may seem silly now looking back, but as a child it can be devastating and detrimental.

Peers were not the only ones involved in constructing such boundaries. A few teachers have been part of the process as well. Amit, a senior in college, described an incident in elementary school: "I was in the AV section and the teacher, she wanted volunteers and I was the first one, and she was like I don't want a brown boy bringing in the TV/VCR. When I told my parents, they said that since we were new to the country I had to learn to turn the other cheek."

Even though much of the ethnicity literature has assumed that the "color line" disappears with increasing integration, the experience of these South Asian Americans indicates otherwise. Kibria's (2000) argument that the boundary of whiteness is contingent upon the marking of Asian Americans as non-whites seems to be validated through these descriptions. The labels attached to appearances, irrespective of specific national origin, reflect attempts by the white children to "place" South Asian Americans within the contemporary American racial framework: if an individual was not white, he or she had to be black (or occasionally, Native American or Latino).

As I mentioned in the last chapter, the parents of the South Asian Americans benefited from the Civil Rights movement because they were able to move to the suburbs during a time when native minorities were still struggling with structural impediments such as residential, educational, and occupational segregation. In the relative absence of a variety of minority populations, the South Asian Americans became "the racial minorities" in these places. The lowering of structural barriers—at least to the extent that immigrants with high levels of education acquired in other countries could access more middle-class jobs and buy homes in the suburbs—was not accompanied by deeper changes in inter-group relations. The South Asian Americans experienced the social costs of such racial boundaries as they were growing up.

Such incidents of racialization have remained etched in these participants' minds. Some of them explain their sense of powerlessness as they were ascribed a master status—the racial status that is predominant in others' eyes—over which they had no control. Akash, who was completing a joint MD/MBBS degree when he was interviewed, elaborated on his frustrations:

As for feeling like an outsider, I felt more when I was younger, much, much younger. The first time I was called "nigger," it was funny because I didn't know what it meant. And it was more in the third grade when people started swearing, because first and second grade no one really swore. In the third grade people started swearing . . . and someone mentioned it to me offhand in that it meant a piece of shit. So I was like okay, you know, fine then you can be a nigger too and I was talking to a white person. . . . And he said no it's because you look like a piece of shit, that's why you are a nigger. And he pointed to his arm. And I spent the whole day, even next, going whoa! I couldn't tell my parents because you weren't allowed to swear in front of your parents. So I'm like I can't say the word, can't tell them someone told me this. And I had to figure out [what this meant], you know, I went to the dictionary and, I was like, "people from Africa?" And I'm like huh? I'm like how does that become me? You know when I look back now I was the only person of color in that school . . . so I couldn't tell any teacher, I don't remember there ever being a teacher of color in my elementary school. And I couldn't tell my parents, so I told my younger brother. So we were like, there must be a word to call white people back. And there wasn't. You know you can look as much as you want, you can pick up maybe this word and you look for it in a dictionary, and you're like no that does not work. And it's a sort of frustration that you just have because there's nothing you can do.

Akash's descriptions closely correspond to the experiences of other racialized groups whose identities are determined by other people's perceptions (Bonilla-Silva 2001; Wu 2002). A key theme in "mainstream" middle-class socialization is the encouragement given to young people to take charge, to "develop a sense of self-confidence, initiative, autonomy" (Rose 1997, 477). Like other minorities, the inability of the South Asian Americans to define themselves in the same racially neutral terms as their white peers, emphasizes their marginality. Raised in middle-class immigrant households that emphasized the "personal achievement" aspect of the American dream, they hitherto operated, often unconsciously, on the assumption that their middle-class status made their racial position irrelevant (Rudrappa 2002). Living outside ethnic enclaves meant that their own friends were white, which reinforced their sense of their lack of difference from white peers. "Considered by the strong sense of individualism inherent in American society, [this] inability to define oneself is the greatest loss to liberty possible" (Wu 2002, 8). Thus, these experiences of "being racialized" have stood out starkly in their minds, because they illustrated the gap between their early taken-for-granted ideas and the reality of their marginalized status. And, as Amit's testimony indicated, for many of them, their parents' inability to understand their racial status in schools exacerbated their frustration and inability to address the situation.

These racial boundaries that define South Asian Americans are critical to how they frame their ethnicity. Not only are they not able to practice symbolic ethnicity, they have to actively deal with their racial marginalization. Their structural integration leads to their specific type of racialization.

CUMULATIVE ENFORCEMENT OF A RACIAL MASTER STATUS. These early encounters at school are not isolated incidents. They were often reinforced through experiences outside school. A sampling of their answers illustrates the varied situations in which the South Asian Americans confronted racialization. Akash, who previously expressed his frustration with racial labeling, Vani, a young white-collar professional, along with Rajeev and Akshay, two college students, described some of these encounters.

AKASH: My parents felt that in the neighborhood, kid's parents treated me differently. My mom tells this story. She said, "you used to come home here to get a drink of water and go to the bathroom. But when your friends came here I would give them Kool-Aid and they could use the bathroom. Why did you always come home for that, why didn't you go there?" . . . and I'm like "I don't know." And it's true. I can remember that when I was in my Filipino friend's house I had no problem using their bathroom.

VANI (who spent her early years in another country): My sister moved to a very high-end area in New Jersey and I am used to hearing I am the nanny or the cleaning lady. I've been finger-printed at the bank, double ID'd, my driver's license wasn't enough, then I'd get my passport, and after that they made me put a finger print on that check. To cash a check for my sister that is only $350! That is completely insane! In H___ you feel more like New York . . . it's a diverse city and I love the fact that I'm not followed in the grocery store and people asking why are you here. And that has been my United States experience, I have been more aware of the color of my skin than anywhere else in the world.

AKSHAY: Many parents will say "I am not a racist, I give money to all these groups," but it is a different story when I go to pick up their daughter for an event.

RAJEEV: One thing I have noticed though that if I drive a car in D___, I get pulled over, while if I go in my friends' car and they're white and they drive through D___, they don't get pulled over. And I just find that really annoying. But that's the only thing I can think is noteworthy.

These types of encounters, in school and outside, cumulatively reinforce the boundaries between South Asian Americans and middle-class whites. Even though these were not daily encounters, they seemed to happen, according to the pattern of their statements, with sufficient regularity. Incidences, such as being mistaken for the cleaning lady, being racially profiled, being stopped while driving through town, or encountering negative reactions/behaviors of friends' parents, closely resemble the experiences of middle-class blacks (Cose 1993; Essed 1991; Feagin and Sikes 1994). Along with the racial labels, these incidents construct a distinction between South Asian Americans and other Asian Americans. Prativa's statement at the beginning of the chapter, as well as the incidents described by other South Asian Americans, attest to how South Asian Americans and other Asian Americans experience different kinds of racism.[2] At the same time, they do not see themselves as black, an issue that is discussed in greater detail later. Thus the intersections of institutional and interactional definitions and behaviors and South Asian Americans' understandings of themselves as not black, yet "not really Asian American," position them in a racially liminal position. This ambiguous position and uncertainty of racial belonging has significant consequences, as we shall see later in this chapter, in how the South Asian Americans negotiate their ethnicity.

GENDERED EXCLUSIONS. The ongoing exclusion experienced by participants in this study is reinforced by their peers' construction of hegemonic masculinities and femininities. Unlike the racial epithets or discriminatory incidents they experienced episodically during their school years, these American teenagers felt marginalized, in a more sustained way, because they did not fit the phenotypic norms of "desirable" masculinity and femininity prevalent in their social circles.

Scholars like Dworkin and Messner (1999) point out that contemporary hegemonic masculinity—the "top rung" of a gender hierarchy which ranks all

other masculinities and femininities as subordinate—is based on the valoriza-
tion of physical strength and athletic prowess among males. Among adolescents, this translates into the attractiveness of "large, powerful, masculine
bodies" (Dworkin and Messner 1999, 343). Fortified by today's extensive marketing, especially through teen media outlets, these images act as symbols that
claim men's aspirations (Messner 1992). This is also a racialized form of gen-
dering: in the media African American male bodies are depicted as uncontrolled and dangerous, while smaller Asian American bodies are designated as
weak and effeminate. In this hierarchy of masculinities, South Asian American
males are different (and subordinate) from whites, blacks, and even other Asian
Americans, who are viewed through the lens of Fu Manchus, or Yellow Perils
(Espiritu 1992; Hamamoto 1994).[3]

The hierarchical boundaries between "normal" and subordinate masculinities are often maintained through aggressive behaviors. Nutan, a male
software engineer, mentioned he had been severely beaten up when he was
around twelve years old. More common were boundaries created through
constant ridiculing and stigmatizing. Among the older males in this group,
being labeled as gay was one way of marking the "nerds" from the "real males."
Akash pointed out that the inept, undereducated, unintelligent, pathetic character of Abu on the TV cartoon series *The Simpsons,* supposedly based on a
Bangladeshi immigrant, provided a popular source of mocking and taunting,
a trend that was confirmed by Kibria (1998). Religious symbols were also a
source of ridicule. Sikh males, who wear turbans as public symbols of their
religion, often faced additional harassment as "diaper-heads," "cabbages," and
other derogatory labels. In her interview, Leela described the experiences of
her brother:

> My brother, well, he wears a turban and we actually brought it up to him
> and asked "if you had the opportunity, would you want to cut off your
> hair?" . . . and automatically he was like "yes" . . . he feels like he is singled
> out here because he is the only Sikh person in school, and his school is
> like 98 percent white American. And I think for him too, he's just, like his
> personality as an individual, he's very quiet and he takes a lot of stuff too.
> He's taken teasing from other students before. My parents had to go to the
> school and he feels like, "Why me? Why do I have to be different?" He's
> like, "I hate it," he's like, "I don't like having this on my head and going to
> school." He's like, "why can't I be just like the other kids?" And, you
> know, I understand how he feels.

Certainly bullying and harassing are not confined to South Asian American males alone, but, for them, it works in specific racialized ways. Not having
a great deal of South Asian American representation within the school's student body means that the labels used against one of them frequently became

the descriptors for most of them. This was exacerbated by the fact that to many of their peers, they all looked the same. Mallika, who had to constantly protect her younger brother from such harassment during high school explained that if the cool group set their mind to intimidate and ridicule these males, by calling them wimps or weird, then such categorizations were quickly adopted by other youth as well.

Connell (1995) has argued that in the contemporary information society, males who control technology and knowledge, that is, the white-collar technocrats, occupy a hegemonic status. Given their trajectory of educational achievements, many of the South Asian American males went on to participate in these types of masculinities (providing fodder for the stereotype of the male "Asian technology whiz"). But during the school years, phenotypic distinctions, expressed through the ideological constructions of desirable types of males emphasized their effeminacy and lack of attractiveness.

A large corpus of gender scholarship has documented how the construction of hegemonic masculinities maintains the intersecting race, class, and gender hierarchies between groups. The "feminizing" of men of a race group contributes to the inferiority of the entire group (Bonilla-Silva 2001; Collins 1991; Mullings 1994). In this hierarchy only "white men are endowed with masculine attributes with which to attract the Asian women" (Espiritu 1997, 95). Since masculinities and femininities are relational concepts and only have meaning in relation to each other, the marginalization of South Asian American males means that females are also marginalized by association.

Like males, females are subject to their own set of pressures. For females the pressure to attain standards of beauty inflict a feeling or need either to be like whites or to project an exoticized, sultry image intended to make them desirable to the "normal" males. In junior high and high school, the norms of beauty are most often based on whatever is typical of whites: light skin, greater height, certain body types, shapes of legs, etc. While several South Asian American females commented during their interviews that recent trends of an increased presence of brown-skinned models in the media, or of Indian women winning global beauty pageants, have slightly eased these "ideals," they still experienced the "white is right" attitude during their early school years. Maya, a junior in college, along with several others, pointed out, "I went to school with Caucasians and I hated being different. No one treated me differently but I hated it. You know about the beauty thing, how girls look at magazines, and I'd look and I was like no one, and I was like 'no one will like me.' I can't describe how much that hurt me, I wanted to be beautiful like my friends and I could never be that."

She also described how many of her friends confessed to bathing over and over again with soap in order to wash themselves "clean and light."[4] Deepa, the physician, who had been labeled a black monkey in school, explained how she tried to fit in with the prevalent gender norms by making every effort to "look white": "Later, when I was twelve, I thought I could do something about how I looked, so I convinced my mother to let me get a perm, to become fashionable. But the hair stylist ended up creating these intense curls, perhaps to fit with my dark-skin, I don't know. What I do know is that among my peers it had exactly the opposite effect than what I intended."

The fervent attempts to be like their peers led several females to work out all the time. Mala, another South Asian American female, said that "I have hips . . . I used to work out all the time" in order to attain the white norms of beautiful bodies. Later, in college, as she developed a circle of friends that included blacks and Latinos, she came to understand that "it was alright to have hips."

Female perceptions of how they were viewed by the opposite sex in forming their first heterosexual relationships in school brought norms of masculinity and femininity into sharp focus. Many females described how they struggled with their "lack of desirability" and feelings of isolation.

SAMINA: Incidents took on new forms of racism as the years progressed. At one point in time I began to look at myself in the mirror from a new angle, and I began to recognize my ethnicity that was clearly visible through physical appearance. . . . I recognized my darker complexion, my ethnic features prevented white boys from taking any interest in me and the very few minorities that were in school were the only ones who would even think of approaching or showing interest in me. In a social setting as in C___, children are raised and conditioned to believe in white as right and anything different is unacceptable and wrong. I can go on with examples of such experiences, but my point is that one can only imagine all the emotions, ideas, and conflicts that flowed through the minds of a child as he or she struggled with issues of race, religion. Such conditions would not have existed in such extremities if I had been brought up amidst minorities. It was only when I was in college, I came to an environment in which a good number of minorities, blacks, Hispanics, Indians existed, and guys began to approach me all the time.

For many, this divisive "color line" persisted in college. Shanthi, a high school teacher, recalled how disillusioned she was when her college roommate, after encouraging her to meet white males, said that she personally would never consider dating someone of Indian origin. Namrata, a university scholar, shared a similar story:

There is a feeling of racism but not in a mean way. It's just like my first roommate and she was American, she was telling me how when she was looking for a guy but how she would just not consider anyone but a white person . . . in general there is this feeling that you will naturally associate with some people and things like that. Then when you are different from everyone you look for something different. . . . And I have so much behind me, that makes me feel so out of place . . . [for example] one time I went to a frat[ernity] party and I was the only Indian person there and no one like spoke to me. Maybe people were less comfortable speaking to me or they didn't want to and I was like this is no fun. But when you are with Indian people you all want to talk to each other. You don't feel so out of place.

Irrespective of what the personal motivations of the white peers may have been, the South Asian Americans clearly experienced these incidents as cumulative. They had been labeled before, and such incidents simply reinforced their earlier experiences. Despite their own expectations of being fully integrated into their white peer groups, these gendered and racialized cues regarding desirable physical appearances and "appropriate" dates act as powerful boundaries between the South Asian Americans and their peers.

In an insightful statement, one of the females who was involved in the *Bend It Like Beckham* discussion, remarked that the news of Parminder Nagra (who played the role of Jess in the movie) being signed up for a role as a physician in one of America's most popular primetime television shows (*E.R.*), was very welcome to her. This meant that she would finally view someone like herself in a role that reflected South Asian American reality, rather than being represented as a cartoon caricature all the time, or not seeing South Asian Americans at all. A few others explained that in high school they rarely thought consciously about these boundaries: at the time the standards seemed normal and inevitable, and their lack of fit was the problem. These ideologies "justify, support and rationalize the interests of those in power: they tell a story of why things are the way they are, setting out a framework by which hierarchy is explained" (Mullings 1994, 266). And, from the vantage point of the South Asian Americans in this study, these exclusions often seemed to be the normal way of constructing life; and, in this scheme, they were forever outsiders.

Overall, the racial labeling and other exclusions contribute cumulatively to the boundaries that South Asian Americans encounter in mainstream arenas of life. Because of their lack of easy fit with the existing race groups, they are viewed and treated as representatives of a variety of race groups. These practices reinforce their racially liminal position. They pay the costs of racial marginalization; at the same time, they are not consistently identified with a "native" racial group. This lack of fit is further enhanced by their supposed un-Americanness.

Fractured Americanness

While many of the racial boundaries described in the previous section define these South Asian Americans as racial minorities according to the structures and ideologies extant within the nation-state, additional mechanisms, often developed in response to global events, also lead to their local status as "foreign" and un-American. The construction of foreignness is also based on phenotypic and cultural components. There are widespread beliefs about "the" phenotypic characteristics of "Americans," and they do not fit that image. Also, since many South Asian Americans tend to look similar to the Middle Eastern population, political conflicts with the Middle East, rather than economic conflicts with East Asia, appear to increase incidents of hate crimes against them.[5] In addition, a series of over-generalized, non-modern traits, and cultural practices are attributed to these second generation individuals. Then, these incommensurable cultural practices are used to mark the ideological boundaries between them and the white mainstream. This construction of foreignness as a form of racialization is very similar to the experiences of other Asian Americans (see Kibria 2000). However, the white mainstream chooses different sets of cultural elements to mark each group as foreign, which exacerbates the perception of the difference between South Asian Americans and other Asian Americans. These local perceptions are influenced by global events so that the interaction of global and local interests is configured as racial boundaries in South Asian Americans' everyday lives.

BEING LABELED AS FOREIGNERS. Like racial labeling, the ascription of foreignness, as Samina's statement at the beginning of this chapter indicates, arises in everyday encounters. All of these participants were asked similar questions. Some also reported "stray" incidents such as being asked to return home "to your own country." Unlike racial labeling, many of these questions about place of birth appeared more "benign" and "natural" to many South Asian Americans; a few had said that since their parents were recent immigrants, it would take some time for "the common person on the street" to think of them as American.[6] However, others like Samina also began to resent and speak out against the constant pattern of questions that emphasized their lack of fit within popular notions of Americanness.

Such "common people's perceptions" of Americanness in terms of whiteness and even black and white, is widely disseminated through the global media. These images then frame how South Asian Americans are regarded in other countries—as non-Americans. As children of middle-class parents and as young professionals, most of the South Asian Americans in this study travel to different nations for education, formal volunteer work, employment, and tourism. Eleven out of the forty-eight participants in this study had lived in other countries for at least three months.[7] Another four had lived abroad for much longer periods of time. While all of the participants had visited their parent's countries of origin, close to three-fourths had traveled to other countries as tourists. There they also experienced ambiguity as "brown" Americans. Anjali described how, when she traveled in different European countries, the tour guides generally asked "where are you originally from?" *after* she had stated she was from America. The steady positioning of herself as "not quite" American continued to emphasize her liminality. The experience of two other participants revealed this same notion. Both had lived and/or worked in other countries for a few years. One of them had lived in an African country where her father had been sent for work. In her perception, people did not take her seriously because of her brown skin and her gender, and she felt that some might have disrespected her because they thought she was "Indian," at a time when Africa had experienced a recent history of expelling Indians. Her only claim to her Americanness was based on the facts that they had "American cars with United States [aid organization] on them," and that she went to an international school. Back at home, she dealt with the "same double standards": no one really thought she was American, and simply assumed she was a foreigner. Another female provided a similar view. Her involvement with some research projects brought her to two Asian countries. While stationed there, she had to constantly negotiate her position as a brown American with a white husband. She said that while she was in an Asian country, she frequently encountered the gendered color line: people were willing to accept white females in supervisory positions, "even though they thought the white females were very inappropriate in their behaviors. They [white females] were given plenty of space. I was not." Furthermore, her "American" husband, a white male, was automatically respected, while she was not. She had to expend a lot of effort to negotiate her position, but felt overall that the representation of "American" as "white" emphasized her liminality and negatively affected her ability to work.

INCOMMENSURABLE CULTURES. Aside from the constant questions emphasizing their differences, South Asian Americans are constructed as foreigners in the United States through the assumption that they have some deep-rooted un-American cultural customs and tendencies.

In the previous section I mentioned how their structural position as "the minorities" in the suburbs allowed others to define the boundaries of whiteness. Another structural shift in the United States—toward multiculturalism—also emphasizes their outsider positions. With the rapid spread of multiculturalism in schools, these young people were frequently called upon to explain the cultures of other nations. As individuals, they were marginalized through their contribution to such multicultural programs, because people assumed they had special insights into other countries in ways that made them different from their peers. It is important to note that along with this expectation of "automatic knowledge" about other societies and their cultural practices, what the South Asian Americans were supposed to explain is often already defined for them according to commonly held stereotypes of "alien" practices. So they rarely receive the opportunity to exercise their agency in defining what they thought to be relevant for understanding these societies and cultures. Here, too, they were deprived of the power to define the situation.

Torres, Miron, and Inda (1999) have pointed out that the new structure of multiculturalism, even though it appears to recognize the multiplicity of cultures within humanity, creates a "set of symmetrically opposite counterpoints (binary opposition one might say), that of the national and citizen on one side, and the alien, the foreigner, the stranger, the immigrant, on the other" (1999, 9). The foreign practices are constructed as pre-modern and traditional, a key counterpoint based on which the modernity of American culture is defined. As "native informants" of these non-American practices, South Asian Americans are caught between fulfilling the role attributed to them and not having the power to challenge the framework that was imposed upon them. The two following statements illustrate this bind. Rajeev, a Hindu, came to the United States when he was three years old. In discussing his sense of being different from his American peers, he mentioned his discomfort about how people perceived and spoke of India: "Like, you know many people would say stupid things about India that was completely untrue and say 'oh yeah this is true.' You know, but no serious racism or no institutional racism, but you know some of my classmates might be extremely stupid and I would just recognize that and it didn't really affect me."

In a similar discussion about feeling different, Ranjit, a Sikh male, described how adults would draw on stereotypes and engage in culturally racist practices while appearing to be culturally sensitive:

> Whenever, like in the 9th grade, we were going through a chapter about India in history class and everything, every cultural topic, he [a teacher] would ask me if I could explain a little more about it. And it was like, they were talking about yeah, well, some regions have, like men have two wives. And yeah, maybe [Ranjit] can tell you more about that. And that was like, that does not make any sense. And things like that, I was expected to explain. Which was like, in my power, as much as I knew, I did. But, like, there was a lot of stuff that I was not even aware of.

Whether or not such practices, like polygamy, actually continue, or are sufficiently widespread to merit the "Indian" label, is not part of this discourse: the controlling ideological mechanisms define how certain cultures should be understood. Scholars such as Gilroy (1993) and Balibar (1991) have pointed out that assertions about the biological bases of race have become somewhat suspect at the end of the twentieth century. Designating people as different is increasingly based on arguments about incommensurable cultures. Hence, these practices that are used to create these differences are often based on dichotomizing modern vs. traditional cultures, independent vs. subordinated individuals, secular vs. fundamentalist tendencies of groups, and ultimately the difference between American and foreigner, distinctions that are evident in Rajeev and Ranjit's statements.

Religion is another source of constructing exclusionary boundaries. Several South Asian Americans referred to newspaper reports of how a large organized Christian group went about vilifying their religions—Buddhism, Hinduism, and Islam—as religions of darkness (Grillo 2001). While a few of them felt this might be yet another attempt to gain publicity for this particular organization, the wider rhetoric about the United States as a country built on Christian values places them in outsider positions: they are constructed as potential recipients of civilizing influences rather than people who actively construct the secular character of the nation through their lives and achievements.

A few South Asian Americans mentioned being teased about weird customs such as "worshipping" cows or fasting during Ramadan. South Asian American Muslims provided the clearest indications of long-standing discourse about their religion as fundamentalist, pre-modern, and detrimental to American interests. Samina explained her long experience of prejudice and discrimination when she was interviewed in 2000: "When I was young there was prejudice against my religious background . . . now when I tell people I am Muslim there is a feeling of fear, there is negativity. First they'll think terrorists, then they'll think Farrakhan . . . what they know is through the media, other countries are made out into very bad people." Several South Asian Americans, of various faiths, explained how these mainstream discourses affected them. Referring to a series of widely publicized books like Huntington's *Clash of Civilizations* (1996), they described the development of a popular discourse about their innate tendency to put religious identity above national identity. There was a widespread assumption that because of their religious affiliation they lacked or had extremely weak loyalties toward the United States. Echoing the statement by Nobel Laureate Amartya Sen (2001), they argued that this ideological fragmentation of their identity into religious versus national identity (for example, Muslim versus American) simply did not reflect who they were. Such homogenous and all encompassing religious norms are also supposed to promote anti-American values such as subordinating women. Consequently, the South Asian Americans felt that they were forced to defend their religion actively, and this conscious effort makes religion more significant (though not in ways described by the critics) in their everyday lives.

However, the gendered cultural imagery, mentioned often as a flashpoint of their "foreignness," was the subject of arranged marriages. This theme, embedded with implications about gender hierarchy, a lack of women's independence, and oppressive families, was pervasively used to emphasize the difference between the free and empowered American woman and the subordinate South Asian Americans. The imagery is based on the stereotype that the typical South Asian American female is one who is forced into arranged marriages and controlled through veiling, payment of dowry, and other customary practices. Samina, a Muslim female, and Alka, a Hindu female, explained:

SAMINA: I get "why don't you cover your hair?" "will you marry someone you don't know?" . . . I am aggressive, outgoing and independent, so hopefully I'll change their perceptions but I also get "maybe she is the bold one."

ALKA: Sometimes, to my friends, I'll say my parents are from India, so I am of Indian background, then they'll ask "Oh did they have an arranged marriage?" Many will be like "Are you here on a scholarship?" or "Is your marriage already set?" or "Will you have an arranged marriage?"

These stereotypical notions of arranged marriages placed South Asian American females in difficult positions because many of them expected to have an arranged marriage, although, as I describe in chapter 4, only two expected to have a marriage arrangement that fit the stereotype: marriage to a person sight-unseen. While the degree of choice was a point of contention within each family, they mostly agreed that the grim picture of total subordination conveyed by the arranged marriage stereotype simply was not true. There were clearly regional and familial variations of what "arrangement" meant.[8] Not surprisingly, the less their family norms fit the stereotype, the more vocal the females were about being irritated with these questions. Anjali, whose parents are from eastern India, argued, "If you think about it, the icon of a fairy tale wedding in the West is the Diana and Prince Charles marriage. It was an arranged marriage of a 17 year old girl to a man 20 years her senior. But somehow that was not seen as her subordination within an arranged marriage. For us, if a family member, rather than a friend, introduces us to prospective partners, it somehow becomes a symbol of all South Asian females' subordination."

In the previous section I described how the construction of subordinated masculinities in schools also affected the females. The cultural trope of the subjugated woman who is forced into marriage includes the idea about the inappropriate male who is unwilling to support the cause of individual autonomy, such as, in this case, a female choosing her partner independently. Thus gender inequality and lack of support for independence and freedom, are supposed to be the mark of the South Asian Americans' foreignness. Of course, South Asian Americans are not the only group that have been marked in this way in the United States; Glenn (2004), among others, provides a detailed history of other groups who have been similarly affected. Yet, South Asian Americans' lack of understanding of the more grounded historical framework of exclusions often means they see their experiences as unique and distinct from other groups.

The use of these images also illustrates the power of globally circulating imagery that are often resurrected for local usage. These stereotypes are reminiscent of the older colonial racialized and gendered rhetoric, which positioned South Asians as an inferior group (Oldenburg 2002; Sinha 2000).[9] Just as controlling ideologies reduced all black women to "mammys" or Jezebels (Collins 1990; Mullings 1994) and all East Asian women to Dragon Ladies or Suzy Wongs (Espiritu 1997), contemporary cultural racism frames South Asian Americans in terms of their tradition-bound, subjugated women compared to free and independent "American" women.

The racialized cultural boundaries are particularly effective because they emerge along with books and a media industry that also add pervasive stories, reports, and images about such subordination and subjugation of South Asian women. Even though the South Asian American females in this study built their white-collar professional careers based on their intellectual, artistic, athletic, and other special abilities, their master status was defined in terms of non-independence and lack of autonomy. As Samina mentioned, her qualities of independence and boldness are simply seen as her American side, something she acquired by her exposure to the United States, a distinction that has been documented by several other second generation females (Bose 1999; Mediratta 1999).

Mallika, who originated from India, pointed out that these selective images circulating through the media, educational channels, and other arenas have made everyone aware of honor killings and dowry deaths in South Asia. She said that few people know that women in South Asian countries have the highest rate in the world of being selected heads of states, the largest number of local legislators, or that they have comprehensive legal rights, such as paid pregnancy leave, a privilege women in the United States obtained only in the later years of the twentieth century.[10] South Asian women also have a long history of activism.[11] Mallika felt frustrated, not simply by these ideologically constraining images that circulate through the mainstream, but because most South Asian Americans do not know about these facts either; they simply accept the one-dimensional rhetoric about their subordination. More importantly, they rarely question this conflation of images of South Asian women with South Asian American women; instead, just as they had accepted the gendered exclusions in school, they often believe in their differences from "real Americans" and speak in terms of "what we do and what Americans do." As Bald has argued "the colonized learn limits which are both mental and physical . . . [once] internalized [they] instinctively know what they can or cannot do . . . thus their marginalization maintains the center" (1995, 111).

LOOKING LIKE THE ENEMY. Being widely viewed to be holding non–American traits can be extremely dangerous during periods of political crisis. United States foreign relations, especially in the Middle East, have often become the lightening rods for determining the racial status of South Asian youth in the United States. When other countries are seen as "threatening" to the United States, politically or economically, racialized individuals who look like "the enemy" to sections of the majority group are subjected to higher levels of discrimination and hate.[12] Becoming visible is akin to having a spotlight turned on members of the group. Those caught in the spotlight remember their vulnerability at being under a significant level of public scrutiny, while those who turn on the light do not hold the impression beyond the moment. Other groups have also been caught in the spotlight: the internment of Japanese Americans during World War II provides another example of racialization, categorization, and punishment, solely due to biological appearance and apparent, immutable cultural characteristics (Espiritu 1997).

Many South Asian Americans described earlier episodes of such racialization. Prakrit, a Hindu, who works for a multinational firm as an engineer, related his victimization during the Iranian hostage crisis. As several United States citizens were held captives in Iran for an extended period of time, all those who "look Middle Eastern" or had names that "sound" Middle Eastern, became a racialized group. He described how he was "mercilessly harassed" on the school bus. His last name was Shah (a very common name among people from Gujarat), so all attributes of "Muslims," personified by the term "Shah of Iran," were attributed to him, and he became the target of taunts, slurs, and attacks. Sumaira, who is Muslim, also echoed this over-generalization, when she detailed some of her experiences in 2000.

> Times have changed a lot, first of all, like if you asked me this question several years ago, I wouldn't have said this, but now because of this whole, um, terrorism and the Middle Eastern crisis with like the Middle Eastern countries, the oil situation, and all of the things that have been going on, the hijacking of planes, Saddam Hussein, it's like everybody—and especially the Palestinian issue that's going on right now. Everybody portrays Muslims as being so bad, and like they're fighting and they're all like I hear jokes all the time about like "Oh you know, you probably have a bomb in your basement or something" like, I mean, not being mean to me, but like as a joke you know. You're just talking, your friends are sitting around and they'll say that.

Sumaira's statement points to the forms of racialization Bonilla-Silva (2001) describes as the new racism. While more individuals recognize the overt taunts as racism, the "jokes" leave the target with a feeling of being victimized, without understanding the underlying cause or how to express her resentment. Since the "Muslim" designation applies to a broad swath of phenotypes, irrespective of country of origin or actual religious affiliation, all South Asian Americans are vulnerable to this social classification.

The aftermath of the terrorist bombings of the World Trade Center illustrates some of these vulnerabilities. Sikh males, whose religion requires them to wear turbans, became (more) visible in the public eye, given the constant media depiction of the 9/11 terrorists as bearded, turbaned males. Even though Sikhs had no connections to "the terrorists," they became targets of several hate crimes. Some radio stations fomented trouble by referring to Sikhs as "cloth heads" and "diaper heads" (*News India Times,* 2002, 10). The first man killed in retaliation of 9/11 was a Sikh male. The killer was quoted in police reports, saying "all Arabs had to be shot" and wanting to "slit some Iranians' throats" (*St. Louis Post-Dispatch,* 2001, A-10). Ironically, the Sikhs who had been targeted as "Hindoos" earlier in the century were now targeted as Muslims. Among the participants in this study, a second generation Sikh felt sufficiently beleaguered to leave college and seek the safety of (his parental) home. Along with the Sikhs, Hindus, Buddhists, Christians, Muslims, and Zoroastrian South Asian immigrants and their children experienced a series of hate crimes for looking like "Middle Eastern terrorists."

Both males and females of Muslim, Christian, Hindu, Sikh, or other faiths, described how they became acutely aware of their surroundings and their vulnerability to attacks from any one in any place. Mallika, who is of Indian origin and not Muslim, reported that she and her partner took it upon themselves to drive to a nearby gas station where a young Muslim youth worked the night shift. She explained how her fears for her partner, "who could be mistaken for Middle Eastern" were extended to include this young man who had been "given a hard time" by many "established" customers. Several other Muslim South Asian American youth also expressed their concern about the heightened vigilance when they were in public places. A Muslim female described how she felt paralyzed with fear the first time she went to the grocery store; she felt that everyone stared at her. After that she could not bring herself to ride the subway in a large metropolitan area for sometime. Many South Asian American females were advised to stop wearing "Indian" clothes for a while; others, like Shaheen, asked their mothers and other acquaintances to refrain from wearing saris or *salwar kameezes* (a two-piece ensemble with a long, shirt-like top over drawstring pants, usually with an additional length of fine material that is draped over the upper body or over the head) because they feared for their safety (see also Khanna 2001).

While the popular discourse on racism often portrays hate incidents as the work of undereducated, working-class youth, the events since fall/September

2001 have involved a greater cross section of people.[13] Shaheen, and a few other participants in this study, reported hearing racial threats on campuses from female students. Suhani, a freshman in college, mentioned,

> People are really ignorant, and they don't bother to find out anything before they say things. Like in my senior year in high school, September 11 happened and a couple of months later this teacher said something like all Muslims are terrorists. And I'm like "don't classify me as a terrorist, do you know its people like you who make us look bad?" Lots of students don't know any better. But a person like her that I looked up to and I respect should recognize what's going on and not label me a terrorist because I am not. And to say terrorism is a part of Muslim culture! It made me so upset that she could say that and she teaches 900 students. If she could say that to me what could she say to the others? And after I made that comment she quickly changed the subject, but she never said she was sorry.

Some structural changes made during this period added to this sense of being pushed into a zone of non-Americanness. The United States instituted a special registration for males between the ages of sixteen and sixty-five who arrived on tourist visas from selected countries including Pakistan and Bangladesh.[14] Two of the participants had grandparents visiting during that time, and they expressed a great deal of frustration about this extra scrutiny. Although one was of Indian origin (which was not a group required to register), and the other of Pakistani origin, they both described how upset they felt to realize how these laws stigmatized their family members as "potential terrorists." One participant of Bangladeshi origin pointed out that if this was an attempt to identify nationalities (rather than religious identities) of accused terrorists, Saudi Arabia and several European countries should be included in this "black-list" register, rather than Bangladesh, which was not connected to any terrorist action. Thus, the broadly defined "watch list," based on the political understanding of Islam, was extremely troubling to these young people, because of what that implied about their position as Muslim (or non-Muslim) Americans in the United States.

Racial Exclusions and Ethnic Binds

The various types of exclusion described in the previous sections affect South Asian Americans cumulatively. Along with racial labeling and profiling, their supposed non-Americanness acts as a bind, restricting their ability to practice their ethnicity in ways of their choosing. This section begins with a description of how such racialization affects their ethnic choices. The first two testimonies illustrate their inability to claim Americanness and the dilemmas of adopting religious identities.

Mallika described an incident that occurred in October of 2001. She was working out in a gym with a friend when a young white male came up to her friend and said threateningly "you look like you could be Osama bin Laden's sister." Her friend tried to explain that she was an Indian, not Saudi Arabian. Mallika realized, even though she and her friend were Americans, this was no longer relevant to the conversation. She felt they could not say they were American or South Asian American. Emphasizing their Indianness, with its association of a mainly Hindu identity, seemed to be the only way of proving their non-threatening character. She later reflected that their responses denied Pakistani and Bangladeshi South Asians the right to use their parents' country of origin as a safety shield in a similar situation. In the emerging discourse about Americans and aliens, where aliens were regarded as bearers of innate and incommensurable cultures, being "Muslim" American was no longer a safe option for her. Given her appearance, the "alien" designation with its implication of a Hindu identity appeared to be the only rational identity for her to pick. Thus she was pushed to privilege one aspect of her identity and submerge others, precisely at a time when she was also being asked to prove her loyalty as an American. Place of birth and citizenship became completely irrelevant to this process of racialization.

Another type of ethnic bind was narrated to me by Shaheen, a Muslim female of Indian origin, who had been very active on her college campus as an anti-racism activist. After the World Trade Center bombing many hate crimes were directed against all those who "looked Muslim"; some people Shaheen worked with on progressive issues on her campus, decided to start a *hijab* (veil or scarf or similar head covering used by some Muslim women) movement. Their flyers explained that this was an effort to stand in solidarity with Muslims and South Asian women. Shaheen described her sense of discomfort and alienation as this symbol was adopted. As a child of Indian Muslim parents, she had never worn or even considered wearing a hijab. She felt that the adoption of the hijab privileged Muslim identities of countries such as Saudi Arabia, and wiped out the diverse backgrounds of Muslims from different parts of the world. The adoption of this symbol is particularly inappropriate because South Asian American Muslims make up 32 percent of the Muslim population in the United States, followed by 27 percent African American Muslims and 26 percent Muslims of Arab origin (Zogby Polls 2001). This last group is more likely to use the hijab, even though there are variations in that group as well (Murphy 2001).

Although Shaheen realized the hijab activists had good intentions, she became very concerned as she watched the more conservative Muslim student groups on campus become the spokespersons for "the Muslim community" as they thanked the activists publicly for adopting the hijab symbol. Even though she and others like her had long been active on campus, their voices were drowned out in this re-invention of cultural authenticity. People like her were constructed as being too American. Shaheen felt very torn between wanting to protest a backlash against people who looked Middle Eastern on campus and not wanting to be part of a movement that reduced her to a cipher. She also expressed that, if she wore a hijab, she would have been in a much more vulnerable position on the streets. So she became "a victim who required protection," while the activists who started the movement became "the enlightened protectors," and were lauded in the local press. The only way she could exercise her agency was by trying to convince the organizers about their "lack of judgment." Like Mallika, her sense of powerlessness and inability to define the situation constrained her agency.

These two incidents, like the themes described in the previous sections, illustrate that South Asian Americans have to emphasize multiple aspects of their racialized identities in order to traverse the racialized terrain of their lives. Neither of these women could claim to be American. In the first case, being American did not absolve Mallika from potentially being Muslim (and therefore a "terrorist"); in the second case, being American meant Shaheen could not represent the "authentic" cultural voice of American Muslim women. Thus their stories reveal how their ethnic options are shaped by these situated constraints and how South Asian Americans have to be able to draw upon many ethnic layers to negotiate their positions in the United States.

NEGOTIATING ETHNIC BOUNDARIES

As they described the many ways in which they were racialized, the South Asian Americans also indicated a variety of strategies they used, individually and collectively, to address their marginalization. This section describes how South Asian Americans negotiate some of the racial boundaries they encounter: they are not only shaped by external ascriptions, but they attempt to change and reshape some of the meanings and content of their ethnicity. I begin with a discussion about the mediating role of racial knowledge. Then I look at the emergent patterns of ethnicity.

Racial Knowledge and Ethnic Options

A number of scholars have described how racial minority groups collectively reconstruct their ethnicity as a way to challenge their stratification in the United States: all the pan-ethnic movements began in this way (for example, Espiritu 1997; Padilla 1985). However, as the previous sections illustrate, for racially ambiguous South Asian Americans, it is not always clear which groups they belong to and on what basis they might be able to develop new ethnic networks. Two more study participants, Aishwarya and Pranata, expressed this feeling of being in-between groups. Aishwarya, of Nepalese origin, who grew up in a university town, holds an administrative job in a university, and Pranata was a student at the time of the interview. Both expressed this feeling of liminality:

AISHWARYA: I always had a difficult time getting on and defining with a group. I mean, I always got along with most minorities but I am not really them, so I am sort of an outcast. I don't belong to the white group. I am not part of the Spanish group because I am not Spanish. I am not really black. So I am really stuck in the middle. You don't belong to the Indian group because you are not really Indian. I don't know whether this is a racial issue that they are forcing on me, or it's just my opinion but you know you don't belong anywhere in that sense.

PRANATA: Being South Asian and growing up in the United States opens up some issues. In my college there is a big issue of diversity and unconscious racism, and one of the big organizations is the black students' organization and they had all these posters about how we need more minority students. But, in my head, I always moved myself with the white majority and in a way it disturbs me that I do it automatically. I am also a minority, but I don't know if I am black.

As Pranata explained, having grown up in the white suburbs, their lives had been segregated from other racial minority groups, just like their white peers. So they rarely developed networks with other minorities during these earlier stages of their lives. Scholars, such as Espiritu (1992) have pointed out that the reconstruction of "collective histories" is often of central importance for bringing together groups that were "previously unrelated in culture and descent" (1992, 3) to form pan-ethnic linkages. The organized efforts increase interaction among previously unaffiliated groups and develop a common understanding of cultures (including histories) that they have in common. At the same time, their coming together provides "real content" to the racialized boundaries that demarcate them as "the same." The coming together of "Asian Americans" or "Latinos" as pan-ethnic groups in the United States (see Espiritu 1992; Padilla 1985; Wei 1993), or black and Asian groups in England or the Caribbean (Anthias 2001a; Gosine 1990; Modood et al. 1997; Sudbury 2001) illustrates similar processes.

A key factor in this process is the construction of a racial knowledge frame (Merenstein 2003). This frame can promote or inhibit the construction of ethnicity in certain directions. With little knowledge of the racial histories of different minority groups (except slavery and the Civil Rights movement), South Asian Americans like Aishwarya and Pranata generally do not see any commonality with the other minorities, especially with blacks. In fact, several South Asian Americans felt that they did not encounter the kind of deep, ongoing discrimination experienced by black and Latino Americans.

Consequently, they did not feel they could claim they were similar—people of color—since the levels of discrimination they encountered were so different. So their choice was to either actively affiliate with other Asian Americans, or to privilege their ethno-national identities within the boundaries of non-whiteness.

The discussion in the earlier sections illustrates how the South Asian Americans in this study rarely saw a connection to Asian Americans; in fact they often bought into the same racialized notions of how Asian Americans are seen among whites. Thus, not surprisingly, they privileged their parents' or forbearers' countries of origin and picked "Bangladeshi" or "Indian" or "Nepalese" or "Pakistani" as significant descriptors of their identity. Even those participants who generally did not think they encountered racism, and who may have migrated from outside the subcontinent, picked these ethno-national identities. Sumi is an interesting example of this group. She moved to the United States from England when she was thirteen years old. I interviewed her just as she was graduating from college:

> In England there was racism, oh gosh definitely. I mean like in England there was a recession and so you needed someone to blame so you blame the Asians. So we were there while the recession was going on and a lot of Indians were targeted and a lot of groups like the National Front and the British National Party, they are racist groups you know . . . and they are looking for someone to blame and if you are an Indian gal or an Indian guy you are a target. Again it is like racial slurs and once, like, I was even chased off a bus and it was scary, you know. I was twelve years old then, running off from two 18-year old guys, I ran down the street and hid so they lost me, but it was scary. . . . Here it's completely different. I've not even seen race as an issue here. I'm not saying it doesn't exist, I just haven't experienced it. . . . When I came to the United States everyone was intrigued because I was from England, so I was into a lot of groups but not into any particular set. You also don't know what people like so I moved around a lot. . . . If someone asks I say I am Indian but I am also British. In England you know there is a lot of racism, so I say I am British but not English, my skin color will tell it all. I live in America but I am not American. . . . In school, there were no Indian groups and your friends can make you feel different. Like I'll go to friends' houses and they'll slip up and say something like "Oh we are not like those people, you know, we are different." And you realize that you are different.

It is interesting to note that while she did not see race as an issue in the United States, Sumi defined herself as Indian first, before she tried to work out the balance of her Britishness (based on twelve years' experience) and Americanness (based on ten years' experience). Her inability to claim Britishness and Americanness lead her to emphasize her Indianness.

Researchers, such as Baca Zinn (1994) have illustrated that as macro-social processes racialize groups, families play crucial roles in teaching children about racism, and thus resist, or at least mediate, the internalization of the messages. However, South Asian families, like other Asian American families described by Kibria (2002), rarely appear to socialize their children about racialization. Instead, "there is a widespread tendency to see Asian American families in narrowly cultural terms—rather than influenced by structural features and arrangements of the society of which they are a part" (Kibria 2002, 41). Thus, their own ideas about where they fit in along with their family emphases lead South Asian Americans towards emphasizing their ethno-national identities.

The complex migration history of this group also contributes to the disengagement with racial structures in the United States. The varieties of racial knowledge and racialization experiences South Asian parents bring from other countries complicate the issue of South Asian parents' understanding and construction of their racial position in the United States. For instance, South Asians are "black" or "Asian" in England (Black Sisters of Southall 1990; Gillespie 1995; Modood et al. 1997), and "banyani" in Tanzania and a range of other marginalized "non-black" races in African countries (Joseph 1999). On the subcontinent, nationality is usually equated to race (Kibria 1998; Robb 1995). Since many of the participants in this study had family members spread over several countries, these multiple classifications complicate their understanding of their social positions within these transnational spaces. As a result, emphasizing their subcontinental origins seemed to be the chosen way of situating themselves across these multiple structural contexts.

Scholars have described how immigrant groups, like West Indians, assert their transnational cultural identity to avoid the stigma of being associated with poor African Americans (Fernandez-Kelly and Schauffler 1996; Foner 2001). For South Asian Americans, labels that acknowledge their transnational affiliations fulfill the same purpose: they can void "being black" if they emphasize their non-U.S. roots and networks. In fact, among the discussions about racial awakening, Amit mentioned how his parents asked him "to turn the other cheek" when he reported how his teacher singled him out inappropriately. These types of reactions underscore parents' attempts to disengage children from what happens locally.

However, more politicized South Asian Americans understand that such labels do not necessarily resolve the tensions surrounding their "foreignness" in the United States. Nor does it solve their marginalization as non-whites.

And they are active, especially through their college years in building pan-ethnic bridges across color lines (special issue of *Amerasia Journal* 2001).

In College and Beyond

Unlike their high schools years, when most of the South Asian Americans were among the very few minorities in the school district, in college, for the first time, they met several people of color. They were able to explore relationships and develop networks across groups of color. Most found the presence of other South Asian Americans in the public sphere comforting, and formed networks that reached far beyond their parents' regional culture, religiously defined, or nation-of-origin networks. Many, among the more ethnically defined youth, developed relationships with other people of South Asian origin.

Others begin to actively breach the boundaries that held them marginalized in high schools. Mala, who had previously explained how she came to terms with her physical appearance once she developed a circle of black and Latino friends, is a case in point: she began to understand different standards she could adopt in learning to appreciate her beauty. A few others, like Samina, found that there were people of color who were interested in dating them. For instance, four of the South Asian America females were in long-term relationships with black men and another was married to an African American. Among the others, one was married to a white male, and two others were engaged to whites. Hence, the rigid boundaries they encountered earlier in school had become somewhat permeable within the dating scene. While the line between whites and non-whites did not disappear (as earlier statements about dating indicated), now the South Asian Americans had more options about who to date, since multiple notions of desirability coexisted with white norms. Most stated that they were more comfortable having a wider circle of friends (of different races) than the networks based on ethno-national identities alone.

The more significant negotiations, described in detail by the South Asian Americans in this study, surrounded their relationship with other Asian Americans. In post–Civil Rights America, most colleges have begun to set up ethnic "cultural" centers. Many of these centers have a specific mission of serving "their" populations, for instance, serving the Asian American population and creating awareness about an Asian American heritage. At least two of the colleges that some participants attended had such centers which were engaged in developing pan-ethnic Asian American consciousness among the different nation-based groups. Some South Asian Americans were drawn to these efforts. Additionally, colleges provided them with new opportunities to study Asian and Asian American histories, arts, literatures, and other aspects of the lives of different "ethnic groups." Such knowledge can help build the framework necessary to develop pan-ethnic networks. At the least, such knowledge often supplemented the lack of family socialization I mentioned earlier.

Even though several participants in the study mentioned they had checked their race category on college applications as "other" and had written in their ethno-national affiliation, some of them shifted from that position and now saw themselves as Asian American. Thus, as colleges and universities have become new arenas for negotiating ethnicity, becoming Asian American becomes one of the many choices.

However, the choices are still set within the racial framework that guides South Asian Americans outside college. For instance, Connecticut is somewhat unique among states with Asian American populations, as Indian Americans alone make up the largest group, numerically ahead of Chinese Americans who are apt to be the largest group in most other places. Yet, several Connecticut-based South Asian Americans felt the Asian American centers were not "their spaces" because they continued to think about Asian Americans according to the mainstream "East Asian" phenotypic framework. Some simply dismissed such "race-based" alliances, saying they found little in common with people of East Asian origin. Abha, a sophomore in college, expressed her uneasiness in the following way: "The term Asian is very broad. Sometimes when I am at this place (an Asian American center on campus) I feel Asian is not me. I think stereotypically of Asians as Chinese, Japanese, Vietnamese. I told someone about going to Asian-nite and they were like but you're not Asian."

Other South Asian Americans developed affiliations with these centers. A few explained that it helped them become familiar with the similar "Asian" family norms, irrespective of whether a person was Korean, Chinese, or from a South Asian country. One individual who was dating a Korean American felt they both respected each other's efforts of balancing their family cultures and their Asian Americanness. A few others described how they became aware of the common Asian American histories through courses they had taken in college and the programs they were involved in. At least eight described their connections to the Asian American label in terms of a political identity. Shanthi explained, "[A]nd something about China comes up, you know, and you're always going to find those people who are Indian saying 'Well that doesn't concern me, I'm not Chinese.' Well, if you're going to fall under the Asian category and come together as a whole it does concern you."

Over the years, there has been a change in how Asian Americanness is constructed via these centers and community-based organizations. One "older" South Asian American female, Hema, who grew up in New York, described how, the first time she went to a pan-Asian event, she felt completely out of place. She went on to point out the degree to which things have changed:

Now there is a big furor, you know, about the South Asian thing. Lots of frenzy around including South Asians in the Census and everything because of the figures, I mean, every pan Asian group is working it's tail off basically to make sure there's South Asian representation . . . it's been remarkable for me to see what's happening . . . the Asian American Studies Programs have to pay attention to this group . . . [even the] Asian American Studies Conference used to get like one in five or six South Asians, now there are so many panels on South Asians.

Despite her observations about the increasing inclusion of South Asians, Hema felt that Asian America still did not centrally accept Hinduism and Islam as part of its religious mosaic. The Asian American identity, according to her, was still "too Christian." Nonetheless, the explicit attempt to include South Asians may influence the trajectory of South Asian Americans differently in the future.

The affiliated South Asian American youth explained that their contacts with other Asian Americans through college led to creation of another layer of ethno-racial—Asian American—identity, that they would "unpack" as needed. As they explored common histories, especially the similarities between the Japanese American internment based on their supposed disloyalties to the nation in 1943 and their own situation, they began to build the interpretive frameworks that attribute marginalization to structural causes rather than their own failures. Along with the development of these pan-ethnic identities, which challenge the constructions of their racialized position, they seem to build a series of political collaborations on campus on issues affecting people of color. Thus, in conjunction with the overt Asian American layer, these affiliations created a submerged "person of color" identity. Akash, who had been "a regular" at two such centers, said that he would consider himself both Indian and Asian, ethnically, and was very active in a number of multiracial issues in his career as a physician. Another male, Faiz, said he felt closer to a community of color and his Pakistani American identity had become less relevant, mainly because of what he had learned through his experiences with such a center. Shaheen, who had described the "hijab incident," was also among those college students who had become involved in activism to challenge racism against all groups of color. Clearly, new racial knowledge has led to this development of other layers of ethnicity among this group.

On the whole, however, the majority of the South Asian Americans in this study had weak or no links to the Asian American organizations. Part of the reason simply is a structural one. Not all colleges have the centers or the courses that help create a racialized framework promoting pan-ethnicity.

However, even on campuses with such offerings, many South Asian Americans simply concentrated on developing friendship networks across national affiliations with other Indians, Pakistanis, Bangladeshis, and Nepalese. While Asian American individuals tried to build both a South Asian presence and develop links to "Asian America," the latter group spent their energy working across religious and national boundaries to build a "South Asian" or "desi" identity.

Desi is a Hindi/Urdu term for South Asian native, a label reflecting both a difference from the mainstream and other established communities of color. As Sunaina Maira (2002) describes the emerging urban desi culture, in the presence of other South Asian Americans, these youth begin to publicly remake and perform their cultures. The construction of this new ethnicity represents both a pan-ethnic dimension (that is, creation of an ethnicity across four national identities), which arises from their specific racialization, and an attempt to exercise their ethnic options by choosing what kind of cultures to emphasize and at what points of their lives.

This desi ethno-racial position symbolically combines parental notions of their children being people with specific country affiliations, while it avoids the pitfalls of being specifically Pakistani, Indian, Bangladeshi, or Nepalese, with their notions of what should be their ethnic culture within the structure of their lives in the United States. For the South Asian Americans in this study, the lack of prior networks of color, their uneasiness about what it meant to be Asian American, and the realities of the racialization they continue to face in their everyday lives, simply made it easier to congregate with "others like themselves." As Rehana, a female of Bangladeshi origin, clarified, having a "desi" circle meant that she did not have to constantly explain herself and her views of the world to anyone—not to her white peers nor to her parents. In effect, those who began to assert a desi identity said that, unlike their parents, their ethnicity was inclusive of Indians and Pakistanis, Bangladeshis and Nepalese, "because we are all the same."

Not all South Asian Americans take on this desi identity as their primary identity. Those who did not embrace the desi identity usually rejected it because of the specific cultural emphases that are merging. While I discuss this issue in chapters 5 and 6, it is important to note that what they were rejecting was a particular combination of music, movies, fashions and a greater north and west Indian and Pakistani emphasis. They felt their own cultures and world views had no place in this emerging culture. However, those who reject this identity do not appear, at least among these participants, to embrace their specific country-of-origin-type affiliation alone. Often, in the course of their conversations, they would explain that what they were rejecting was the emerging desi culture, but they actually worked hard to maintain ties with other South Asian Americans, irrespective of their specific country of origin.

Thus, though in somewhat rudimentary form, two overlapping ways of resolving the contradictions of their liminal positions appear to be emerging among South Asian Americans. One form emphasizes the American desiness, across the several nations of origin, the other builds multiple additional layers, along with South Asian Americanness. The second position is illustrated by Faiz's statement:

> Many labels are appropriate right now. Earlier, in high school, it was Pakistani. There I would say Pakistani American. To a person like yourself who is educated and South Asian, I would say South Asian, but I wouldn't say it to you if you were educated and you were white. Then I'd say Asian American or American of Asian decent. Where were you born, it doesn't mean anything, it's where are you most at home. I don't know I'm more comfortable with South Asian deeply. I see it as an outside perspective when I read books like [Vijay Prashad's] *Karma of Brown Folk,* and stuff it's like that. I can relate to that but as an outsider looking in. I can see how it happens but it's not my whole life. There is this constant juggling back and forth. Especially through my work now. I work at youth work. At a conference where they are talking about South Asians I can relate more to that than East Asian. Growing up in Hartford, which has a large Puerto Rican population is different from growing up, say in Enfield. Certain issues are being brought together. But I know I've related better with African Americans and Jamaican Americans than I have with Anglo-Americans. The constant struggle with me is who do I affiliate with and it is constantly changing, it's never constant.

Given the various tensions that Faiz tries to balance, the only type of ethno-racial identity possible for him is this multilayered one that changes with the situation while it engages multiple structural margins.

Overall, this discussion of how individuals attempted to negotiate their ethnicity indicates that South Asian Americans add additional layers to their ethnic identity while they are in college. These layers provide a way to disassociate themselves from their marginalized position within the all-encompassing white middle-class framework. They are able to exercise their agency to choose either a more culturally defined desi or a more instrumental South Asian American identity, or even to construct a combination of the two. They also have opportunities to form larger political affiliations with other Asian Americans and diverse persons of color to collectively challenge many of the boundaries that are common to these groups. This bridge building and activism makes them more conscious of their history as Americans. Although the multiple layers are tied to a series of structural constraints, maintaining these layers allows them some individual "choices" about which sets of layers they can emphasize and in what context. At this point in time, as larger numbers of South Asian Americans become adults and shape their ethnicity, they are building varieties of multilayered ethnicity in response to the extant social structures.

CONCLUSION

The main focus of this chapter was to describe the reasons why the South Asian Americans in this study chose a hyphenated identity. Their accounts show the different types of overt and covert racial boundaries that structure their experiences, and place them in racially ambiguous positions. In spite of being part of middle-class America, in terms of their residences, education, and professional affiliations, they are consistently "marked" as non-whites and as non-American. The hyphenated labels they use, at least the non-American part of the label, are reflections of these realities.

The pervasive, ongoing experiences of racialization also illustrate that we cannot simply assume, as the segmented assimilation model indicates, that maintaining ethnic group networks arises primarily because of rational economic motivations of the group for getting ahead in society. While those reasons may play a role in why individuals maintain some types of ethnic group networks, the sense of powerlessness that the South Asian Americans expressed repeatedly, indicates that we need to look beyond the motivations of ethnic groups. Many of the experiences that the South Asian Americans narrated appear to fit the predictions of the racialized ethnicity model. They clearly experience racialization in ways that are specific to their position within the mainstream institutions and they appear to be negotiating pan-ethnic and ethno-national group identities. Indeed, as later chapters show, there are increasing collective efforts to develop these ethnic identifications.

However, the meanings of these hyphenated labels also encompass influences other than racialization in the United States. The racialized ethnicity model does not, as yet, systematically consider the effects of participating in global networks and segmented consumer markets. As the next few chapters illustrate, these are also important influences on their choice of hyphenated labels. As racialization processes and the consequent negotiations shape their experiences in the node, the transnational field contributes further to the construction of their ethnicity: these multilevel processes influence the left and right sides of their hyphenated ethnic label. As I illustrate which layers of ethnicity become salient and how South Asian Americans negotiate these layers in the next few chapters, it will become evident that we have to go beyond nation-based influences to fully understand the ethnic experiences of groups like the South Asian Americans.

In sum, this chapter showed the crucial role racialization plays in keeping the South Asian Americans "ethnic," in spite of their integration in terms of residences, education, and related facets of their lives. Their experiences of racialization lead them to negotiate multilayered, fluid, and dynamic ethnicity. The common "more pan-ethnic" layer becomes relevant to the second generation of Bangladeshi, Indian, Pakistani, and Nepalese Americans because they are affected by broadly similar processes of racialization. The convergence of local and global processes influences their experiences, and they, in turn, draw on multiple sources and contexts to fashion their ethnicity.

CHAPTER 3

Maintaining Meaningful Connections

Samina (speaking about her visit to India): It's great to be among people who look like you.

Namrata: Family, they're always there for you . . . if I was in trouble, my uncle from Australia would get on the plane and he would be there for me.

WHEN SOUTH ASIAN AMERICANS like Anita, who was quoted in the last chapter, spoke of "having culture," they generally referred to a subset of cultural practices. These are marked through external ascription or racial stereotypes to construct the boundaries between them and their white peers. Since the "marked" culture arises within the structural context of the United States, along with the marking of phenotypes, Samina's comment above shows how individuals use their experiences in other places to try to disengage from the racial ideology (about the normative white standard) prevalent in the United States. Namrata's comment indicates another dimension of their ethnic experiences: South Asian Americans participate in family networks across several nation-states. This global dispersion of families is related to the migration histories I described in chapter 1, but more important to this discussion is how their transnational family ties influence their ethnicity. This chapter demonstrates that the participation within these transnational family networks is not based on any essential cultural traits. South Asian Americans have to creatively weave resources available from such transnational networks (along with balancing the challenges that arise from such family participation), in order to balance their Americanness and South Asianness. I show that South Asian Americans actively use their transnational family networks to subvert and challenge some of the racial constraints they encounter in the United States. At the same time, their social position relative to these other structural conditions influences how they think of themselves in terms of hyphenated labels.

Rather than focusing on the private sphere of the nuclear family in the United States, I follow feminist scholars who have suggested we look at the intersection of the "public" world of laws which govern the movement of people of various nationalities to different countries, and the "private" world of families for understanding the experiences of individuals in immigrant families (for example, Ferree 1990; Kofman et al. 2001). Using the South Asian Americans' descriptions of their families—which encompassed members beyond the nuclear family—I discuss how and why they maintain such memberships, along with how their ethnic options are affected by their membership in this transnational web of relationships. Apart from speaking about aspects of their cultures that were marked as "un-American," South Asian Americans asserted that their way of "doing family" was culturally different from other groups. Being part of transnational family networks implies *they* are able to emphasize their ethnicity in specific ways, including their ability to claim that their family connections are deeper and more sustained than many other groups. Like many other immigrant groups and their children described in the transnational ethnicity literature, their ability to use global communication and information circuits to manage geographically dispersed networks allows them to mitigate some of the effects of being non-white in the United States and other countries. They are able to transcend some of the structural constraints they encounter in maintaining family connections or celebrating family events, by reconfiguring their lives within a more global context. Thus, transnational family networks are a critical resource in this process of negotiating forms of ethnicity across countries.

Although some of the transnational literature suggests that individuals can easily move between countries to configure their lives as transnational villagers (Levitt 2001), this chapter shows a different picture. The second generation is structurally positioned differently from their parents in the United States and these other countries, and they encounter a series of other structural constraints that act as additional ethnic binds.[1] In other words, this chapter shows that transnational spaces are not neutral contexts; South Asian Americans have to contend with social structures in all the countries which make up their transnational horizons. These structural constraints make them realize the limits to which they can claim the non-American part of their ethnic label. In the last chapter we saw that South Asian Americans privileged their ethno-national identities in order to balance their nuclear family socialization and their racial liminality in the mainstream. In this chapter I show that far from recreating the cultures of their ancestors through their participation in family networks, to develop this ethno-national layer, the South Asian Americans are sifting and selecting cultural practices to reconstruct them in ways that best fit their lives within these multistructural contexts. My analysis includes a discussion on transnational weddings and how this emerging "cultural" form illustrates some structural and cultural dimensions of South Asian American ethnicity. Overall, this discussion shows that their participation in these extended family networks makes them feel American along with providing them with new resources to build up their ethno-national side.

TRANSNATIONAL FAMILY FIELDS

Although the South Asian Americans in this study describe their experiences in other countries as "private" family affairs and focus primarily on relationships within families, their individual accounts illustrate how national and global politics impinge upon these family experiences. As I present their interpretations of their difference from their white peers based on the type of family they belong to, who makes up their family, as well as their "cultural" understanding of family closeness, I show how structural influences channel such understandings. Their descriptions indicate a pattern of nodes and fields that constitute this network: the nuclear family is the node and located in the United States, but the extended family is a field of relationships. The grandparents, uncles, aunts, cousins that play an important part in South Asian Americans' lives are spread across many countries. To South Asian Americans these family fields serve as sources of identity, acceptance, and support. Thus, South Asian Americans attempt to maintain meaningful connections with this larger, transnational network.

In this next section, I highlight two facets of such globally spread family fields, which are important for this discussion. Both facets illustrate the nature of the transnational context and how it influences the experiences of South Asian Americans. First, the multiple nationalities of family members affect the ability of South Asian American kin to easily gather for visits and family celebrations. Extra effort involved in arranging visits clearly sets this specific family structure apart from those families within the United States, whose grandparents and other significant relatives are not subject to similar restrictions. Second, the ongoing reliance on technology, punctuated by periodic visits, influences how South Asian Americans "do family," and this in turn influences their ethnicity.

Geographic Diffusion of Families and Related Nationality Issues

The family field of the participants in this study—the places where significant family members live—includes India, Pakistan, Bangladesh, Nepal, England, France, Germany, Middle East, Nigeria, and Australia. Some, as I mentioned in the introduction, had family members who lived in more than one South Asian country.

While the South Asian Americans in this study referred to these people primarily in terms of the family relationships, and conceptualized "doing family" across a transnational space, this space is not free from structural restrictions. The various nationalities (including citizenship status) of different family members affected their movement between countries. Thus, cousins from

England did not require a visa to visit family in the United States; but those from India did. Family who lived in different African countries often faced the possibility of having to travel to another country to get to a United States embassy for their visa. Just as the ease of travel by family members differs, depending on their location in particular nation-states, the length of time people from other countries can visit is also variable. While a six-month visitor visa to the United States was standard until 2001, the length of stay is now determined by embassy officials, based on the particular nation-state's position vis-à-vis America's security concerns, and the profile of the visiting person.[2] For example, the new registration laws for male visitors between the ages of sixteen and sixty-five from Pakistan and Bangladesh which caused so much frustration for some of the South Asian Americans in this study, are part of these new security measures.[3]

Nationalities of family members are also very important if they wish to migrate to the United States under family reunification laws. According to United States immigration laws, *family* is defined primarily as the typical United States nuclear family: parents and their children make up the family. Unmarried siblings and parents of the migrants (that is, aunts/uncles and grandparents of South Asian Americans) are considered to be extended family and have to wait for longer periods of time, even after the primary migrants (South Asian first generation immigrants) sponsor their migration to the United States. The waiting period of any family member varies by relationship and country, depending on the quota established by the United States. On average, Indian spouses of legal residents wait for a couple of years, versus ten years for unmarried siblings; a parent's waiting period can last anywhere between two and ten years. Married siblings of the first generation migrants cannot be directly sponsored for migration (that is, their parents have to sponsor them). If family members are British or French, then these waiting periods are significantly shorter.

The ability of South Asian Americans to move also depends on political relations between countries. As American citizens, they can freely travel to the European Union, but require visas to travel to all four South Asian countries. In India, as foreign adults, they are subject to special registration laws if they stay for over three months.

These differing restrictions contribute to the pattern of multicountry locations of family members, though small groups move between countries through protracted family reunification schemes (Kofman et al. 2001; Rex 1995). These multicountry regulations that restrict "spontaneous" or even relatively easy gathering of family members is one of the main reasons why the South Asian Americans have felt different from their United States–based peers. The participants repeatedly said that they could not "do family" in the same way as their peers.

DOING FAMILY. The geographical distance and multicountry restrictions on travel shape the nature of interactions of members within this family field. Given the dispersed geographic locations and the political conditions of travel, South Asian American families use a variety of mechanisms for maintaining connections with each other.

Cheaper telephone calls and airfares, and the rapid spread and use of electronic mail, facilitate ongoing communication in the family field. This situation differs greatly from earlier in the twentieth century, when migrants' letters took months to reach their families "back home." In fact, only two of the participants mentioned writing letters themselves, though some said their parents wrote the letters to which they added messages. Now, as communication technology becomes more accessible, it is possible to call countries in South Asia for less than fifty cents per minute on regular phone lines, even less using a phone card. Calls to Europe are often cheaper than in-state United States charges, so letters are being replaced with direct calls to loved ones. While all the families of the South Asian Americans in this study used e-mail in the United States (though the level of use varied among members), access to e-mail varied by location among family members in other parts of the world. Those in Europe and Australia had equivalent access, while those in South Asian countries had less. Class and age also played a major part in which family members in South Asia were likely to use the internet. Some of the South Asian Americans participated in e-discussion lists which include most people all over the globe and/or log on to chat rooms at pre-appointed times over weekends. More technologically adept family members exchange video clips, event pictures, and voice files (for instance, younger children lisping words). Most use a combination of methods.

There is an interesting pattern in how various technologies have broken down the "traditional" pattern of who stays in touch with whom. The bulk of the phone communication is by the parents, who then inform their children about what is going on with other relatives. But the narratives of the South Asian Americans show an increasing trend of *directly* staying in touch with selected members in the family field via e-mail. Calls are usually to closer family members (that is, cousins) in Europe. E-mail is generally preferred when dealing with places where there is a significant time difference, especially to South Asia or Australia, which are nine to fourteen hours ahead of the United States. Use of these means of communication also increases the "range" of conversations because of the ability to communicate with several people simultaneously. As Namrata explained,

[W]ith the internet and stuff we email each other all the time. My grandfather [in India] has it, my uncle [in Australia] has it, and my aunt in the Middle East has it, so all the news gets to everyone . . . with cousins in

England and here . . . birthdays and so on, family members will e-mail me. My mom isn't super efficient with e-mail so she used to dictate to my brother, but my uncle may say "so how are things?" and I will sit and write one long page on what's going on with us. I don't know whether it makes me feel more Indian but it is about being more close to family members.

Clearly, in this instance, a greater proficiency with technology creates new channels of communication between family members, overriding the age-based interaction repertoires that govern face-to-face meetings. The forms of greeting and address are more informal, and everyone in the family becomes responsible for communicating with others in the field.

The growing sophistication of technology also opens up different forms of "cultural" participation in family life. One participant, Anjali, described how her uncle had sent a picture of his forehead on the family mail-list to remind his cousin (Anjali's aunt) that *bhai-phota,* a ritual where sisters bless brothers, was fast approaching. Her aunt, who lives in France, replied with suitable wishes for all of her cousins. Knuckolls (1993) has described how South Asian cultures emphasize lifelong closeness of brothers and sisters (including cousins who are referred to as brothers and sisters) and these ties are ritually celebrated through the year. Yet, given their geographical dispersion, it is harder to maintain such rituals (if families do not resort to the standardized card and gift giving). For Anjali, this novel idea of virtual *bhai-phota* was appealing because it combined the technology she was most familiar with, and upheld her status as an "older sister" who could "bless" all her cousin brothers and all the younger children within the extended family. She realized there were endless opportunities for such virtual participation.

Depending on the financial position of the family, frequent travels to various countries—especially to South Asia where more of the larger family tends to be located—as well as visits by relatives from other countries to the United States, also facilitate the maintenance of closer and meaningful connections with family members. Among the South Asian American participants in this study, the average gap between visits to South Asia appeared to be between two and three years, although a few said they visited every year. These visits to family allowed them to not only spend "quality time" with certain individuals, but also to participate, even if only episodically, with other rhythms in life.

NAMRATA: I am so glad I have the opportunity to go back to Kerala and see what it is like, because it is so different from here . . . when I go to Kerala, there is a whole different side to life . . . life is so much more simple. We go out, we visit family, we stay with our grandparents so they are not running around all the time so I can take time and enjoy things more, to sit outside, my grandmother and I will walk outside and we'll go "the coconuts are ready" and something like that. I get to appreciate nature and it is a strong strong family bond.

This process of developing a familiarity and understanding of other's lives and a sense of sharing in collective experiences and a font of memories fortifies the bonds between these far-flung family members. The other ongoing forms of virtual participation reinforce this sense of "common participation" in family life. Set within the efforts of the first generation to provide regular remittances of money to support and care for the elderly, to cover expenses of family illness or family events, such as marriages, and rite of passage rituals, the activities of the second generation cumulatively reinforce a sense of very close family bonds.[4]

MEMBERSHIP IN THE FAMILY NETWORK. South Asian Americans' illustrations of these family ties raise a crucial question: Are these ties or connections based on virtual participation, weak ties? Are they mostly symbolic, that is, without any real influence on South Asian Americans' lives? On the contrary, the study participants demonstrate deeper and more ongoing ties. Their descriptions indicate the range of family members they recognize, their awareness of their position in this structure of relationships, and their familiarity with and adoption of the "ethnic" understanding of families. These indicators fit what are generally described as close-knit networks, even though network members are not geographically proximate (Wellman 1999).

Each of the South Asian Americans in this study—whether of Bangladeshi, Indian, Pakistani, or Nepalese origin—included people beyond parent and sibling units in their descriptions of "family." The most detailed chart was illustrated by Deepa. This former valedictorian, whose mainstream organizational memberships read like a "model American" dossier, was able to document a network of over fifty people, spanning the United States, India, England, and France. Similarly, another male of Indian origin listed forty family members across several countries. Other South Asian Americans indicated a variety of vital relationships (people they felt they could call on if needed), typically including grandparents, and a variety of uncles, aunts, and cousins. Frequently, they listed people in the United States first, then mentioned paternal and maternal grandparents, aunts, uncles, and cousins who lived in other countries.

These South Asian Americans generally used culturally specific terms to indicate these relationships (among kin and fictive kin) even if they otherwise claimed little fluency in their parents' native language(s). They were able to identify specific relations between people, and explained each person's fit within the network. Their descriptions of family closely resembled the understanding of nuclear families in South Asia (Purkayastha 2002a). Typical "nuclear" families consist of a couple and their children, the male's parents and unmarried siblings, and, sometimes, his married brothers and their families, as well as unmarried aunts and uncles. Other relatives—married siblings and their families, the wife's family, uncles, aunts, and cousins—who do not live in the same household, are also considered as part of the family. Indeed, all the major South Asian languages demonstrate intricate and nuanced family relationships that cannot be adequately translated by using English words such as uncle, aunt, cousin, or grandparent. For instance, a child addresses his/her aunts and uncles in ways that indicate whether they were their father or mother's siblings such as *mama* or *kaka, pishi* or *masi* in Bengali, one of the languages spoken among some Hindu Indians. They also have specific terms for identifying the age relation of these family members to their parents (whether they are older or younger), such as *jetha* or *kaka,* and they have the ability to indicate degrees of emotional closeness such as *pishi* or *pishimoni* or *pishibhai.* Irrespective of religion, which can influence the actual terminology within the same language, these intricate *relationships* seem to be equally important to all the nation-based groups. Selina, who is of Bangladeshi origin (where Bengali is the national language), pointed out how these relationships also interact with age hierarchies. Her mother's youngest siblings are closest to her in age and she enjoyed a very close relationship with them. She used a Bengali term that can best be translated as a "teasing type" of relationship. She felt these relationships could not be adequately captured by any English term, because a similar range of love, closeness, and duty that these relationships represented, simply did not exist as a social fact within the English-speaking world. Terms such as cousin, aunt, or uncle do not specify such a variety of nuanced relationships. As part of the English-speaking population and world, one could be closer to or more distant from a cousin, but there would be no specified degree of institutional recognition of "shades of cousinship" that are based on age, gender, mother's or father's side of the family, and other socially significant statuses.

On the whole, the South Asian Americans' descriptions reflected both their cultural understanding of such families and their participation in these networks. Along with their perceived difference from their "average American" peers whose salient family members live in the United States, this adoption of a cultural frame, that includes a wider set of members as "the family," is another facet of their perceived difference from their white peers.[5]

FAMILY FIELDS AND ETHNIC RESOURCES

Why do such relationships endure, despite the geographical dispersion of the family field? Historically, the institutionalized marginalization faced by earlier generations of migrants in multiple countries had led many South Asian groups to actively maintain family networks as one of the most significant sources of support irrespective of the country they lived in. As Rex (1995), Cohen (1997), and others have argued, such groups create internationally dispersed diasporic communities in which family connections are actively maintained, though often in modified forms (to fit their specific local needs), as a basis of resources for enhancing their local social locations. In many ways, a similar pattern is evident among the South Asian Americans in this study. Their statements indicate their reliance on their "family experiences" to mitigate some of the negative attributions used against them in the United States, and to develop alternative frameworks for disassociating themselves from such structures of marginalization.

Among the main boundaries the South Asian American sample described in the last chapter, were the negative meanings ascribed to their phenotypes, as well as the constructions of their "not-quite" Americanness. The participants in this study mentioned the geographical limits of American racial categorization: in South Asia they were not phenotypic minorities. They mentioned how they knew from extended family experience that the stereotype about their oppressive family cultures was not true. They also described having a greater range of supportive family members, and an increased awareness of the global horizons of their lives, as some of the main resources they draw on from their family networks. (However, the next section shows that they also become very aware of the limits of their cultural South Asianness.)

The Limits of United States Phenotypic Categorization

"Family fields" provide a major source of affirmation regarding the limits of the specifically American structure of racialization. While South Asian Americans in this study are not immune from negative racial categorization in Europe (as we have learned from the discussion on *Bend It Like Beckham* in the postscript of chapter 1, and the reactions of tour guides depicted by Anjali in chapter 2), their experience in South Asia are different. Most of the South Asian Americans mentioned that one of the key advantages to visiting any of the South Asian countries was that the people looked very much like them. They were not made to feel inferior or suspect in banks, hotels, streets, or other places they traversed in the course of their everyday lives, merely due to their general appearance or skin color. Two South Asian Americans provided a slightly different view about the reactions to phenotypes: one Nepalese American and one Bangladeshi American pointed out that those who looked "more oriental" were likely to be seen as "foreigners" in countries like India and Bangladesh. They became aware of this while visiting relatives, and when people on the streets assumed they did not know the local language. However, without the attendant political construction of themselves as "the enemy," these incidents did not seem to create any deep sense of frustration. Since family visits shield them from most other forms of classification and hierarchy prevalent in these countries (as I discuss later), the absence of American-style racial stratification is a significant source of comfort for these South Asian Americans. Overall, the pattern of these descriptions indicates that claiming part of an additional identity that does not lock them completely into American racialized positions is a strong incentive to maintain a hyphenated label.

REJECTING THE NOTION OF OPPRESSIVE FAMILIES. Another critical "ethnic resource" for the South Asian Americans in this study, was their perception of the role of their families in their lives. Since much of the cultural marginalization of South Asian Americans is based on stereotypes of arranged marriages and other such cultural practices, strongly suggesting the oppressiveness of South Asian families, they often draw on personal experiences to disengage from these controlling symbols.

Almost all of the South Asian Americans defined their extended family relationships in terms of greater closeness and an increased sense of mutual obligation. South Asian Americans, whether they were of Bangladeshi, Pakistani, Indian, or Nepalese origin, and irrespective of religious affiliation, emphasized these family ties.

ABBAS, A MALE OF PAKISTANI ORIGIN: For us, family ties come first.

PRATIVA, A FEMALE OF NEPALESE ORIGIN: I feel like there is a lot more stress on family and consideration on what you do for each other is endless. That's the major thing. Within the immediate family the devotion to one another is more intense, even within the extended family the love is endless, the duties are endless.

MALLIKA, A FEMALE OF NORTH-WESTERN INDIAN ORIGIN: In my family there is this huge push about extended family. It's like a village raising children. I have experienced it and I identify with it, it's a part of "who" I am. That unity of my family is a very typical South Asian thing. I too put a huge emphasis on that.

NAMRATA, A FEMALE OF SOUTH INDIAN ORIGIN: [F]amily, they're there for you all the time. If I had a problem my uncle will fly from Australia and he'll be there. There is a strong sense of responsibility toward each other. Even when we were in India the past year and my great-uncle was ill—he is my grandfather's brother, and his kids are in Africa—since we were there, you know, we were the ones staying in his house making sure he was well taken care of. . . . When your family will do that much for you, the least you can do is keep in touch.

VARSHA, A FEMALE OF WESTERN INDIAN ORIGIN: You want to keep family, even if you go your separate ways. . . . I have three sisters and we are very close and if I didn't talk to my sister for three months, that would be very weird. If you don't make time for it it would not happen. Like for us, if we didn't talk to family in India, how would you know what's going on? You were brought up to be a part of the whole.

REHANA, A FEMALE OF BANGLADESHI ORIGIN: One thing that I really admire about our culture is the central importance of family. That we don't just give up. We really fight as far as we can and see things through. If you can't handle something you are not alone. I have my parents and brother to help me through it, and I feel stronger. That is a major flaw in American culture.

These statements show how South Asian Americans draw on their transnational family experiences to create new interpretive frameworks. Several participants also described how, in the aftermath of September 11, 2001, they received anxious phone calls from all over the world inquiring about their well-being, as stories of hate crimes against Middle Easterners *and* South Asians received extensive media coverage around the world. During a time when they felt very vulnerable in public places in the United States, such phone contacts served as a source of additional support and comfort.

The near unanimous assertions of the South Asian Americans in this study about the positive aspects of their family contrast sharply with the pervasive rhetoric in the United States about families that are oppressive and about subordination of females.[6] The next chapter illustrates that this understanding of deep ties and mutual support does not inhibit their negotiation of gender, race, religion, and other boundaries that particular nuclear families try to impose upon them. Nonetheless, they are able to reinterpret families in more complex ways, moving beyond the unidimensional discourse of oppression. As Taylor and Whittier (1992) have pointed out, for any marginalized group, the construction of a positive identity means trying to withdraw from the framework of the dominant society while creating new self-affirming values and structures. Clearly, the South Asian Americans reinterpret what is used against them, reflecting on their own experiences as a standard for the rejection of the "oppressive families" stigma.[7] This redefinition often leads some South Asian Americans, like Rehana, to compare their families to that of their peers in ways that *their* families become the norm and those of their peers "flawed," a course that is not uncommon in building cultural nationalisms (Omi and Winant 1994).

GLOBAL AWARENESS. To show their difference from their white peers, at least a third of the participants interpreted these family ties and obligations in another way: they pointed out how interactions with this larger family network have kept these South Asian Americans *more globally aware.* South Asian

Americans like Amit, Namrata, Suhita, and others described this global awareness in terms of their perceptions of the consumer culture in the United
States, and their resistance to the pressures of consumerism which drives so
many American lives.[8] Others spoke about their global consciousness to show
how it influenced their decision where to live or work, in a context that
extends far beyond the boundaries of the United States. In the ordinary course
of their lives, this global awareness and thinking in terms of horizons that
extend beyond the nation-state emphasize their difference from their peers.
Pratibha explained how difficult it was to explain her position to some of her
friends, "He'd be like 'where do you see yourself living when you are older,
you see yourself living in America right?' And I'm like 'I don't think I want to
live in America all the time.' And he's like 'What? But this is the best country
in the world!' And I couldn't have him understand there's so much more to the
world than America."

A significant number of these South Asian Americans actually lived and
worked in other countries for periods longer than three months. Their family
networks frequently acted as resources in easing their lives in some of these
countries. Deepa and Soma, among others, explained how they worked in
some South Asian countries as part of their formal medical training, and as
physician volunteers to widen their own experiences of practicing medicine
in other places. In both cases, fictive kin who were in the medical professions
in these countries facilitated these arrangements. Even when they lived in
countries with no family networks, their long history in visiting several countries regularly, acted as "prior training for handling different encounters." In
sum, their experiences in the family field provided a resource for them in
thinking about global possibilities of their educational, volunteering, and work
lives.[9]

The participation in the transnational family fields positively influences
their ethnicity in many ways. Multiple facets of ethnicity are constructed
through their awareness of phenotypic "normality" in other parts of the
world, and in how they see themselves as American *and* culturally different
from many family members, while maintaining shared relationships of love,
support, and "deep ties" with family around the world. Along with their global
awareness, they use their transnational family experiences to "mark off" their
own versions of difference, and to build mechanisms for rejecting some of the
more racist interpretive frameworks used to maintain boundaries against
them. The similarity of these processes—the forms of racial boundary construction in the United States and the lessons learned from participating in a
transnational family field—are universal to all the South Asian Americans,
irrespective of their specific nations of origin. This "common experience"
makes it easier for them to come together at their colleges and universities as
"one group."

Balancing the Challenges

The transnational family field acts as an extended source of support and mutual obligation and it provides an alternative framework that South Asian Americans can use to address everyday cultural boundaries. But it also poses some structural challenges to their notions that as individuals of South Asian origin they are "all the same." At the forefront of these challenges is their ability to balance their perception of being "all the same" and the realities of the political conflicts between India, Pakistan, and Bangladesh (and the sometimes uneasy relationship between Nepal and India) that resonate through their families. The second challenge is that they also have to negotiate exactly how they are Bangladeshi or Pakistani or Indian or Nepalese.

SOUTH ASIAN CONFLICTS. In the discussion of the movie, *Bend It Like Beckham,* two of the three females spoke about the animosity between Indians and Pakistanis, and how they were socialized to reject each other. Within South Asia, the partition of the Indian subcontinent in 1947 led to an unprecedented level of migration in two directions. Hindus tried to cross to India and Muslims to West and East Pakistan. The history of families with relatives in these South Asian countries (initially India and Pakistan, and then later India, Pakistan, and Bangladesh) is intertwined with political histories of intercommunity violence and dislocation as each "religious" group moved, as refugees, across the newly created political boundaries (Nandy 2000).

Less recognized but equally important are the political schisms between Bangladesh and Pakistan. Suhani, a student of Bangladeshi origin, explained the reason:

> I was wondering about one thing. I was talking to my dad and researching the 1971 war between Bangladesh and Pakistan and I know India helped us win the war. But there was genocide. I was wondering why no one knows about it in the United States. I would have expected the United States to do something. When I read about Auschwitz and lots of people died. But nobody cares about Bangladesh. For me I am so surprised that a country can do a genocide, they killed them and slaughtered them. My father was in that war. That's why he came here. And I'm like "how can this get covered up and no one says anything about it?" Three million people, and they killed the intellectuals first. Not like anyone cares. Three million people in nine months that were killed. And you have the Holocaust and a complete genocide where 10 million people were killed in six years. Imagine if it [the genocide in Bangladesh] went on for longer. And nobody cares.

The histories of these conflicts continue to reverberate shaping their ethnic identifications in specific ways. Amidst the efforts of groups of South Asian

Americans to create a more pan-ethnic South Asian Americanness, some of these "family" histories intervene and emphasize their differences. The theme of animosity toward other religio-national groups is discussed in the next few chapters as well.

Larger political factors are also influential in molding their experiences when these South Asian Americans visit South Asian countries. Some of the South Asian Americans described how larger geopolitical issues impinged directly on their family lives. For example, while this book was being written, a participant contacted me again to tell me about an incident, which, she felt, captured some of the complexities of her ethno-racial identity. She was going to India, with her mother and her siblings, to visit her mother's family and to enjoy some sightseeing in different parts of India. When her mother went to get their visas, she was asked about her husband's original nationality. (All the members of this family are American citizens.) Since the participant's father was originally from Pakistan, the family went through an agonizing wait to find out whether they would get "permission" to visit their relatives in India! As a Muslim woman in the United States and particularly after September 11, this participant was acutely aware of her marginalized status in the United States. The new rule requiring (non-citizen) males from selected countries (including Pakistan), between the ages of sixteen and sixty-five, to register with the Immigration and Customs service was already in effect. Now she became aware of how, in a post–September 11 world, the United States was not the only country that was singling out Muslim men and Muslim families for special scrutiny. India's geopolitical problems with Pakistan were being expressed through the extra inspection of patriarchal family connections of Muslim visa applicants. For people who had family ties to more than one country, these political relationships of several countries essentially impinge on elementary activities such as visiting family.

Once she was in India, this participant did not encounter any negative incidents. Her phenotype did not mark her as an "alien" (as it does in the United States). If she was treated as an outsider at all, it was as a "Delhi-ite." Since people from Delhi are perceived as very "westernized" by people in other parts of the country, this level of outsidedness did not bother her at all. In fact she said she felt rejuvenated by this trip because she was able to connect to her family and really understand her heritage as she traveled to many Islamic (and other) historical sites.

Another participant, who is a Hindu, who had family in Pakistan, described a different type of marginality. Unlike the previous participant, she arrived in Pakistan during a time of political tension.

When we went to Pakistan for the first time, I was seventeen and my brother was fourteen, they had a fight. Some Pakistani fishermen had been captured by India and then released. So we got off the plane with them screaming "Pakistan Jindabad, Hindustan Murdabad" [long live Pakistan, down with India]. My brother and I didn't get defensive, but we knew we were not Pakistani, but my father is Pakistani but he knew we would not be on that side . . . and having the name I have, no one would call me in public. And my father's sister was like "I'll call you "Saveena," and I'm like "what?' And my mom's like "we are not going to scream your name in public . . . we were going to a market to shop for cloth," and I was like "what if you call me by my real name." But you know how the markets are open, and what if someone grabbed you, what would we do? With my brother they just used his term of endearment [which is not as religiously coded] . . . anyway it was all very confusing, because they'd call me and I would not answer. . . . I also have never been so stared at, so I went home and put on a salwar kameez [to avoid standing out].

While the political incident with the fishermen had contributed to the extra volatility of the context for the second individual, the general theme of political constraints these individuals have to face is clear from both stories. To the extent that national security and community boundaries are increasingly being expressed as religious identities, having family in more than one country becomes a problem. The second individual had to figure out how to merge with the crowd, change her name, don the local clothes to become less conspicuous in that place. Despite the difference in context, the outlines of this story are very similar to the experience of Mallika and her friend at the gym when they were accused of resembling Osama bin Laden's sister. Those females too had to figure out how to become less conspicuous.[10] In each case, these larger politics also made their religio-national identities more salient than they had ever been. It is also clear that these external influences often make it more difficult to maintain openness toward multiple countries; instead there is pressure to choose one or another affiliation, developing and hardening boundaries to create "essential" identities, where no such essentialism existed before.

These national politics influence the lives of South Asian Americans in one other way. While several European countries have allowed dual citizenship facilities to people of selected nationalities, countries like India are just beginning to offer similar political statuses to persons of Indian origin (PIO). The new political PIO status comes with new rights/privileges to hold property, to invest, and to access some of the premier educational institutions of the country.[11] India has proposed extending dual citizenship to people of Indian origin who live in the United States, Canada, England, Australia, Ireland, Finland, Netherlands, and Italy—subject to security concerns of India (Khan 2003). The other countries on the subcontinent are prominently absent from this list. The addendum regarding the security concerns—much like the new restrictions in the United States—is most likely to disproportionately affect people like Samina, who have families in more than one country, and are already marginalized in the United States due to their religious affiliation. This is not a new development, because a similar set of stringent restrictions was applied earlier against Sikhs during the 1980s movement for a separate Sikh homeland, Khalistan (Kishwar 1998). These forms of political restrictions on selectively defined ethnic groups act as additional hurdles as South Asian Americans in the United States try to construct pan–South Asian American identities.

Moving Beyond Essential Cultural Identities

Although both external ascriptions and family experiences strengthen the South Asian Americans' links to the South Asian part of their hyphenated identity, being part of this network does not solve the other aspect of their racialization, their social position as "not quite American." Their marginalization on the basis of their "essential cultures" in the United States as Indian or Pakistani or Bangladeshi or Nepalese is balanced by their experiences of not quite fitting these categorizations within the family field. Many of the participants in this study spoke about how people would automatically know, based on their clothes, apparel, and deportment that they were from a different country. So while they might resemble other South Asians in terms of phenotypes, they did not feel they were "the same." Their "extended families" often emphasize this distinction as well.

PRANATA: Even though here we are considered Indian, when I go back for a visit, everyone introduces us as American.

SHAHEEN: [W]hen I do something differently, they'll go "forgive her because she is American."

SUHITA: I used to say I am Nepalese, I am Nepalese, but I don't know if I said that because everyone told me I was. But when I went to Nepal everyone said I was American and I was angry because I thought I was Nepalese. But now I am really in-between Nepalese and American.

Suhita's frustration points to the complex ways in which external impositions of essential cultural identities have to be negotiated by South Asian Americans. All three statements indicate the extent to which they had internalized the idea that they were "Indian" or "Nepalese." Even though the motivation for such categorization differs, United States–based external ascriptions and nuclear families have pushed these South Asian Americans toward identifying with their root "cultural" identity. In direct contradiction to their encounters in the United States (or in other parts of the world), their experience in South Asia indicates that they are *American*. They are seen as individuals who, in spite of similarities of phenotypes, practice the culture of their nation of residence, in ways that make their practices different from the South Asian local practices of culture.

While these South Asian Americans asserted how they were culturally different from other Americans in how they "did family," they also mentioned how their extended family would try to impose different cultural norms, most often in terms of limiting their ability to "do their own thing." Family members, parents, and others, who wanted them to be accompanied by others when outside the homes, often opposed their decisions to go out by themselves, specifically if females wanted to stay out late at night. Confronted with these types of evidence of their cultural differences from South Asian natives, the ideological framework about their deep-rooted South Asianness in the United States no longer holds such powerful implications for South Asian Americans. Their participation in these larger fields with diverse interpretive frameworks forces them to reconcile these opposing categorizations of their ethnic identity. While they retain their ethno-national identity layer, it often tends to be fragmented. And, they develop an additional awareness of their Americanness that is salient in this context.

Apart from their increasing awareness of their Americanness, South Asian Americans are brought face-to-face with a variety of cultures in each country as well as their own position relative to these cultural mosaics. Choosing one particular culture as the main form of their ethnicity, a form that can be claimed as a "national" label—"I am Indian American or I am Nepalese American"—requires them to engage in creative ways with their ethnicity. Namrata, who spent several months in a course on classical dancing in a different state of India, explained, "When I go to Kerala, I don't notice how different I am, I am always with my family. And I understand the language, so it is no big deal. But when I went to Orissa, I didn't know Hindi or Oriya, I didn't know the people. . . . I felt so completely like an outsider." Other South Asians also pointed out that what their parents emphasized in the United States as their specific South Asianness often did not fit the cultural reality on the ground in the South Asian countries. One of the participants, Shanthi, who had years of Indian classical dance training in the United States and felt well-attuned to "Indian" culture, described her disappointment when she found her cousins did not share her interests:"It's kind of funny because when I go to India and they are all listening to American music, and I'm like 'what are you doing, you have such beautiful music here and you have all this beautiful stuff here and you just don't appreciate it.' "

And so, South Asian Americans often have to resolve these issues of what constitutes "authentic" cultures in these countries—the hiatus between their parents' versions and their own experiences—in order to pick from these cultural repertoires. Whereas fluency in English in the United States can bring various ethnic groups like the different South Asian Americans together, the multilingual character of the South Asian countries means that picking cultural expression and practices of one or two linguistic communities is never sufficient to build commonality among people who come from a vast array of linguistic (and regional cultural) groups. These tensions are explored further in chapters 5 and 6, but it is important to note that the multilingual, multicultural character of each of the South Asian countries means that these South Asian Americans have to confront the reality of the fragmented version of their "cultural connection" to these societies.

Theoretically, little attention is paid to this phenomenon as scholars discuss ethnicity in the United States. Questions about ethnicity and culture in the United States have generally related to acquiring proficiency in English, in order for "ethnic groups" to be able to integrate into the mainstream. Such theories do not capture the South Asian Americans' reality. They are already fluent in American English, as are most of their parents, but their lack of proficiency in the multiple languages of South Asia brings them face-to-face with their limited experience in "the cultures" of these different nation-states which are supposed to be ingrained in them.

For the South Asian Americans in this study, exactly *how* they are Indians or Pakistanis or Bangladeshis or Nepalese becomes a central dilemma for them. Are they more Bengali, Gujarati, Marathi, Malayali, or Punjabi than Indian, more Sindhi or Baluchi than Pakistani, more Sylheti or Chatgayiya than Bangladeshi, or more Newari or Gurung than Nepalese? Linguistic proficiency in any of the regional languages is not sufficient to claim Indianness or Nepaleseness. Because of its unique history, which I narrated in chapter 1, Bangladeshis are the only group that can claim a nationality on the basis of a widely spoken language. However, this dilemma is not about language alone. About half of the sample said they spoke their parents' language fluently, the others had varying degrees of proficiency. A few did not know any South Asian languages at all. Nonetheless, as Namrata pointed out, knowing one language is not sufficient in multilingual countries such as India. Anjali, who belonged to the non-fluent group, mentioned that most people did not understand her heavily accented Bengali, so she often spoke English to her older relatives and cousins. It was a problem for Anjali to go out by herself, because she could not communicate. She could only go to the more high-end shopping centers and restaurants, where people spoke English. She also was not able to follow local jokes or understand much of the literature written in the regional language, even though she had read many of the translations. She said her idea of "Indianness" that she had claimed as part of her hyphenated label was based on her middle-class family's Bengali culture. Her Indian ethnicity was actually quite fragmented.

Participants like Partha argued it was perfectly possible to have a deeper understanding of *an* ethnic culture (in his case a Bengali culture which spanned Bangladesh and West Bengal in India) without identifying with emerging "Indian" or "South Asian" ethnicity in the United States. He felt the emerging South Asian Americanness was too influenced by Hindi/Urdu cultural understandings and the cultural practices, histories, and memories of *these* linguistic communities. Several Bangladeshi Americans also echoed this sentiment. Nepalese Americans spoke about their dilemma: How Indian movies and fashions are major influences in the lives of their peers in Nepal. Yet, situated in the United States, they often had to look harder for what is *Nepalese*—itself an amalgam of multiple religions and cultures—to avoid getting drowned in the growing tide of Indianness in the United States. A few others, less introspective about the links between families and larger political, historical, and cultural processes simply equated their family cultural practices to "Indian" or "Pakistani," and talked about their adoption or rejection of certain aspects of the cultures of these societies.[12]

Thus, due to their experiences in their transnational family networks, the construction of ethno-*national* identities is not generally based on an uncritical acceptance of broad national cultures. Instead, the South Asian Americans go through a process of sifting: identifying aspects of their regional and/or familial cultural repertoires that are more meaningful to them, and then negotiating how these particular aspects of ethnic culture contribute to their fit within their family fields *and* the United States.

In *Modernity at Large,* Appadurai (1996) argues that the scholarly conflation of modernity and a global influence of Americanness, along with the assumption that globalization implies the rapid spread of American culture, fails to adequately address other regional sources of modernity and cultural hegemony. The content of culture—what is marked or mobilized as "ethnicness"—is rarely based on cultural myths, symbols, rituals, and practices of single nations. Rather, it arises from sets of structural relationships within and between "nation-states, multinationals, diasporic communities as well as subnational groupings" (1996, 33). Thus what the South Asian Americans are likely to pick as ethnic is dependent on balancing what they are familiar with through their families and what serves their needs within this larger context of "interpenetration of nations" (Abelmann and Lie 1995, viii). As Das Gupta (1997) concludes from her study of the second generation Indian Americans, constructing hyphenated identities entails a process far more complex than a simple balancing of two parts—one "ethnic" and one "mainstream American." For South Asian Americans, it requires juggling and balancing different sets of conflicts, and complex layers of local, regional, and national cultures that do not always fit easily, to create the ethnic part of their hyphenated identities.

The construction of ethnicity through this process of sifting and managing of conflicts provides the fluid and inessential quality of their ethnicness. The hyphenated identities of these South Asian Americans are formed of complex sets of layers that do not always converge or overlap and often remain fragmented. While their structural positions in the United States and in these other countries create shared experiences, their cultural commonality has to be worked out actively in order to strengthen their ethno-national and more pan-ethnic South Asian American identities.

TRANSNATIONAL WEDDINGS

The discussions in the preceding sections illustrate the larger patterns of how South Asian Americans configure their identity within a transnational context. In this section, I focus on weddings to show how multiple structures, various types of family ties, and the efforts of South Asian Americans to balance the opportunities and constraints they encounter, are leading to the emergence of "new" cultural forms that were similar among all of the participants. The attachments South Asian Americans develop with their families, along with a wish to practice their ethnicity during some important times of their lives, seems to be leading to a shared pattern of organizing "Indian" or "Pakistani" or other South Asian American weddings (also see Leonard 1997). Among most South Asian American families, the emphasis on marrying within certain ethno-national and religious groups also means that families seek marital partners through their transnational networks, a subject which is further discussed in chapter 4. However, irrespective of whom South Asian Americans marry, their ability to organize weddings and related events across multiple countries demonstrates one shared aspect of how they practice ethnicity.

Weddings are occasions for the gathering of family and friends, regardless of race or religion or rationality. However, for the South Asian Americans, travel restrictions that apply to many of their family members often make it almost impossible to hold weddings in the presence of extended family members in the United States. While their fictive kin are a source of support in the United States, their ongoing participation in transnational family fields and the close relationships with many extended family members steers many South Asian Americans toward exploring forms of weddings that cross national boundaries. While there is also a significant financial advantage in getting married in a South Asian country—with each dollar translating to forty to eighty units of local currency—all of those who adopted these transnational forms emphasized the need to have their relatives at their weddings as their primary motivation.

The exact form of these weddings varies: many first get married in the United States, then organize a wedding reception in India, Pakistan, Nepal, or

3.1. Guests at a wedding in Pakistan. Photo by Sabiha Vahidy.

Bangladesh. Others get married in a South Asian country, even though both partners reside in the United States. Some get married in both countries using different combinations of religious and civil ceremonies. Typical to the age range of the South Asian Americans I interviewed, four got married while I was conducting this research, and at least a dozen others attended weddings of cousins in India. Many had photographs of these weddings and/or receptions. A few of the participants talked about weddings where at least one reception was held in a South Asian country, another in a European country, along with parties in the United States.

Arvind, who had recently started a white-collar career in insurance when I interviewed him, first drew my attention to this type of wedding. His fiancée, whom he met in college, was born and brought up in the United States, while Arvind spent his early years in India. He said he wanted to go to India to get married for two overlapping reasons. His primary motivation was to ensure a proper wedding ceremony. His father had been to a Hindu wedding in the United States and was shocked at the priest's lack of knowledge regarding the Sanskrit prayers.[13] He felt the priest was making a mockery of the whole ceremony. Thus, it was important for Arvind to have a ceremony that was conducted correctly and in a dignified manner. Second, he wanted to be able to fully enjoy the wedding, without any restrictions on what could be done in public places. He said,

3.2. Wedding attire for family members at a Pakistani wedding. Photo by Sabiha Vahidy.

Here, with my friends and other people, it doesn't have the charm that I notice. My brother and my sister both got married in India. So, the thing that we had, the traditional stuff . . . from firecrackers to dancing in the middle of the street, it was just fantastic for me. . . . And also there's this other whole bit about the fire, that you can't light the fire in most places here, but that is the key to our ceremony. . . . And [his fiancée] is already there, three months in advance so. . . . I mean she has her own dreams so she may have more answers for you, whatever she wants to do, she can't do it here obviously with the financial limitations, with the timing, with school. Also the rituals preparing for the wedding . . . they go to dances and ceremonies and this and that, so she'll appreciate that in India. . . . People [are] just so amused at work when I mention that I'm getting married there. For me, I don't have to do much, but my biggest problem is, should I have an elephant or a horse?

Not all weddings, even in India, involve horses (or elephants) and firecrackers. Nevertheless, any "traditional" wedding requires the presence of several relatives and often the entire neighborhood. Even though the "modern traditional" weddings among the middle class are held at private halls, built for this purpose, since land-use laws are not configured in the same way as the United States, many of these halls could be in the middle of residential neighborhoods. The public displays—the music, the illumination, the flower-decked cars or animals (depending on the regional culture and class background of the family), and other aspects of the celebrations—are common to all four countries.

Many of the family rituals—irrespective of religion—are similar as well. Several Bangladeshi Muslim participants described the all-female ceremonies (which are very similar to those practiced by the Hindus in West Bengal) that

3.3. Mehendi design on the hands and feet of a bride at a Pakistani wedding. Photo by Sabiha Vahidy.

are part of weddings, and require the presence of many people. A Nepalese participant, Suhita, explained how the role of the younger sister-in-law is crucial for setting the tone of the relationship between the groom and the rest of the bride's family, and she looked forward to the opportunity to play this role. Samina talked about a ceremony she had witnessed in Pakistan, in which younger relatives hid the groom's shoes on the wedding night, demanding a ransom in exchange the next morning. Such wedding ceremonies, which are common among a number of South Asian cultures, require a group of younger people to ritually engage in the spirited and light-hearted exchanges between the "groom" and his new relatives. Other rituals emphasize the love, duty, respect, and support of the extended family, such as aunts, uncles, grandparents, and other older relatives.

Arvind's statement hinted at several problems in trying to hold such a wedding in the United States. First, the costs make it difficult to get entire families to come to the United States. Tourist visas from India are prohibitively expensive for most people, as are the plane fares. It was unquestionably cheaper for Arvind's family and his fiancée's family to go to India. Second, with ongoing visa restrictions, no one can predict if a family member will be allowed to visit the United States for a wedding. Since weddings are designed to include a variety of relatives in many formal roles over several days, they also require relatives to be available for several days, sometimes more than a week. This is often not possible in the United States, where there is a general expectation for weddings to take place on weekends, and relatives participate in clearly defined and time-designated events. In South Asian countries, where various cultural groups often follow their own calendars on deciding on auspicious dates for weddings, few weddings are held on weekends. In those countries, while workplaces might follow Gregorian calendars (with exceptions made for observing religious rituals, such as Fridays for Muslims), social calendars follow whatever is true of the culture. (And people are legitimately expected to take time off from work for these weddings.) Third, Hindu wedding ceremonies are performed around an open fire, a custom that is widely restricted as a fire hazard in most wedding facilities in the United States. Furthermore, many groups (for example in northern and western India and Pakistan) have traditions that include arriving at the place of ceremony in a wedding procession accompanied by a great deal of dancing and music. Such customs are also prohibited in the United States. These constraints led Arvind's family to organize a "traditional" wedding in India, a choice made by other participants in this study.

The importance of family participation was very evident in the case of Anita's wedding. She and her partner had both come to the United States when they were infants. Although her fiancé had not visited India frequently, she visited almost every year. When she insisted on having a traditional wedding in Kolkata (Calcutta), both of their families went to India for the ceremony. She said she decided to arrange the wedding in India because most of her relatives, irrespective of where they lived in India or in other countries, could attend the wedding there. Anita had traveled to India several times by herself and had made a documentary on "top rung" female executives. She was already familiar with places of importance for wedding arrangements, the stores to buy clothes and other accessories, and where to get custom stitching for clothing, etc. Even though she was fully capable of organizing this wedding herself, she got various relatives involved. Thus, she upheld the fundamental principle of traditional weddings by creating a role for everyone. She often called one of her aunts in Kolkata to manage the inevitable differences of opinion between family members about the best way to conduct different details of the wedding. She explained that the advantage of holding the wedding in Kolkata was that the older and younger relatives could participate in different matrimonial ceremonies for an extended period of time. She scheduled her wedding during a time when most schools were on vacation, so extended family from the United States could take their "family vacation" time to attend this wedding. And, the ceremony could be performed correctly: in front of a fire, with the traditional *alpana* (floor design) at the wedding site, and a priest conducting the wedding in the Bengali Hindu manner.[14] The religious ceremony, the "noisy" merriment, the socializing, and the food, could all be planned in a common spot in the middle of a residential neighborhood, the way most Bengali weddings are celebrated. Typically the groom's family organizes another gathering within two or three days of the wedding ceremony. In this case, her husband's family organized their reception at a prestigious hotel in Kolkata, and the festivities carried on for a week, in the "traditional" manner.

Later, Anita and her husband organized a reception at a lake front country club in northeastern United States for their friends who were unable to go to India for the ceremony. Then their parents jointly hosted a similar reception for the rest of *their* friends (the fictive kin) in the United States. Here, too, Anita avoided the problems of having to make travel arrangements and acquiring visas for her relatives if they were to come to the United States. Essentially, she was able to circumvent all the restrictions that Arvind mentioned. In India, she organized the type of décor and environment that she wanted. In the United States, businesses are beginning to appear that offer South Asian wedding accessories, wedding consultants, as well as priests who conduct "Hindu weddings." However, these services often best reflect the ethos and cultures of west and north Indian cultures, rather than the cultural specificities of India and the other countries' multiple cultures. Anita wanted a Bengali atmosphere, Bengali food, décor, and ambiance. With the support of her relatives from multiple places, she was able arrange the wedding to her specifications in

3.4. A scene from a wedding in India (note the fire in the lower left corner). Photo by Annapurna Sinha.

3.5. A wedding reception at a country club in the United States. Photo by Annapurna Sinha.

Kolkata. So, South Asian Americans, like Arvind and Anita, who are relatively entrenched in their family fields, are able to organize these major events in ways that best fit their versions of doing ethnicity in contexts that transcend the boundaries of nation-states.

These transnational weddings illustrate a crucial way in which South Asian Americans negotiate their ethnic preferences. When they favor a wedding with relatives, this transnational form lends itself to balancing the restrictions on the travel of family members by bringing a part of the wedding, be it the ceremony or the reception, to South Asia. Even among those whose weddings are held in the United States, the subsequent reception in South Asia adds an extra "ethnic" emphasis to their weddings. But there is a degree of choice in exactly which part of the wedding is performed in which country. It is a "choice" that needs to be worked out in order to balance travel restrictions and the location of family members around the world (with multiple school and work schedules), relative to the degrees of closeness of and obligations toward the family field and the financial status of the family.

While the emphasis on involving relatives might suggest some expressions of "cultural authenticity," these weddings, at a structural level, have begun to resemble mainstream weddings in the United States. These weddings typically separate the religious ceremony from the reception; each reception combines a dinner with formally organized seating arrangements, music, dancing, and speeches in a "desirable" setting. Several South Asian American weddings I attended in the United States followed this format. Abandoning the simultaneous wedding and informal socializing format, South Asian religious ceremonies are conducted in one place (a religious institution, a banquet hall or in a home, depending on the religious and regional variations). An abbreviated version of the pre-wedding rituals takes place in the homes of the bride and groom. The receptions are formally organized by professional staff at the facilities (instead of relatives) and are often held in a hotel or country club. Since many of these clubs and hotels do not allow "ethnic" catering, the main dinner is mainstream American fare.[15] Even the couples who got married in India, came back and organized receptions in this format in the United States. Thus, in some ways the weddings in the South Asian countries link a transnational "private-ethnic sphere" to the "public arena" in the United States.

Not all South Asian Americans have the level of ties that allows them to ask relatives to organize weddings. Indeed many affluent South Asians (on the subcontinent) have also begun to use a combination of wedding consultants and relatives to organize these celebrations. For the affluent groups (and many of the South Asian Americans in this study fall into this category by the standards of the subcontinent because of the relative strength of the dollar to the South Asian currencies) tourist facilities are beginning to offer wedding packages just as in the United States. Since many of these "top" sites are often converted castles or other heritage sites, the packages offered by these places, along with the presence of relatives in the country who are likely to come to the wedding, make this an attractive prospect for some South Asian Americans.

One South Asian American made an interesting comment about this nexus of tourism and weddings. She had attended the wedding of her cousin held in a castle in India. A number of these castles in northern and western India (and in scattered locations of the other countries) have now been transformed into tourist hotels. Each offers a "slice" of Indian life (including grand wedding packages) to all those who can afford the prices.[16] She described how her cousin's white college friends had gone for the wedding: "[L]ike we were at the wedding. The [major elected official of an Indian state] comes and they are taking pictures and they are like, oh get all the white people, get them for the pictures. You know it is going to be in a tourism guide or something."

She went on to say that "all the girls" yearned for such fairy tale weddings—complete with castles, gorgeous clothing, and jewelry, elephants, camels, and live musicians—a description which closely approximates the images of "princely India" marketed in the west. As these historic buildings of the subcontinent are converted to tourist sites where consumers can experience slices of culture/history, it is not inconceivable that other South Asian Americans, who have few family ties, may nonetheless opt to hold their wedding in such sumptuous surroundings. As middle-class consumers they would be adding an "ethnic accent" to their weddings, much like the other middle-class folk in the United States.[17] Clearly, for many of these South Asian Americans, these grander weddings are more affordable on the subcontinent *and* they acknowledge—real or symbolic—family ties.

Overall, these weddings illustrate that ongoing, often virtual, participation in ethnic family networks promotes the thinking about global horizons of their lives. Such "ethnic" practices cannot be adequately described by simply dichotomizing modern non-ethnic American and traditional ethnic life. These weddings reflect situated cultural practices: they are possible because the restrictions in one country may be balanced by increasingly easy access to another, and by growing sophisticated circuits of communication technology, which makes it possible to maintain meaningful family connections through virtual communities. These weddings are also *racialized* forms because, despite a growing belief in greater openness toward multiculturalism in the United States, what is allowed, as multicultural celebration, often has to fit what is "normal" for white natives. Both, the host of restrictions that some South Asian Americans avoid by transporting their main wedding celebrations to other countries, as well as the altered structure of weddings in the United States, illustrate that the rules of practicing cultures have not changed substantially to accommodate these "South Asian" practices.

CONCLUSION

This discussion on the structure of transnational families and how they influence the ethnicity among South Asian Americans illustrates several issues that are being debated in the ethnicity literature. First, the data in this chapter show that far from being neutral arenas, transnational spaces are structured through multiple sets of national restrictions on movement of people of specific gender, religion, nationality, etc. The South Asian Americans in this study are not able to move equally freely between the countries. Their own movement, as well as the movement of their family members, is contingent upon the legal-political relationships of several countries. Second, there is a debate about whether or not cultures developed in transnational spaces draw upon place of origin as the main signifier of ethnicity (see Anthias 1998). The data here show that South Asian Americans actually come to realize their lack of "essential ties" with South Asian cultures because of their experiences in that region. They are constructed as American within this field. Rather than developing commonalities because of cultures shaped by places of origin, the commonality within each national group (for instance, within the Indian or Pakistani groups) and between the groups (for instance, between Nepalese and Bangladeshis) appear to be influenced by their structural position—they are enmeshed in transnational family networks and they are marginalized in the United States. In fact, the information in the last chapter and this one shows that they develop aspects of their Americanness *and* their South Asianness *in both regions*. Thus, they have both American and ethno-national layers, and they share the commonality of having these two layers with other South Asian Americans. Third, most of the literature on contemporary ethnicity does not pay as much attention to the complexity of the ethnic side. This chapter also shows that because of the multilingual, multireligious, multicultural structure of most of the South Asian countries, choosing an ethno-national identity means working through the complex cultural and political issues that make up such identities. Thus these ethno-national identities are not already defined cultural templates which are transmitted through family socialization. Instead, the ethno-national part of their hyphenated identities is composed of complex, often fragmented layers, which reflect intersections of family cultural orientations, strength of their regional cultures within the ethnic community in the United States, as well as sociopolitical events that take place in different parts of the world. Overall then, the layer(s) of ethnicity developed through such family fields clearly illustrate its dynamic, rather than essential character.

The discussion in this chapter also highlights several nuances for understanding contemporary ethnicity. First, historical and contemporary global restrictions on non-white migration (which influences where family members are located), and contemporary sociopolitical events (such as riots or political conflicts) shape the transnational family field. The efforts by South Asian Americans and their families to subvert these constraints and restrictions sustain family fields. This chapter shows that while most South Asian Americans in this study had "deep ties" to their family networks and consequently felt more familiar with the field, not all members have similar levels of ties with family. Some ties may be more indirect and symbolic than others, as in the case of the South Asian American who primarily saw India as a context for a fairy tale wedding. In the absence of racial boundaries in the United States, such contexts may become more neutral backgrounds for practicing more symbolic forms of ethnicity like white-ethnics. At present, however, given the racialized context of their lives in the United States, this field provides resources and supportive networks that shape South Asian American lives. Second, while much of theory regarding ethnicity/culture focuses on private spheres of family as the main arena of ethnic socialization, and source of the nation-of-origin ties, the South Asian American experiences show how the family sphere and the larger geopolitics intersect, both within and across nations. Thus, for them, "doing family" across national boundaries requires a series of new innovative practices to balance multiple geopolitical contexts.

Overall, the experiences of the South Asian Americans in their transnational family fields show that both institutions—family and state—remain important for understanding contemporary ethnicity in a globalized world.

CHAPTER 4

Constructing Ethnic Boundaries

NEGOTIATIONS AND CONFLICTS
OVER GENDER, RELIGION, RACE,
AND NATIONALITY

Pranata: A lot of our connection to Indianness, you know, is from the temple. . . . I have mixed feelings about [the temple] 'cause I don't think it's necessarily a religious place. It's more of a social thing. I think the social aspect is really important and that's needed. But it's kind of hard 'cause it wasn't just the idea of being Indian, but also being Hindu . . . but it's just going to the temple I never really felt, it didn't necessarily affirm my feeling Hindu or anything . . . it just felt forced in some way, like "here are your people why don't you talk to them." And it's also a difficult position especially because, for my parents, this is a place that they know. I would go and see some of my friends who are Indian but in some ways I am not part of it. I am still friends with some of them, like [Shanthi]; she's probably the only one I have felt some level of ease with. But it's a weird place and also, I didn't participate in the dance like every other girl does, and I think in some ways that maybe also made me feel a bit more estranged or, I don't know, weirded out.

Maya: Yes, it seems like there is a double standard in the Indians, like the second generation especially, because your parents are from India they follow those rules. But the guys definitely have an easier time than the girls do . . . my friend's brothers don't care what they do but, but our parents are more strict with the girls, like my parents were like don't get involved with any guy. Even my guy friends will tell me don't mess around. But they mess around though. But they want to marry someone who is completely pure; it's so unfair . . . what happens to the girls they are messing around with?

THE ROLE OF nuclear families in socializing the next generations is well recognized in ethnicity literature (Bacon 1996). However, much
of this literature tends to conceptualize families as separate cultural worlds,
instead of worlds that are structurally and culturally related. In this chapter, the
discussion of South Asian Americans within their nuclear families moves away
from ideas about two cultural worlds identifiable by stable sets of socially
shared meanings and practices. Instead I look at how emerging cultures are
affected by the interaction of social structural processes at the node (that is, in
the United States) and the transnational field. I show that families are not simple, solitary units; they are institutions beset by competing interests of members who are positioned differently (Hondagneu-Sotelo 1994). Set within
intersecting transnational, national, and local structures, families construct a
variety of race, religious, gender boundaries which generate conflicts and
negotiations that shape South Asian American ethnicity.

This chapter examines *what* exactly is presented as "our culture" by
nuclear families in the United States, *why* certain versions are emphasized, and
the *conflicts* that arise between generations as particular versions begin to dominate the definitions of ethnic cultures. As the earlier chapters have indicated,
the first generation primarily emphasizes ethno-national identities; this chapter shows that they emphasize certain aspects of ethno-national identities that
are linked to *their* structural position as middle-class, non-whites in the United
States. This partially explains the puzzle several second generation participants
encountered in South Asia: what is taught to the second generation as "our
culture" by their parents in the United States, does not always fit local cultural
practices in South Asian countries. Families in the United States selectively
emphasize particular versions of these ethno-national identities, that is, they
pick from a shopping cart of ethnic understandings and practices. Since the
middle-class first generation is not a unitary group, several versions of ethnicity emerge, although some versions gain more widespread recognition and
acceptance than others.

What happens within families cannot be separated from what happens
outside families, and this chapter also shows how emerging emphases within
families and ethnic community organizations converge and diverge to create
hegemonic and alternative repertoires. The attempt by some sections of the
immigrant generations to construct "superior cultures" overlaps, to a certain
extent, with the efforts of many religious community organizations to emphasize superior *religious* cultures. The confluence of the interests of some of these
families to define superior cultures by drawing gender, race, religious, and
nationality distinctions, with the interests of those in power in formal religious
establishments creates a hegemonic version of ethno-national culture. (I
henceforth refer to this as hegemonic culture and the family-and-religious
community nexus that promotes this culture as the hegemonic group.) To

what extent the family/community versions of ethnic boundaries converge or diverge from transnational family versions, or the boundaries established through mainstream racialization processes, becomes a crucial factor in influencing second generation ethnicity. The interest among the South Asian Americans to create South Asian American or desi identities, which I described in chapter 2, implies building and maintaining networks across groups that are being constructed as distinct and separate by the hegemonic groups in all four nation-based communities. The degree of opposition they encounter from the first generation as they build these South Asian American identities influences how the South Asian Americans in this study think of the content and boundaries of their ethnicity.

In this chapter I show that while they are generally appreciative of the close ties within their nuclear and transnational families, the second generation are also critical of many aspects of the cultures their parents wish to instill in them. I focus on three arenas that the participants mentioned most often: their conflicts with parents over high achievement, their efforts to avoid internalizing the hegemonic versions of culture, and their negotiations of the gender regimes that entrench hierarchies between males and females. These arenas are not distinctive; they intersect and shape each other and cumulatively introduce a range of class, gender, religious, racial, and national boundaries within the meanings of South Asian Americanness. For ease of discussion I consider them separately as I analyze how the South Asian Americans experience and resist many of these boundaries.

Constructing "Superior" Cultures

Most of the South Asian Americans described how their nuclear families socialized them, overtly or subtly, into a sense of a distinctive and superior family/ethnic culture. For many, this superiority is constructed within the parameters of the classic United States immigrant success story: their parents work in white-collar jobs, and as the census data shows decade after decade, they are more educated and more affluent than most other groups including native whites (see Barringer et al. 1995; Narayan 2004). This achievement is then attributed to their cultures of hard work and supportive families. This is a story of "individual" achievement *par excellence,* where all structural issues— their migration as highly educated immigrants as race-based laws were dismantled through the efforts of African Americans and other racial minorities—are wiped out to emphasize how superior cultures lead to positive outcomes.[1]

How these ideologies work through various types of families and the ways in which the second generation interrogates these over-generalized versions are described in the following sections. Before we look at the conflicts, it is important to understand the structural context in which the first generation constructs its "superior culture" narrative. After all, why is there a need for immigrant families to talk about their superior cultures, when their structural position as middle-class folk with upper-tier jobs is no different from that of equivalent white groups? The emphasis has to be understood with reference to the mainstream racialized construction of "minorities" in terms of achievement and cultures. A black-white racial discourse in the mainstream often defines racial minority positions in terms of poor cultures of minorities (see Massey and Denton 1994 or Omi and Winant 1994 for summaries of these arguments). Other groups are simply assumed to fit this structure, even though middle- and upper-class Asian Americans are racialized in ways that are different from those belonging to the lower classes (Ong 1996). The mainstream racial ideology blames the cultures of racialized minorities (especially their work ethics and "non-traditional" families) for their lack of success in an "open" United States society. The model minority rhetoric about South Asians and other Asian Americans is one building block of this argument; the achievement of the various Asian American groups is held up as an example of the effect of "good cultural values."

The South Asian first generation's constructions of superior culture are based on exactly these racial standards. When they emphasize their superior culture as an outcome of their "good values," they often use the same criteria—work ethics and strong families. Some families deny the structural dimensions of racialization as well as the ideology that stigmatizes their children as holders of non-American cultural characteristics. They do not see the contradiction between their children's achievements as testaments to their "good American values" and their stigmatization as non-Americans. Others recognize racialization, but they attempt to ignore it by socializing their children to "turn the other cheek." A small section understands these barriers and challenges the superior culture rhetoric in the ethnic communities.

Yet, what the ethnic community can use to define these superior cultures is always an open question. Mainstream entities co-opt some aspects of cultural knowledge (for instance the co-optation of yoga which is discussed in the next chapter) for sale and profit; at the same time, other entities regularly denigrate practices such as dowry deaths and honor killings, characterizing these as *the* cultural norm. So the immigrant generations' attempts to claim certain cultural practices as *purely* ethnic practices is often problematic. Like other racial minority groups they attempt to define an affirming culture as a way of challenging the dominant group's definition, but their claims are drowned out by the claims of the dominant groups. These denials or the downplaying of the role of racialization often set the stage for family conflicts. Since South Asian Americans visit and maintain connections with various South Asian countries, they are able to use their own knowledge to challenge some versions of ethnicity promulgated by sections of the first generation.

Conflicts

According to South Asian Americans, the notion of a superior culture is based on the superior achievement profiles of this group in the United States. Linking high levels of achievement (in education and occupations) as the outcome of South Asian values—hard work and strong families which are tied by strong bonds of love and obligation—South Asian parents place an "unusual" emphasis on getting good grades and building upper-tier careers. Having arrived as highly educated migrants, the parents of the South Asian Americans in this study often emphasize achievement in terms of a narrow range of white-collar careers in medicine, technology, law, and the sciences.

Kader, a male of Bangladeshi origin, explained how he was studying engineering because his parents wanted him to do so. His passion was politics and he personally would have preferred a political or diplomatic career. He was planning to join the United States army in order to keep his future options in politics open. Others described similar pressures. Namrata, who is a presidential scholar at her university, explained that one major difference between her peers and her was the standard her parents expected of their children. "[A]lso in terms of studies and such. We just know more is expected of us. And we have to do well. Like my parents are always telling my brother if you don't do well you'll just be a bum and you can't do that and we won't support you, although they will. But they are always pushing."

Most mentioned how this culture of achievement was upheld as a community. Many said there was too much competition and pressure based solely on whose children went to the Ivy League colleges. Some explained that such achievement standards were normative within their transnational families. Educational achievement is of central importance to educated middle-class families in South Asia, where it is the single most important route to entering coveted occupations. Others thought this emphasis was a function of their parents' lives in the United States. They were in white-collar jobs and they refused to think beyond this box.

According to these South Asian Americans the emphasis on achievement set them apart from their friends. In schools they were set up as different since they were constantly asked to put their education first. Since many of them were trying to appear socially "normal" according to their peers' standards this emphasis was often interpreted as "unusual pressure" by the second generation. Some, like Rehana, pointed out that it set up achievement competition among ethnic peers; they constantly tried to out-do each other instead of building networks of support against a common pressure of racial marginalization in schools.

Both males and females were subject to these "superior achievement" pressures, although there were some gender distinctions. Most males felt that there was a lot more pressure on them to keep to the white-collar professional or managerial career track. Prakrit explained, "I became an engineer. I followed the path. But I see my cousin, she's at Harvard. She was working for Bill Bradley, she was working for human rights and I see her making the right choices . . . a lot of the women, more so than the men [are politically engaged]. Maybe they are more aware of their mother's struggles. But their economic security helps too."

Given the contemporary range of hegemonic masculinities, many South Asian families push males toward white-collar technocratic occupations (Connell 1995). Masculinities organized around technical knowledge—which make up the occupational world of the new middle classes and are based on the global control of knowledge—are typical of many of this subset of parents, and, set up as "the" achievement target of the males.

Families clearly differed in how they socialized females within this cultural achievement norm. Some South Asian Americans felt their families provided them with fewer educational opportunities compared to their brothers. Others said there was *greater* pressure on them than the males because they were aiming for white-collar professions that were still sex/race segregated. A few mentioned that because their mothers made more money than their fathers this simply raised their parental expectations about what "South Asian girls" achieved. Pranata, who described her parents as more egalitarian than many other parents within the community, felt there were no overt barriers, but there a was a subtle gender distinction.

> Both my mom and dad's side of the family really emphasize education as being something that's important. And education for the women as well. . . . I can work hard in school and I'm not treated different than [her brother] . . . I've had a lot of opportunities and privileges of being equal or on par with the boys in my family and I think education has played a big role in that. I think that's been a big step. But in some ways it's still like oh but you're still a girl. . . . I can go into a career, into whatever I want and that's great, but it's almost expected of the boys. I think, in some ways, if a girl does it, it's an accomplishment.

Several said they grew reconciled to these pressures later, but it was hard to meet these standards when they were growing up. The following statements illustrate their experiences:

PRATIBHA, A NEPALESE AMERICAN SAID: There are conflicts with parents. When I was growing up my parents thought I was a bad girl. I had good grades, but it was never good enough. I used to envy my (white American) friends; their parents were so nice to them. Like this one girl made brownies with drugs in it, and her mother only made her write a poem of atonement.

NAMRATA, WHO SPOKE ABOUT HOW THEIR PARENTS PUSHED HER BROTHER AND HER-
SELF TO ACHIEVE, ALSO SAID: [high achievement was emphasized among
South Asians] . . . whereas for an American person, being average is okay.

To what extent are the standards actually different from the standards of
the mainstream middle class? Is "being average" okay for "an American person"? After all, scholarly work on middle-class cultures describes how emphasis on success is a normal part of "standard" middle-class orientation (for
example, Rose 1997). Nor is the parent who asked her child to write the
poem of atonement the typical "soccer parent." What makes such insistence on
achievement *ethnic* in character?

I would argue that experiences with racialization affect the motivations
and understandings of both generations as they draw a line between what is
ethnic and what is "American." Some parents subscribe to the existing racial
ideology and try hard to succeed as "model minorities"; they distance themselves from those who they see as the "real" minorities. Much like the segmented outcomes described by Portes (1995a) and Zhou (1997), in the minds
of these parents, becoming a "racial minority" instead of remaining an "ethnic
minority"—which is based on denying racialization and emphasizing a distinctive culture—would be a sign of downward mobility. However, given their
racialized position, in spite of their denials of racialization processes, their story
of "success based on their superior cultures" has to be proven through their
successful raising of high-achieving children. Thus, there is an ongoing pressure on their children to be better, smarter, more high-achieving compared to
their white peers. But other parents, who do not necessarily subscribe to the
racialized idea of a model minority culture, also realize more pragmatically
that being a racial minority requires being better than the rest of the playing
field in order to achieve the same outcomes (Fong 1998; U.S. Civil Rights
Commission 1992). Thus, this second group of parents also emphasizes high
achievement. Both groups use a country-specific South Asian cultural norm
argument to insist upon high achievement standards.

The insistence on high achievement within this ethno-national cultural
framework intersects with how second generation South Asian Americans
understand their social identity. If middle-class South Asian parents emphasize
achievement in ways that reflect their *middle-class* ethnic understanding of
good parenting, their interpretation is often at odds with the framework of the
second generation. The first generation's interpretation bundles expressions of
their closeness, love, and obligation with the time, energy, and financial investments that they make to ensure higher achievements by their children. As we
saw in chapter 2, the second generation is constantly exposed to the racial discourse about non-American families that do not allow too much freedom and
independence to individuals (and the corresponding implication that white

families provide such freedom and independence). Their internalization, or even partial internalization, of that perspective frames how they see their own parents imposing these achievement standards on them. While many of them were willing to work toward these high standards, they also interpreted the efforts of their parents as "excessive" degree of control that their ethnic parents exert on their lives, a degree which is, in their minds, different from what happens in average white families. Just as their white peers rarely distinguish between different classes of racialized individuals (that is, race is their master status), whites appear as a monolith to the second generation. These South Asian Americans did not appear to pay a great deal of attention to what happens to children of parents with similar educational and occupational backgrounds. More importantly, the "average American person" in many of their minds, is, not surprisingly, the "desirable" male and female who was set up as the normative standard by which they were judged negatively in high schools. (The high-achieving white peers are seen as exceptions to "the norm.")

The emphasis on this link between culture and achievement overlaps with the racial characterization of blacks and Latinos in sections of the mainstream as "low achievers with poor cultures." It also separates middle-class South Asian Americans as a "culture group" from others *within* the South Asian community who don't fit these middle-class standards.[2] The first generation members who act on the assumption that they are model minorities often deny racism vigorously, using much of the same racist talk to "educate" the second generation about their "misguided" notions on race. I was witness to one such exchange where a middle-aged male and an elderly female lectured a panel of five South Asian Americans (including three participants in this study) who had spoken on different dimensions of racialization that affected their lives. The first generation female said racism had disappeared, while the male said there had never been any racism in the United States and these panelists had just picked up a lot of wrong-headed notions from their schools. (Such views, as I discuss later, are further institutionalized through some hegemonic community groups.)[3] In general, other parents do not subscribe to such views and are critical of such overt racism among sections of the community. However, even those who do not participate in such explicit racism often ended up on the exclusionary side in the perception of their children, because they emphasize an ethnicity defined by achievement *without providing the race socialization* that challenges the "poor cultures, low achievement" racial ideology.[4]

The emphasis most South Asian families put on the *family network* as the most important source of support, also distances South Asian Americans, if inadvertently, from other United States–based communities of color. Most South Asian Americans pointed out that their families were always there to help them with all kinds of problems. Their socialization of dependence on families is no different from how other racial minority groups depend on their kin for their survival and the well-being of their families. Certainly, Taylor's (2002) book, among others, documents how various racial minority families in the United States continue to maintain "non-traditional" families such as dual households (an early variation of the current multinational households of the South Asian Americans), fictive kin, and other strategies as networks of support. But the South Asian Americans in this study explained that this emphasis on family support, especially transnational family support, is often presented to them as a unique characteristic of South Asian cultures. This emphasis on "family alone" influences how individuals deal with adversity, including racial marginalization; such coping becomes part of a private strategy—enacted within the transnational "private" family sphere—rather than building up a collective resistance within the public sphere in the United States. Thus, very few South Asian Americans have been socialized about the need to transcend the boundaries between communities of color in an attempt to challenge these boundaries in the United States. In common with other Asian American families described by Kibria (2002), the meanings of families and ethnicity are constructed in cultural terms alone.

The discourse linking superior achievement and ethnic culture is usually presented in country-specific terms and is one of the ways in which parents highlight the importance of ethno-national identities. The reactions of the South Asian Americans to these standards reflect the degree to which they understand the problem of such "culture only" ideologies, and the extent to which they are willing to conform to or reject these embedded boundaries. Most appear to simply select those parts of the ethnic repertoires, that is, the shared understanding and cultural practices that fit their lives. Since they are enmeshed in multiple boundaries, what they negotiate with their parents also reflects how these other boundaries intersect in their lives. The conflict, then, is about the degree of permeability of the boundaries of South Asian American identity that their parents wish to inculcate.

CONSTRUCTING ETHNO-RELIGIOUS COMMUNITIES

The ideas about superior achievement and South Asian cultures are upheld through a combination of family and community norms and controls. As these immigrants with new religions settled in the United States, the temples, gurudwaras (Sikh religious places), mosques, and churches often begin to act as the foci of ethnic communities. Unlike ethnic enclaves where the presence of others often acts as a collective form of social control, such as the Vietnamese American community described by Zhou and Bankston (1998), for the geographically dispersed South Asian Americans, constructing community is harder. Since religions like Hinduism are not organized, in India or

Nepal, as congregational communities that require regular attendance in religious institutions, new practices are often introduced to create more uniform and centralized religious communities. The dimensions of this religious diversity and syncretism are apparent when we consider that even now, 15 percent of the Indian population officially acknowledges practicing more than one religion (Nandy 2002); in addition, there are extremely varied forms of worship among those who claim to primarily follow one religion. So creating more uniform ethnic religious communities, in ways that keep members within the folds of centralized religious institutions, is a particular challenge for many religious groups from South Asia. Nonetheless, in the absence of a variety of secular spaces for ethnic community members to gather, the religious institutions become synonymous with "community spaces." This has significant repercussions on the second generation's ethnicity.

Since Hindus are the majority group among the South Asian Americans, it is instructive to look at what is happening among them. Pranata's statement at the beginning of the chapter describes the role of temples in the United States: they act as places for gathering, and for inculcating ideas about "your people" to the second generation, often in gendered ways. For example, according to Pranata, it was normative for the girls to dance. The emphasis on performance is tied to building ways of doing cultures across multilingual subgroups that make up the Hindu community. Performances rank high on this list. Maira (2002) has described how mostly females learn classical dancing while the males may play musical instruments. Such emphases can build up particular types of within-group networks, for instance, networks among females who perform in these dances, versus the females like Pranata who feel like outsiders. These repertoires help develop a sense of who the insiders to the group are based on who is most visible in these places.

As religions are structurally transformed in the United States (often to fit the policy requirements for not-for-profit corporations) they take on a more centralized homogenized character. This transformation often provides new political clout for some hegemonic groups to define *their* notions of "South Asian" (usually Indian, in some exceptional cases, Indian and Nepalese) culture through temples.[5] While there is a *general* middle-class emphasis on achievement and superior cultures among families as I discussed in the last section, some groups become hegemonic by using their "official" positions in religious establishments, to construct a narrower ethno-religious identity, using the same discourse about high-achieving cultures (Kurien 1999). These common frames are used to draw many families into these narrower notions of ethnicity. The more successful a group is at creating these centralized networks, the greater its power to define "the community." Thus, even though other groups exist within these religious organizations, the hegemonic group becomes the public voice of "the community."

The form of ethnic culture promulgated by the hegemonic group is based on some crucial transformations of Hinduism. Despite the hegemonic group's rhetoric about the unique and superior culture of South Asians, it vigorously attempts to structurally transform the religion to fit the dominant American form and then popularize it through official bulletins and through temple-based programs aimed at different generations, as "culturally authentic." As Saxena (2004), among others, points out, Hinduism is organizationally a decentralized spiritual system: Hindus have no fixed forms of worship, no specific texts that everyone reads, and no specific deities that are venerated by all. Systems of belief in India and Nepal can range from deity worship, to abstract spirituality, or even atheism. Since these variegated beliefs also vary by region, culture, family, and an individual's preference over her life course, setting up temples as congregations with homogenized forms of worship represents a major transformation (Yang and Ebaugh 2001). The insistence on temple-based forms of religio-cultural practice also leads to centralization of power. Along with this transformation, a range of activities that closely resemble Christianity such as Hindu Sunday schools, gift-giving tree ceremonies during December, programs on "how to do puja," and Hindu camps are introduced.[6] The emerging centralized form in the United States then re-inscribes one form of worship—a temple-based, Brahmin priest–mediated form of Hinduism—as "the" Hindu way in the public eye. It also sets up formal barriers against people who are not members of this religion as well as informal barriers against those who do not believe in such Brahmin priest–dependent forms of Hinduism.[7]

Since this transformation—going to temples on weekends, sending children to Sunday schools, engaging in priest-mediated forms of congregational worship—begins to resemble the practices of the Christian mainstream, it is interesting to analyze what is defined as ethnic and superior. Apart from the "belief" in different gods, a new ideology of superiority is constructed by sifting through history, selectively emphasizing some aspects, and ignoring others. Newsletters often emphasize the ethic of care and the theme of strong families as the core of ethnicity. Two-parent households with very low rates of divorce are a major theme, as are duty, love, and obligation to family with a special emphasis on the care of the elderly.[8] In addition, such newsletters extol glorious epochs of history and achievements, creating a new version of a shared history as a binding force of an "Indian" community. In keeping with the purpose of a religious organization, these "historical" accounts focus on a Hindu civilization (sometimes including aspects of Jainism, Buddhism, or Sikhism), but overlook the contributions of Muslims and Christians. This transformation of a variegated spiritual system into a congregational religion in order to make it fit the requirements of the United States, opens up a space to create a centralized hierarchy and to institutionalize the power of the hegemonic group, who become spokespersons for "the community."

As they reinvent this new form of "traditional culture," the hegemonic group is dependent on two hierarchies to maintain power: gender and nationalism. First, the roles of males and females are clearly demarcated. Females are lauded as the keepers of tradition, the guardians of the private sphere, and are responsible for the well-being of the community through their successful socialization of their children into this ethno-religious culture; that is, they are given significant symbolic space, assigned most responsibilities in the homes, and given very restricted access to the public power that determines the directions of the community. Males are expected to keep up the tradition of high achievement and act as spokespersons of "the community"; this hierarchy is evident in ethnographic studies of temple-based ethno-religious communities (Kurien 1999; Rayapol 1997). Thus, in families that already practice overt gender distinctions, the emerging community repertoires reinforce ideas about what is "natural" for the community.

Second, this use of religion in the service of (ethno)-nationalism, to borrow a phrase from Madhu Kishwar (1998), creates sharply defined boundaries between Hindus and Muslims and requires separating histories and cultures to fit essentialized identities.[9] On the one hand, since temples claim Indianness, Indian Muslims are left out of this emerging form of Indianness, as are Christians, Sikhs, and others. On the other hand, these clearly demarcated identities that emphasize religions as primary forces also fit well with emerging racialization trends in the mainstream where Muslims are vilified, and Hindus less so. These fragmented identities can create a sense of safety for those who subscribe to this ideology of religious fragmentation.

However, during the interviews, it became apparent that while the South Asian Americans in this study were aware of the hegemonic religious assertions of Hinduism, the vast majority of them, like Pranata, were not active participants in the process.[10] At the most, many of them went with their families to "a Diwali show and dinner" but the emphasis was on a form of sporadic socializing rather than ongoing participation in an ethno-religious community. The non-participation of the second generation in "religious activities" was recently apparent as one of the temples conducted a "youth survey" that tried to find out why the Hindu second generation did not attend the temple regularly. In the survey, being Hindu was defined in terms of ritualistic practices and congregational participation that reflects the hegemonic group's ethos, a pattern pointed out to me by some parents who are critical of this hegemonic ethno-religious community.

Temples are not the sole guardians of religious assertions of ethnicity. Groups that practice other forms of Hinduism continue to exist. Anjali, who is of Bengali origin, explained that she has rarely gone to the local temple. Her family members (who live in different parts of the world) practice different versions of Hinduism. The majority of her family members emphasize a "high civilization" version of Hinduism, with its intellectual (instead of ritual-dependent) understanding of spirituality; they emphasize individual responsibility for transcending all forms of social boundaries and uphold a holistic vision of the universe over specific forms of practice. Anjali said when she was younger her parents took her regularly to the Christmas service at a Vedanta society in New York City, and emphasized the version of Hinduism that was *formally inclusive* of multiple religious traditions. Clearly, her family practice of religion places her as an outsider to the emerging hegemonic version of Hinduism.

Other South Asian Americans who practice more syncretic forms of religions encounter similar boundaries. For instance, the Newars among the Nepalese practice a syncretic form of Buddhism and Hinduism and the insistence on "pure Hinduism" by temples creates boundaries between the hegemonic form of Hinduism and the Newar version. Indeed, all Nepalese Americans are also marginalized by this hegemonic version which conflates being Hindu with being Indian, effectively ignoring people with roots in the only officially Hindu country in the world. Indeed, all the Nepalese Americans echoed Pratibha's expressed wish (recorded at the beginning of chapter 2) to be known as members of their *unique* society.

Anjali also described the conflicts of her regional cultural group with the local temple, which exemplify some of the ways in which patriarchy is upheld through the efforts of the hegemonic group. This temple features many gods and goddesses, but the goddesses are represented as consorts of the gods. In her regional culture, however, every major Hindu celebration focuses on a goddess, with the male gods in very secondary positions. The main celebration—Durga Puja—shows the goddess, on a lion, killing a brawny, powerful male demon. When the Bengalis proposed putting this image in the temple, the executive committee of the temple sent back a letter asking for a female icon "with pleasing features."[11] Anjali said that Bengali celebrations continued to be organized in rented halls, and the use of the neutral space allowed people of other religions, including Islam, free access to these religio-cultural celebrations. She described many instances when this celebration engaged the efforts of Bengali Hindu Indians and Bangladeshi Muslims in the cultural program that is centrally featured during this time. Aware of her own family history of moving as refugees during the partition of Bangladesh, she remarked how the bonds between Bengalis were being kept up despite traumatic political experiences many families experienced. In contrast, she said, at the Hindu temple, where the majority of the families had been far removed from the actual experience of the partition, people were now actively engaged in dividing Muslims and Hindus.

Each nation-based group among the South Asian Americans has a number of other ethnic sub-groups based on other aspects of identity (see Khandelwal 2002; Leonard 1997), however, the emerging emphases among the hegemonic groups appear to be similar. The construction of such rigid religious boundaries is not confined to Hindus.[12] The Muslim South Asian Americans of Bangladeshi origin expressed a similar concern. They described the Pakistani version of Islam as the hegemonic version (although there are variations among the South Asian Americans of Pakistani origin) and distanced themselves by explaining that the language and cultural practices the hegemonic group followed were distinctively different from their practices. Most of all, they expressed an outsidedness to the gender norms that are enforced by the hegemonic version of Islam. Selina, who is of Bangladeshi origin, explained that even among the more benign set of practices, all these religions restricted the role of females.

The growing power of such hegemonic groups also has to be understood with reference to the context in which they emerge and flourish. Since they are the ones who most often voice and enforce aspects of culture that the mainstream defines as "different or traditional" (as opposed to modern cultures of the United States), they often have most access to the media as representatives of the ethnic community. Others, more egalitarian, whose ethnic practices are based on permeable boundaries, are less obviously "ethnic" and they rarely get similar publicity. For instance, several first generation South Asian women have been very active in promoting competing notions of tradition (for example Abraham 2000; Dasgupta and Das Dasgupta 1996, 1997). They have actively challenged these conservative notions of ethnicity, gender, religion, and nationality.[13] They have also actively challenged the earlier white-feminist notion that minority women can become empowered only through distancing themselves from their "traditional" cultures. While there is a growing literature on gender issues created and disseminated by these other groups, it was clear, from my interviews with this study's participants, that these ideas (and groups) were not widely recognized by the South Asian Americans. The few who were aware of these other groups and versions either knew about them because their families were involved, or through what they had encountered in colleges (and their own activist networks). Thus in their minds, the hegemonic, conservative position represents "the South Asian perspective," and they define themselves in terms of their degree of compliance with, or distance from, the hegemonic form.

In sum, the recreation of ethno-religious communities in the United States is often accompanied by the homogenization of religious practices and centralization of the authority structure in religious communities. Hegemonic groups in these communities construct an ideology of superior civilization to draw in families who are looking for ways to collectively construct affirming cultures that act in counterpoint to the racialization of their cultures, irrespective of whether these families deny such processes or acknowledge them.

But the hegemonic versions also attempt to further fragment South Asian Americans on the basis of religion, nationality, and gender. As Shah (1997), Yuval-Davis (1994), and others have pointed out, the reconstruction of ethnicity among minorities often leads to the ascendance of conservatives as the public voices for the group. These constructions of ethnic boundaries through ethno-religious communities further exacerbate some of the conflicts over gender, nationality, and race within families.

GENDER REGIMES AND CHOICE OF PARTNERS

The confluence of the family and community impulses, and how these intersect with larger structural processes, is most evident as we examine the different gender regimes among this group. This discussion is centered on dating and choice of life partners and illustrates how these constructed boundaries play out in the lives of South Asian Americans.

The relative freedom of these South Asian American females to choose their partners is the main point of conflict between the generations. The boundaries parents have tried to impose were based on how they defined "our group" in terms of religion, nationality, and race: these ideas often developed, as we have seen in the previous sections, in interaction with the mainstream and ethnic community. In matters of dating and partners, parents have used their superior achievement standard to send messages about homogamy, varying on whether this meant people of the same class group, or more specifically defined religious, nationality, and race groups.

Three groups—which represent a constellation of practices rather than clearly distinctive groups—are presented here to illustrate how the surveillance and scrutiny of female behaviors produces different forms and boundaries of ethnicity. It is important to note that this cross section describes these middle-class participants, and that the inclusion of other class groups could alter the "groups." The first group, which I refer to as the "essential-ethnicity group" is at one end: their parents do not allow them to date and expect them to accept arranged marriages. These are arranged marriages that uphold caste, religion, linguistic group, region of origin, class hierarchies, and the primacy of parental decisions in choosing spouses. All these participants equated their family norms with being "the" Indian, Pakistani, Bangladeshi, or Nepalese norms. The middle group, which I refer to as the "bounded-ethnicity group" consists of South Asian Americans whose families try to enforce strict scrutiny of females' dating and sexual relationships, but do not expect as strictly defined forms of endogamy as the first group. In many cases, the South Asian Americans from these families subvert these norms by not mentioning their dating practices or relationships to their parents. The third group, which was much larger, numerically, than the "essential-ethnicity group," but not as large as the bounded-ethnicity group, does not encounter such surveillance or scrutiny of female behaviors or absolute restrictions on out-marriages. I refer to them as the "pervious-ethnicity" group.

The Essential-ethnicity Group

Varsha represents the conservative end of the continuum for females among all the South Asian Americans. Her parents expected their daughters to go through arranged marriages with men of their caste group in India. Since caste groups are always very specific to region, religion (in terms of which kind of Hinduism is practiced), and linguistic groups in India, this meant that they were expected to marry people from specific villages in one part of India, whom they had not met previously. Her older sister had married someone chosen by her parents from this village and Varsha, who was very close to her sister, had witnessed her sister's struggle to make the marriage work. Varsha clearly saw this form of marriage as "the Indian" norm and said she did not mind getting married this way. However, she did add that she negotiated the meaning of the arrangement, rejecting her parents' focus on their ancestral village as the only source of potential partners. She said, "Personally I don't mind an arranged marriage as long as my parents don't force me to marry someone I don't like. . . . I told my parents I'll get married to an Indian but you better look at countries other than India. There are very few educated people in our caste in India." Among males, Satyakam (who is of Hindu, Indian origin) and Abbas (who is a Muslim of Pakistani origin) described their intentions to uphold "traditional" norms. Satyakam felt that he had to uphold his caste tradition especially because Indians in the United States increasingly ignored it. To him, a key way of upholding caste distinctions was through carefully chosen marriage partners, and his parents would take care of the choice. Abbas also felt the arranged marriage system had worked for "his culture" for thousands of years so it would work for him. His mother would return to Pakistan and pick a girl for him. Although his parents would ask if he had someone in mind, it would ultimately be their decision.

Although all three were expecting to go through this form of arranged marriage, there is a significant distinction between how Varsha and Abbas explained normative behaviors of males and females.

ABBAS: Dating in Pakistan is different. . . . I tried to become American when I came here . . . my sister gave me a new car. She gave me everything that was possible, nice car, clothes everything. I did date and messed around during my high school. But when I went to college I realized I was not doing it for myself. I was doing it so that people do not hate me, or dislike me, so I tried to act like them . . . rolling up in the car and driving around with nice rims and wearing baggy clothes. I never smoke or drank because it's not something I approve of. But still, I did other stuff . . . guys can have sex, but for Pakistani people having sex is a big big thing. If a girl kisses someone they are going to regret it all their lives. But a guy can have sex and forget about it the next day.

Varsha described the effect of such gender distinctions in marriages. She said her male cousins followed the same norm. "In my family the role of women is totally messed up. I have a younger brother and he is totally spoilt and he can do no wrong, it's like he is male so that's alright. . . . My cousin got married and the way she [his wife] acts, it's 80–20 in their marriage because only he makes the decisions. It's not like he does not respect her, but she doesn't speak up. She wants to go to school, but she won't say it."

A series of gender distinctions are apparent in these statements. Abbas, who, like conservative males of any group, enjoyed the male privilege of "doing other stuff," assumed that upholding the "Pakistani" norm depended on controlling female behaviors. As the female who would suffer the consequences of such gender hierarchies, Varsha attempted to negotiate with her parents. Abbas or Satyakam felt no need to negotiate the standards with their parents since they expected their lives would be similar to the lives of Varsha's cousins, with very unequal power relations between the male and female partners in the marriages.

The greater control of females and the reliance on over-generalized notions of ethno-national identity is often imposed through closed networks. Any attempts to negotiate their position by members of this group involves negotiating the meaning of their ethnic identity and getting their families to accept an expanded notion of who belonged in the group. This is exactly what Varsha was attempting to negotiate by lobbying for a partner who had grown up in the diaspora.

The Bounded-ethnicity Group

The second group's enactment of their gender regimes comes closest to earlier scholarly descriptions of living in two worlds (for example, Bacon 1996). They differ from the first group because they are subject to restrictions on dating (which is often used synonymously for premarital sex), but they are allowed some choice in who they marry. All the females in this second group were very critical of the unequal gender regimes in their families. While some described the different chores they and their brothers performed in the household as proof of their parent's sexism, most mentioned different curfews and unequal freedom to drink and date as the main points of conflict with their parents. Maya, a female, said, "Yes it seems like there is a double standard in the Indians. Like the second generation, especially because your parents are from India they follow those rules. But the guys definitely have an easier time than the girls do—my friends' brothers don't care what they do, but our parents are stricter with the girls, like my parents were like 'don't get involved with any guy.'"

Most of these females said that as they got to college, they started subverting these parental strictures. However, two of the females described how the males within the group would try to uphold the "ethnic community norms" and become "protective" of the females' behaviors. By reinventing an extended family role of fictive brothers or cousins who are supposed to "support and help" sisters, in an authoritarian way, these males start becoming protective of "their females."

Meena, a Hindu from New York, said: The guys are more protective. The girls do it too, but they don't talk about it. The guys want to show it. They want everyone to know they are taking care of the girls. And the girls like it too. I know I like it although after a while it gets to be too much. My friend's boyfriend is very protective and she just loves it.

Alka, a Hindu from Connecticut: In my group the guys will try to integrate, but there are some extremities. Like my guy friends will get very protective of us especially if we are talking to strangers that are male, and do the older brother syndrome. Which like no other girl will go over to another girl and threaten to beat her up . . . [Q: What is the elder brother syndrome?] They'll come and stand next to you instead of letting you finish the conversation, they'll give that person the third degree, they'll tell that person you are not available, even if you are. They'll definitely hover over you; they'll be in your space and later ask you thirty questions about how you felt through the whole thing. I've seen it happen. It's funny. Can be degrading. It's also reassuring. It's all of those.

I described the cultural closeness of brothers and sisters in the last chapter and mentioned that these norms were extended to fictive brothers and sisters as well. In these situations, however, the cultural symbolism was being used without the associated cultural controls. Being a brother to a sister involves participating in ongoing androgynous (even feminine) norms of caring and help (Knuckolls 1993). But these "fictive brothers" are not expected to enact the more feminine norms. Thus, the androgynous aspects of culture are transformed into ultra-masculinist "norms of protection" which act as ways of exerting control over females. Depending on their particular family socialization, some females accepted these behaviors as normal and, as Meena and Alka point out, even appreciate such protection.

Most others, like Maya, who is quoted at the beginning of this chapter, were irritated by the double standards and often distanced themselves from these "too ethnic" networks.[14] Several South Asian American females mentioned how the behaviors of these males to "claim their females" led to fights in South Asian American parties. While most authors emphasize the control of females by ethnic communities, I would emphasize that the control of females has to be understood in relation to the transformation of masculinity in these communities. The power differences are greatest when females are controlled and males are free to try on ultra-masculinities. This is the transformation the two females described. For males who are marginalized in the mainstream as undesirable, control of females within the community becomes a primary means of enacting masculinity (see Connell 1995 or Messner 1992 for a detailed conceptualization of these masculinities). Not all males engage in these forms of doing masculinity, but, as Messner (1992) has described, the relative access to other social forms of power appears to be related to which males participate in supporting or opposing these forms of control over females.

Unlike the males, most females in the second group spoke about restrictions on dating. However, both females and males dated, and, in keeping with parental restrictions, they did not tell their parents about these activities.

AMIT, A CHRISTIAN MALE: The few dating experiences I had were under the table so to speak. My mom is traditional and she's like keep your mind on studying, studying, studying . . . my father is like you don't want to get involved with girls till you are married. It's culture and tradition I guess.

SUMI SAID: Like my parents know that I am capable of lying to them. They know him, you know, but it's hard. Its like he is South Indian and he is Christian, and I'm Hindu, it's the whole thing you are Hindu so you have to marry a Hindu.

ALKA, A HINDU FEMALE: A lot of people don't tell parents their true feelings. My struggle is that I always have to tell them the half-truth; I'm not going to volunteer any more information. They know not to ask because they don't want to know the answer. But they know where we stand and what we do. [But] . . . I won't exactly tell them hey mom I'm dating a guy and thinking about having sex with him. That's my struggle.

While I did not solicit opinions from the parents of these participants, I became aware of the extent to which this "don't ask, don't tell" policy helps to maintain the first generation's illusions about their children's lives through my own participation in a number of social events in these communities. During much of the conversation about the educational or occupational achievement of the second generation, parents whose children were in college would often advise couples with younger children to shield their children from the "American" practices of dating, drinking, and engaging in premarital sex. Irrespective of what their own children did, the persistence of this story across social settings built up the ideological framework of what constitutes South Asian-ness. However, it was clear that while the second generation acknowledge these "South Asian norms," they subvert them anyway.

Shanthi, a Hindu female, is a case in point. When I interviewed her she was dating a member of another religion. Her parents were unaware of this. She said that most often her fictive kin would approach her parents and tell them about "possible matches," so she had asked her mother to ask them to contact her directly. During the course of this research, Shanthi broke up with her boyfriend and married someone who she met through the community match-making system she described. (She too organized a transnational wedding like Arvind and Anita in India.)

Although the strictures against dating in the second group are similar to the norms in the essential-ethnicity group, the form of arranged marriages and their individual roles in it are somewhat different. Shanthi's experience illustrates that parents filter prospective partners, and this second group gets to choose whom they want to marry from among the prospective choices. Most of these South Asian Americans insisted that they had a formal role in voicing their opinions. Since many of this group were dating secretly, they expected to marry through arrangement *if* they had not found anyone they really liked. The form of arrangement they had in mind was very different from the form described by Abbas or Varsha. Amit, who is Christian, said, "They are going to try and introduce you to someone, friends of friends. It's not like you won't see her, you get to know them, and then if it does not work out it doesn't work out. Someone that's good for us, especially if you don't know too many Indians."

Prospective partners are typically located through transnational networks in the United States, Canada, or United Kingdom, and sometimes from South Asia. These choices are determined by similarities of class background, religion, nationality and, if possible, by linguistic group/regional cultures. Often broad groups that are similar in terms of nationality and religion, but not necessarily in terms of specific regional or linguistic cultures, are acceptable. The transnational family field becomes a critical source in such searches. Many echoed Amit, who said that being a geographically dispersed minority group meant that they were unlikely to meet someone like themselves within the course of their daily activities. So the prior filtering worked well to bring them in contact with eligible persons; after that they could make a decision based on their personal preferences. One female remarked that the "thirty-point matches" many of the dating services advertised on television for non-ethnic Americans was a mirror image of what went on in her community. According to her, the impersonality of the dating service versus the personal time investment of her parents and family members was the only difference between these "love" and "arranged" marriages.

For many of the South Asian Americans in the first and second groups, their families attempt to construct superior cultures—characterized by achievement and strong families—in gendered ways. Males are encouraged to attain white-collar technocratic positions and become good providers, which makes them eligible matches. In contrast, the pressure on females to achieve is accompanied by strict scrutiny of their freedom to date and freely find marital partners, so that the emphasis is that they become high-achieving but chaste wives. The control of females ensures homogamy within patriarchal family systems.

Apart from subverting their parental strictures, the South Asian Americans also indicated that their parents' ability to control them through the "South Asian culture" frame is mediated by their own knowledge of what they consider to be "typical" behaviors of females in South Asian countries. Sumaira and Alka's responses are typical:

SUMAIRA, A FEMALE OF PAKISTANI ORIGIN, SAID: I went to visit my cousins for this holiday. I'm wearing my traditional clothes with my family, and we're going to my cousins' house. My cousin's wearing jeans, and a t-shirt, and they're speaking to me in English, so are my aunts and my uncles. And I mean, not all of them are like that—I'm just giving you one example—so I'm just like, it was so weird. I was just like, look at me, still retaining my culture, yet my own people living in their country and never, ever lived anywhere else, are doing that.

ALKA, A FEMALE OF INDIAN ORIGIN, SAID: They [an ethnic organization] pull all the stereotypes of an Indian teenager. . . . And in India I've gone to clubs and girls will wear halters and I've stayed out till four and slept over at [her mother's friend's son's] house.

While many parents attempt to clearly separate "South Asian" norms from "American" norms, many of these second generation females (and some males) see these norms in far more complicated terms. They argue, like Alka and Sumaira, that they are subject to greater scrutiny because of *South Asian American* norms, That is, the norms of their ethnic communities in the United States. But they also use their parents' framing of "American" to argue that, as females brought up in America, they are unlikely to follow South Asian practices. Given these different frames of reference, many of these South Asian Americans felt comfortable with adopting different behavior sets for different (family/community and mainstream) arenas and they often invested a great deal of time and management skills in keeping their dual lives separate.

Although they often used their "Americanness" as an argument to challenge gendered restrictions, it became clear that members of this second group were less apt to challenge ethno-national and ethno-religious boundaries.

Several Hindu South Asian Americans, who were strongly influenced by hegemonic norms, said they would never date Muslims. Meena provided an insight into the extent to which some South Asian Americans of this second group are socialized to operate within the boundaries.

> It's so funny they [referring to an Indian group] don't like Muslims but two of my friends are Muslims. One of my best friends is Muslim . . . its very ghetto, they are so overpowering and scary. . . . Mostly with girls its like I will never go with a Muslim. Like it's a fact that Pakistani guys are good looking. But the Indian Hindu girls are like they may be good looking, but there's no future there, because I refuse to be with a Muslim . . . its not like they're not friends with them, but not girl-guy relationships. . . . Pakistanis because of their culture, they don't party so they don't go to these meets. They don't drink when they go to parties, so they don't mix in terms of groups. My friend is Gujarati Muslim, but we don't consider that Gujarati, we just consider her a Muslim. We are like we have two Gujaratis in the group. Then we're like wait, two? Of yeah, we forgot about her.

As a number of scholars have argued, the gendered expectations of females to uphold "tradition" often means females are expected to uphold the boundaries between "Indian" or "Pakistani" or "Bangladeshi" or "Nepalese" in attempts to keep them "within the community" (Anthias and Yuval-Davis 1989; Das Gupta 1997; Rudrappa 2002). The success of the combined efforts of some families and the hegemonic community group is evident in Meena's description of upholding these boundaries.

Those who transcend these boundaries are severely censured. One participant whose husband is black explained how her immediate family rejected her when she told them she was going to marry her long-time partner. While they had relented slightly with time, she still felt a degree of outsidedness. More devastating for her was the realization that she could probably never take her husband home to visit her extended family on the subcontinent, because they would not wholeheartedly accept a black American spouse either. Another participant, who married a white American, said her parents had no problems with her choice. Her extended family on the subcontinent welcomed him. However, the second participant felt that if her own partner had been black, it could have been a problem in her extended family too.

"Race" is not the only point of contention. Sumi, who is of British Indian origin, described "all hell broke lose" when her cousin married a Pakistani. (Later Sumi's father began to bond with the nephew-in-law, but the girl's parents did not relent). A couple, one is Muslim and the other Hindu, described the different types of difficulty they faced. Apart from the mainstream vilification of Muslims, a number of community and family issues made their partnership more challenging. Although both of them construct their ethnicity like the third (that is, pervious-ethnicity) group their statements provide a clear indication of how social control and censure operate in the communities.

THE MALE PARTNER: [Speaking about difficulties] [N]ot between us but outside. The good part is that neither of us is attached to [our religions]. But there are certain times like when my father passed away, there were some rituals that she wanted to do but she couldn't do it . . . it's a hard adjustment. Yet as I get older there are certain things that I won't argue against.

THE FEMALE PARTNER: I have been brought up to respect what's going on without impeding on it and I do that. At the same time I was wrestling with myself thinking what is wrong here, why aren't the women allowed to do what the men are doing. . . . From my standpoint there was definitely a history of conflict from my family point of view and within the context of the larger community. Like when I'm speaking to another South Asian they're like wait a minute you are Hindu and he is a Muslim so what do your parents think . . . do they know? Those were some of the first things I remember being faced with.

THE MALE PARTNER: The value for us is that we are not so entrenched, but we are aware of it. I can see how it could become an issue in future if one of us became more religious. . . . I don't understand her religion and I sense the tension coming at me. At times like marriages you sense you are very different. Also rituals like mourning. . . . I didn't know what I was doing but I went along. So that's a core difference.

The challenges described by this inter-ethnic couple illustrate that the animosities between India and Pakistan (and among Hindus and Muslims), which other South Asian Americans who have traveled to the subcontinent have described, continue to affect them in the United States.

Nor is religion the only point of contention. Another female's experience illustrates another facet of this problem. Both of her parents are of Indian origin, but her father is Muslim and her mother a Hindu, and she describes herself primarily as an Indian Muslim. Her boyfriend in college was Muslim, but he was of Pakistani origin. Because of her boyfriend's association with the Pakistani students organization in college, as well as her own dislike of the "Indian clique who ran the Indian organization," she began to join in the activities of the Pakistani organization. Her parents were extremely distressed because, in their minds, their Indian identity was being jeopardized by her drift towards Pakistanis. The difficult position of this female and her parents was exacerbated by the hegemonic Hindu group's efforts to conflate Indian with Hindu, leaving the Indian Muslims in a liminal space. Ultimately she broke up with her Pakistani partner and got engaged to a Jewish person.

Thus, among this group, some South Asian Americans challenge some of the gender boundaries using an argument about their Americanness, while maintaining the ethno-religio-nationalist boundaries imposed by the first generation. They covertly transcend these boundaries by constructing two simultaneous, somewhat dichotomized realities. Others breach the religious, nation, *and* racial divides by creating friendship networks, and sometimes marital partnerships, and remove themselves from the ambit of the first generation hegemonic groups.

The Pervious-ethnicity Group

The third group is composed of second generation persons who described their ethnicity in terms of choices. A few had encountered opposition in their families to dating other minorities or people of other faiths, but their families had changed their perspectives over time. The rest did not encounter similar restrictions on dating or choice of life partners. Their parental notions of their ethnic identity were not contingent upon the extra surveillance and scrutiny of female behaviors. Pranata, who earlier explained that she was not subject to any overt gender distinctions at home, described her struggles with understanding what the "Indian" norms were.

> In some ways I see my father's side of the family as being more traditional with things. And also just you know, I'm really amazed at what my mother did . . . just having to leave home and come to a country she didn't know. I just feel like, women within the South Asian culture have had to endure a lot. I think now, they've been silent in some ways for so long and even though some of them aren't so silenced now . . . it's just really showing me South Asian women can be empowered and do things for themselves and I think in some ways that's made me identify with my culture more. Also seeing my mother get more involved in [women's issues] has made me feel more comfortable with the idea of being empowered. For my mother having her own career and all these interests that she has and developing them has definitely made me really proud of her, but also be like if she can do this I shouldn't feel like I have to hold back. But I think [this idea of South Asian marriages for women] has definitely gotten confused just 'cause . . . when people think of Indian women they think of them as being submissive and all this. And I think having an education has, in some ways, made it hard for me to relate to that position. And it gets really confused I think . . . like my father's mother, she did control the household but it was within the domestic realm and my grandfather was the one with the last word . . . and it's changed so much now. And I think also, in some ways the experience that I've had hasn't been the typical Indian family you know . . . [when] people think of being an Indian woman they think

of an Indian woman in a village in India who's in a situation of domestic violence. That does happen here, I'm not saying that it doesn't, but it's a different picture than the life I've had.

Pranata struggled to separate the different ideological constructions of Indian womanhood (in the hegemonic community in terms of women's family roles and the mainstream in terms of subordination) with changing roles of females within her transnational family. She clearly saw ethnicity as dynamic rather than based on unchanging tradition; she had witnessed her parents getting more involved with people of color issues and she did not think of her ethnicity (and theirs) as a sharp break from tradition. She tried to find some continuity between the norms her parents were subject to in India, the trajectory of her mother's life, and her own position as a high achieving Indian American. She said that several of her family members had married people of other groups (white Christians and Jews), so her choice of partners was not restricted like it was with some other people she knew.

Selina, who said that she had deliberately adopted a very ethnic persona (in terms of fashions and style) during her high school years to separate herself from her white peers, and that she was highly critical of the gendered practices of most religions, married a white-ethnic American. She said the commonality of values worked for both of them. Her experience was that both her parents and the ethnic community had been accepting of her choice. Her extended family on the subcontinent made her husband feel sufficiently at home so that he was visiting them on his own at the time I interviewed her. Anjali, also, described her family as an amalgam of intermarriages between Hindus, Sikhs, Muslims, and Christians and many nationalities and linguistic groups.

Most of the parents in this third group seemed to be willing to ignore "the" community's ideologies and allow their children—females and males—to make their own choices. Mala is typical. She said their parents had no problems with her dating and were willing to confront anyone who spoke badly of their daughter. "My cousin's husband, he hates me because he thinks I am too liberal. He told my father how could you allow your daughter [to date] and my father was like that's my daughter that's my business. That took care of that . . . like the guys I go out with, as a formality I'll ask my mom can I go out, she'll never say no. Hasn't said no for years."

The South Asian Americans whom I categorized in this group not only separated themselves from the hegemonic versions of "South Asian" cultures, but they often described the content of their ethnic culture in different terms. Deepa, for instance, had set her mind on marrying someone of her linguistic background so she could avoid dealing with the cultures of other South Asian groups, which she often found to be too restrictive and ritualistic. However, she met someone through work who belonged to a different linguistic background but shared her cosmopolitan values; when they decided to get married, neither of their parents had any problems with their choice. Partha, who is of Indian origin, also said that the regional cultures of many South Asian groups were very ethnocentric and he preferred the greater openness and universalistic values of his own sub-cultural group. Kader, who is of Bangladeshi origin, echoed his interpretation. Partha later became engaged to a white woman, who shared the "cultural values" that he defined in terms of universalism. His family welcomed her.[15]

Clearly, the boundaries of this third group's ethnicness are not as sharply demarcated as the second group, but it is problematic to assume this is simply a sign of its members' greater integration into mainstream America. I would argue that for this group, paying heed to how they define their cultures makes it difficult to fit them neatly into dichotomized categories of "ethnic cultures" or "mainstream" cultures. Their social identity is based on a rejection of the emerging narrow ethno-religious constructions among the hegemonic community group, as well as the racial *and* nationalistic standards by which they are framed in the mainstream, that is, whether they are culturally American or not. They construct their cultures in more universalistic terms: a sense of social justice, and a commitment to weakening social boundaries between people (of nationality, religion, race, gender, etc.). The construction of their cultures weaves strands from a global world and they referred to an array of global thinkers who influenced them; Rabindranath Tagore, J. M. Krishnamurthy, Khalil Gibran, Maya Angelou, and Isiah Berlin were the names mentioned. It is difficult to describe them as ethnic in the sense of being a group that is *different* from the mainstream, or to describe them solely as integrated Americans, since their universalistic version of culture resembles the cultures of some *sections* of the mainstream only.[16] Their negotiations of ethnicity involve transcending the hegemonic communities *and* national horizons. Their understanding of culture and their social consciousness spans a transnational space.

NEGOTIATING ETHNIC BOUNDARIES

The existence of multiple boundaries—in the mainstream, within the transnational networks, and within their communities and families—generates ethnic repertoires that coexist and clash, creating bridges and chasms among the second generation study participants as a whole. A few trends are clear from their discussion about their family conflicts suggesting increasing challenges and negotiations of racial, gender, and religious boundaries.

First, their discussions on families indicated that the South Asian Americans have begun to reject the overt racism of some of their families. Maya, among others, said, "What I hate most about Indian people is they call blacks by this name and Chinese people by this name and they talk down. I hate it. I

don't care if people call me Indian. But the racial undertones [of first genera-
tion] I hate that."

Prakrit illustrated another dimension of this overt prejudice. He described
how "a group [of 'Indians'] from Africa talk against Bangladeshis, Bengalis,
Pakistanis, and blacks." He pointed out that even if groups that had been
expelled from some African countries remained bitter toward those Africans,
it was hard to excuse their rejection of all *black* groups because of their prior
history. Their prejudices were now being expressed in another structural setting, in ways that fit the hegemonic community version in the United States.

Their rejection of these attitudes is consistent with their attempts to build
more diverse networks of friends in college that I described in chapter 2. They
move from an all-white friends group during their high school years to friends
of diverse racial backgrounds during their time in college. Overall, their discussions indicate that most consider *their* ethnic boundaries to be more permeable than that of the version circulated by the hegemonic groups. At least
their statements indicate that they remain more open to building multiracial
ties, similar to the trans-ethnic black and Asian identities that have been developing in the United Kingdom (Anthias 2001a; Sudbury 2001).

Second, there appear to be two ways in which South Asian American
females challenge and negotiate gender inequalities. The convergence of the
hegemonic gender norms *and* the mainstream characterization of subordinated "South Asian" females guides the understanding of many females in the
essential-ethnicity and bounded-ethnicity groups. These groups appear to
accept this ideological construction; they focus on gender boundaries their
families impose upon them and subvert the strictures through their dating
behaviors. In addition, they argue and demand more equality with their
brothers within their families in matters of chores, curfews, and are sometimes
able to "bring their parents around." In contrast to the first two groups, those
in the pervious-ethnicity group are not as constricted by their family norms
(and are disengaged from the hegemonic community norms). They appear to
focus more on interrogating the racialized mainstream construction of subordinated South Asian women. They also challenge gender inequalities, but
focus on intersecting hierarchies, instead of focusing on gender boundaries
alone.

The discussion in this chapter also shows conflicts over the ethno-
religious content of their ethnicity. At least, in terms of potential marital
partners, more South Asian Americans (of the essential-ethnicity and
bounded-ethnicity groups) are willing to stay within the boundaries set by
their families. The effort of the hegemonic Hindu groups to separate themselves from Muslims is paralleled by the construction of Muslims as a separate
group through several current policies in United States and other countries.
Religion and nationality also remain schisms within transnational family

fields. Thus, the confluence of these three levels in marking boundaries between Muslims and non-Muslims appears to be a potent force in fragmenting ethnic identities on religious grounds. While some South Asian Americans have breached these boundaries, the relative power of the non-hegemonic groups to keep this boundary permeable in the future will determine the degree to which religious boundaries remain salient to the construction of ethnicity.

The evidence from this chapter also illustrates what is common to the experiences of all South Asian Americans. They all have parents who emphasize achievement, all parents are ardent about their ethno-national identities (albeit in very different ways). They all share common experiences of having family in different countries and share the experience of being open to or influenced by sociocultural influences across nations. To the extent they are racialized as "the same," these common experiences, even when the specifics differ, can act as tools to build more pan-ethnic ties. These common experiences were mentioned by South Asian Americans when they described how they were all the same. Just as the emphasis on religious identities is likely to further fragment their pan-ethnic ties, their ability to move beyond parental and/or community notions of essentialized culture is likely to depend on the success of their pan-ethnic projects. So a central challenge for these South Asian Americans is to navigate through the parental, community, and mainstream influences, and find more politically neutral ways of enhancing commonalities. The next chapter shows that, aided by a growing global market of ethnic consumer products, they gravitate toward consumption and performance, books, movies, dances, music, and fashions, to define their ethnicity. By choosing these building blocks to "do culture" they are able to avoid some of the constraints that are imposed upon them.

CONCLUSION

This chapter focused on the conflicts with the second generation South Asian Americans and their parents over gender, nationality, religion, race, and class boundaries that were being produced through their nuclear families (and ethnic communities). The chapter further confirmed some of the processes that were evident through the interactions of the second generation with their transnational family field discussed in the previous chapter. We also saw the intersections of the public and the private: the mainstream structures, ethnic community interests, including the emerging hegemonic versions of ethnicity, and how these intersect with family practices. This chapter also confirmed the theoretical perspective that ethnicity is not about the transmission of cultural templates through the generations. Instead, ethnicity is actively constructed within situated contexts. Just as their transnational family experiences create layered ethnic identities, so do their experiences within the United States.

Diversity and difference is central to the experience of being ethnic and the South Asian Americans maintain a fluid and contextually informed sense of ethnic identity.

The discussion in this chapter focused on the construction of ethnicity through the demarcation of, and engagement with, a series of gender, religious, nationality, and race boundaries. Many first generation families emphasize their "superior cultures" as a way of creating distinctions between themselves and other, less high-achieving groups in the United States. In the process, they also deny the reality of other South Asian Americans, whose profile does not quite fit this superior achievement profile. And they attempt to set themselves apart from other racialized groups. Not all first generation South Asians subscribe to such ethnic identities and there are struggles and negotiations over which version "wins." The groups that become hegemonic and are able to disseminate their templates of "our ethnic culture" most widely gain this power because they most closely approximate some of the mainstream expectations. Within the families, there are a series of struggles over the different boundaries. Ethnicity emerges, not simply as a matter of homogenous culture, but through a series of struggles of groups and individuals, in communities, and within families. These individuals and groups are located in different structural positions and are simultaneously engaged in carving out the contours of ethnicity. Thus, their ethnicity reflects an amalgam of these divergent *and* overlapping processes of negotiations.

This chapter illustrates that many groups draw on "nation-of origin" frames to define their ethnicity as many of the diaspora scholars predict (for example, Cohen 1998). Yet, two trends in this chapter suggest a different way of understanding these frames. First, what exactly constitutes "common origins" is not pre-given. Groups refer to political entity and/or cultural or symbolic entities depending on their particular circumstances. It is clear that most of the first generation South Asians were not actually using the pre-partition history as a way of describing "traditional" common origin (that is, the versions that would have to be inclusive of Indians or Pakistanis or Bangladeshis, depending on which ethno-national group asserts their "origins"). Instead, the contour of this "place of origin" which inspires identification with "the ethno-national identity" is being recreated along religious and nationality lines. Many of the problems that South Asian Americans with family in more than one nation encountered, as I described in the last chapter, are also local-level problems of fitting into these ethno-nationally identified communities. Which ones do they belong to, and which aspects of their identity tie them to these communities? Second, nation of origin also suggests all individuals equally participate in such real or symbolic nations. But the boundaries that are emerging through the hegemonic versions of ethnicity clearly exclude many people from equal participation in these ethno-national identities. Thus, even though groups may promote ethnicities that tie them with nations-of-origin, the nature of these relationships is stratified. Division and difference mark the claims about who falls within the purview of common origin and in which way, and, this is a reflection of their structural positions within these communities.

The main theme of this chapter was the boundaries that are produced through nuclear families and how the second generation negotiates these boundaries. Clearly, all members of families are not equal, and ethnic families, like other families in the United States, are sites of struggles and cooperation to determine how individuals should live their lives. Even though ethnic families often claim "our culture" as the reason for imposing certain boundaries, the presence of three types of families and how they interpret their ethnic cultures shows a great deal of variation in the types of boundaries that are produced and how these shape ethnicity among the second generation South Asian Americans. The motivations, ideologies, and practices of South Asian families would multiply if we consider the newer South Asian immigrant groups as well. Irrespective of the form of negotiation these South Asian Americans adopted, they breached and subverted some of the boundaries and shaped their version of ethnicity.

As Wollett and her colleagues (1994) found from their study of Asians (of South Asian origin) in London, groups that are subject to multiple boundaries maintain a fluid and contextually informed sense of ethnic identity. A similar pattern seems to be evident among the South Asian Americans as well. Thus, this chapter confirmed some of the patterns evident from the previous chapters: South Asian Americans maintain multiple layers of ethnicity to deal with these structural contexts within which they are enmeshed. The specific shapes and forms of ethnicity they build, which is the subject of the next two chapters, is influenced by the types of boundaries they encounter in these intersecting contexts.

CHAPTER 5

Ethnic Practices, Cultural Consumption

Meena: "I was not at all Indianized till I met Reena in tenth grade and she introduced me to Indian films and music."

Namrata, who is of Indian origin, said: "I think the second generation created our own Indian culture, it's a fusion, it's like American culture with an Indian theme to it."

Saira, who is of Pakistani origin, said: "I watch a lot of Indian movies, because that's gonna let me keep hearing the language, and at home we actually got a satellite dish, we get the channels from there now, so when I'm at home I'm always watching like the news and Urdu, and seeing like all the things going on, and watching TV shows and everything from there. We like the desi stuff, like Indian and Pakistani together, we call it desi, D-E-S-I."

THIS EXPLORATION OF South Asian Americans' reasons for choosing hyphenated identities has focused, so far, on boundaries that result from social relations that constitute nation-states, ethnic communities, and nuclear and transitional families. I have illustrated how racialization processes and hegemonic ethnic community forces use "essential culture" frameworks (albeit in opposite ways) to construct ethnic boundaries. Nuclear families emphasize ethno-national identities; in contrast, their transnational family experiences make them realize they are "culturally American." South Asian Americans negotiate their ethnicity amidst these often-contradictory constraints and opportunities: even though they are pushed to privilege their ethno-national identities in college, in the company of others in the same general structural location, they try to construct more pan-ethnic South Asian American identities.

This chapter documents the influence of another set of forces—the global industry in selling cultural products—that provides South Asian Americans with "neutral" cultural tools—fashions, music, movies, books, and related items—

for building bridges across nations-of-origin boundaries. These tools also seem to help them navigate, at least on the surface, the gender, religious, race, and nationality chasms embedded in ethno-national forms of ethnicity. The quotations at the beginning of this chapter illustrate the emerging shared interest in music and movies among Indian and Pakistani Americans. This chapter shows that all four groups—Bangladeshi, Indian, Nepalese, and Pakistani Americans—appear to be developing "fusion" or "hybrid" desi culture that is based, not on deep essential cultural characteristics or practices, but on shared consumption of material cultural items.[1] The South Asian Americans use these material cultural items for constructing ethno-national *and* more pan-ethnic identities.

In this chapter I illustrate how these "neutral building blocks" shape ethnicity. Globalization scholars have pointed out that the growth of the industry for producing, marketing, and selling cultural products allows contemporary groups to construct and display their ethnicity in new ways (for example, Appadurai 1996; Halter 2000; Lury 1996). The convergence of these economic globalization forces with sociopolitical openness toward multiculturalism in the United States has led to the increasing accessibility of art, music, movies, books, and fashions. These in turn have become a major influence on how lifestyles, including ethnic lifestyles, are being organized in post-industrial societies such as the United States. This idea of lifestyles implies a series of practices, mostly outside formal work hours and work spaces, that allows people to display their choice of identities. The process of construction of such lifestyles appears to suggest that all groups have the freedom to equally exercise their choice about which kind of identity-based lifestyles they can build (Lury 1996). Indeed, like other middle-class Americans, several participants in this study saw themselves as exercising autonomy in what they choose to consume and to what degree they wish to emphasize their "distinctive" cultures. Earlier studies on blacks in the United Kingdom show that groups marked as racial minorities are rarely able to transcend their master status; they can, however, try to control the meanings and understandings of the content of their cultures (for example, Anthias 2001a; Gilroy 1990). This chapter shows a similar process at work among the South Asian Americans. The racial boundary between them and the mainstream persists, but they use these items to create "their own cultures." And, contrary to the predictions of the globalization scholars who see such emerging globalized cultural forms as mechanisms through which the structural constraints of nation-states can be traversed (for example, Appadurai 1996), this chapter shows that South Asian Americans are drawn into more globalized structures of racialization. In fact, the global industry of selling cultures is contingent upon their remaining "ethnic." They are targeted by segmented identity marketing initiatives: as a range of companies creates their desire for specific ethnic products, their subsequent consumption patterns appear to confirm their "essential" cultural preferences, which, in turn, implies they will continue to be considered as segmented markets. However, the need to create larger markets means that increasingly larger numbers of individuals, across countries, are being drawn into segmented markets and to marked identities.

This chapter is organized into three sections. I first describe the shift toward a post-industrial economy as well as the greater sociopolitical openness toward multiculturalism in the United States, and what this means for middle-class, non-white groups. Then, I describe how their consumption of material cultural items from a global market and their emphasis on performances helps these South Asian Americans build more pan-ethnic identities. In the last section, I discuss the implications of these ethnic practices in terms of the advantages they gain by emphasizing these building blocks, as well as the inequalities that remain unresolved through such practices. While consumption practices develop and sustain ethnic networks, the primary focus in this chapter is on these consumption practices. The ethnic networks are discussed in greater detail in the next chapter.

The Use of Cultures for Organizing Society

While the far-reaching effects of the Civil Rights Movement in the United States are correctly credited with creating a social ethos of greater openness to cultural pluralism in the country, this period has also witnessed the growth of economic motivations for promoting multiple cultures. The social organization of this openness toward multiple cultures has created new spaces for practicing multiple cultures in the United States, just as it has created new restrictions on what may be practiced, under which conditions, and through which forms of expression. In this section I briefly discuss the economic and political underpinnings of this controlled openness toward "cultural groups" in the United States.

Zukin (1995) and Sassen (2000), among others, have described how the shift toward a post-industrial economy in the Euro-American countries has led to the increasing emphasis on the production of knowledge and services. A specific part of the production of knowledge has been the development of a strategy for marketing cultures. Art, music, and ethnic celebrations are transformed into items for sale through gentrification projects, ethnic parades and festivals, tourism, and the creation of consumer tastes for a variety of "cultural" products. Tea or coffee is no longer just a beverage; the consumer also buys the image of the misty hills of Darjeeling or of Juan Valdez. The production sites and purveyors of such ethnicity are no longer only businesses in ethnic neighborhoods or products from "home countries." In the United States, art districts, performance centers, festivals, heritage trails, and museums, have become important sites for constructing and selling cultures. Old ethnic areas or sites of historical events, such as the underground railroad, or Chinatowns, are repackaged and reframed as consumable items on heritage tours. Museums are no longer simply monuments of philanthropy or high civilization. They are production centers of the modern economy: creating tastes, as well as identifying, packaging, and marketing cultures and cultural items for consumption. Thus the production of ethnic cultures is increasingly a mainstream economic and political activity.

As the selling and consumption of cultures becomes increasingly central to the economies of Euro-American countries, companies with a global reach through cyberspace target groups of consumers by appealing to their "fundamental" identities. These companies may be located anywhere in the world, just as their marketing targets could also be located in any corner of the world. Issues of citizenship, political affiliation, and other differences are wiped out in these appeals to fundamental identities as companies try to create and sell to new markets. For instance, South Asian Americans can buy "South Asian" music produced in the United Kingdom by companies such as Sony (Sharma 1996). The Mumbai-based film industry in India—Bollywood—which produces the largest number of movies in the world, increasingly markets its movies globally and is creating a new genre of movies that claim that "the hearts of 'Indians' anywhere in the world remain Indian for ever."[2] A rapidly growing range of "South Asian" designers in India, United Kingdom, and a number of other countries are beginning to offer ways of expressing South Asian identities by adopting certain kinds of fashions. Similarly, new tourist packages allow South Asian Americans and their parents to re-experience their "home countries." Castles advertise themselves as settings for perfect weddings (as we saw in chapter 3) and family events, and "textile tours" offer new ways of experiencing histories and contemporary social activities along with the more traditional tours of "princely India."

Scholars, who study the influence of these processes on individuals, point out that the availability of these consumption items has led to new ways of participating in societies. Traditional sources of identity which have been related to nationality, family, long-term employment, and relationships to people in geographic proximity, are now being replaced by more fluid identities based on the construction of lifestyles (Hebdige 1979). The hallmark of being a citizen of post-industrial societies—in the sense of what makes a person culturally American or British—is the ability to exercise individual choice, in other words, free of the fetters of family or other loyalties to consume items and construct lifestyles. Hirsch (1977), among others, argues that individuals are no longer judged by how well they do their duty to the nation but by how well they exercise their capacity to make a consumer choice. This form of social identity has been labeled "consumer citizen" (Canclini 2001). An individual's identity is a project defined by the possession of desired goods, and the pursuit of framed styles of life (Bourdieu 1984) that are structured through patterns of consumption. These shared patterns of consumption also allow commonalities of lifestyles to develop across nations. The idea of a global village is based on these notions of choice and shared consumption (McLuhan 1964). People seek to display their individuality, sense of style, and distinctiveness from other groups through the choice of a particular range of goods that delineate their lifestyle, while they bond with others who display similar lifestyles. The economy of selling cultures enables people to pick from a global range of products to build these lifestyles (Giddens 1999).

Harnessing that appeal to ethnically identified products has been one of the most successful marketing strategies in the post-industrial global economic order. Ethnicity "has a built in appeal that should make Coke and Pepsi envious. Madison Avenue could not have conspired to make a better and more appealing product" (Waters 1990, 154). The growth of this modern consumer capitalism has led to targeting segmented ethnic markets in ways that "ethnics" can satisfy their urge to "celebrate" their heritage through what they consume. "Markets offer greater awareness of ethnic identity, and offer immediate possibilities for cultural participation" (Halter 2000, 6). Middle-class ethnics are ideal targets. They are confident about expressing their ethnicity through their consumption. The middle-class Irish, for instance, can be targeted for buying Celtic designs, Irish crystal, linen, or for flying on Irish airlines to go back, as a contemporary airplane advertisement extols, to their "mother's home," thus keeping a sense of Irishness salient through ethnic consumption. Racial minority groups such as South Asian Americans are also increasingly drawn into similar forms of consumption as a primary avenue for expressing ethnicity. Music, movies, fashions, books, and heritage tourism (where the South Asian Americans and their parents travel to experience global family roots) are among the building blocks of this form of ethnicity.

At a macro-societal level, the production of culture for global markets has been paralleled by the growth of multiculturalism within the United States. The Civil Rights Movement challenged notions of biologically innate proclivities of races. However, the shifting discourse on race, as I discussed in chapter 2, is often framed in terms of cultural differences. The form of multiculturalism that has emerged has shifted the public discourse to the realm of cultures alone, specifically to an emphasis of the equality of cultures. People are assumed to be free to celebrate their cultures in their homes, while a series of ethnic celebrations, in schools and other public arenas, allows public expression of these multiple cultures. And, as "cultural items" are sold through mainstream outlets, people are free to express their cultural distinctiveness through consumption. Promoting multiculturalism politically overlaps with the contemporary economic growth strategy in post-industrial nations.

The ability to fashion one's own lifestyle based primarily on what one consumes indicates new ways in which individuals and societies are woven together, but there are at least two aspects of this economic and political multiculturalism that negatively affect racial minorities. First, this chapter shows that while South Asian Americans are becoming avid consumers of cultural products, the underlying structural arrangements that mark their "ethnic practices" as un-American have not changed to re-position them as *American* consumer citizens. As I discussed in chapter 2, while schools and other institutions attempt to become aware of and understand cultures as part of the multicultural ethos, South Asian Americans continue to be structurally positioned as native informants for South Asian societies. Without a change in the underlying racialized ideological framework of thinking about "other" cultures as deep rooted, unchanging, and essentially non-American in their core values— the clash of civilization perspective—South Asian Americans remain "South Asians" in the United States. Their preference for these products appears to indicate—both to the mainstream and to many South Asian Americans themselves—their essential ethnicness. In other words, the structural arrangements that categorize ethnic groups solely as cultural groups render the hierarchical aspects of ethnicity invisible through this form of economic and political multiculturalism (Bonilla-Silva 2001).

The second related issue is about *public* expressions of cultures. Performances, fairs, parades, and related events have to be carried out in controlled settings, fitting into the rules of what can and what cannot be public performances. The rules are often based on embedded notions of safety and security based on white middle-class notions of what is acceptable (Zukin 1995). Cultural events are held during times selected according to school or town calendars that best reflect the lives of the majority group. In chapter 3, I described the frustrations of the participants who were unable to organize their weddings in ways they considered to be appropriate, because of a variety of legal restrictions on "the proper" use of public places. The well-publicized conflicts with the Chinese communities in New York and Mayor Giuliani over the right to use fireworks during the Chinese New Year are other examples of these restrictions (Williams 1999). While colleges and schools encourage public displays of ethnic cultures, groups are only allowed to showcase their cultures by wearing "native" clothes, bringing cultural foods, and showcasing dances or music or other arts. For instance, when Indian college groups attempt to organize Diwali celebrations in colleges, this celebration has to be re-cast as an event where students gather in ethnic clothes, perform dances, songs, or fashion shows.[3] However, during a focus group discussion with several graduate Indian (foreign) students pointed out that in India, Diwali is primarily a *public* festival and open to all intrepid individuals (of any religion) who want to set off fireworks. In the United States, given the structural impediments, South Asian Americans have to turn to *performing* cultures (Mukhi 2000).

Thus, political and economic multiculturalism offers new opportunities and constraints for doing ethnicity. In the next section, I discuss patterns of South Asian American consumption of fashions, music, movies, books, and the effect of such consumption patterns on their ethnic options.

ETHNIC CONSUMPTION, ETHNIC PERFORMANCES

I indicated in chapter 2 how coming to college represents a distinct stage in the lives of the South Asian Americans because now they have the opportunity to collectively build and assert "their culture" with other South Asian Americans. This is a time when they are able to transcend some of the ethno-national identities they may have taken for granted earlier. The following statement describes some aspects of this process.

PRANATA: The guy in the movie [*American Desi*] kind of was where I stood with [my ethnic identity]. He ... was a little bit more apathetic than I am, but he didn't really care about, at the beginning of the film, the idea of being Indian ... when he went to college, he was just kind of whatever about it. [But] he meets this girl that he really likes who's South Asian as well, and she knows all about these Hindi film songs and about the movies and they have to work on this cultural event together. And through liking her he also learns that ... not everyone is going to respond to it in the same way, and the way you look at your culture doesn't necessarily mean you're ashamed of it. . . . I think in that way, it just, it was nice for me to see because it kind of made me think, oh, you know there are other people who feel the way I do.

In some ways, colleges serve one of the functions that ethnic enclaves played in the lives of earlier immigrants: South Asian Americans, who lived dispersed lives before, are now more likely to find other South Asian Americans and collectively practice ethnicity. But the mere presence of these peers is not a sufficient condition to build these bonds, nor does it resolve whether ethno-national identities or more pan-ethnic versions are likely to become more salient. The diversities—especially of religious practices and regional cultures—and conflicts that I described in the last chapters do not promote automatic ways of building meaningful networks. As Pranata indicates, South Asian Americans arrive in college with very different ideas about *how* they are Indian or Pakistani or Nepalese or Bangladeshi, along with a great deal of ambivalence about whether they are "South Asian" as their racial experiences suggest. However, they often end up developing South Asian American commonalities through their emphasis on fashions, music, movies, and books as the main signifiers of their ethnicity. While this chapter shows that not all South

Asian Americans adopt this form of asserting ethnicity (the primary reason why I chose to avoid using the label "desi" to describe the entire group), nonetheless, this form provides some advantages. They do not have to choose between ethno-national and pan-ethnic identities: their consumption patterns can be framed as either identity depending on the specific context. In this way, these ethnic cultural products act as neutral building blocks of ethnic identity.

Since this form of doing ethnicity conforms to the public rules about doing cultures, South Asian Americans are able to build a public form of South Asian Americanness that Namrata referred to at the beginning of this chapter. Maira (2002) has described South Asian American events in colleges as a sort of "coming out" for this group. In the presence of other South Asian Americans, many of them begin to explore ways of publicly asserting their South Asian Americanness—building a collective ethnic form across religions, regions, languages, and often ethno-national differences, through a common set of signifiers, such as fashions, music, and dances. Unlike the times when their parents took them to attend or participate, often reluctantly, in ethnic community events, in colleges they can express "their cultures" in the mainstream.

In urban areas, clubs also organize evenings that primarily cater to South Asian Americans. These other arenas simply extend the number of public places where their South Asian Americanness can be asserted. These different public arenas influence the emphasis on consumption as a way of asserting ethnicness.

Fashions

Fashions and music are the main identifiers of "ethnic events." Meena, who had grown up in a suburb of New York, described the "Indian" college scene based on her experiences in New York City. She explained that since she had always attended mostly white schools (including a private school), her sense of what was Indian became more formalized in college. Many others echoed Meena's story of being introduced to Indian films and music by another South Asian American. They described how their Indian or other ethno-national identity developed through acquiring material cultural items. Others mentioned the *additional* possibility of becoming South Asian American through the same process.

Coming together for college-based or other events provides South Asian Americans opportunities to "put on ethnicity," and, from their descriptions, it was evident that this is exactly what they did. Even if they had been reluctant to wear "ethnic" clothes before, many of them prepared for these South Asian events by planning their wardrobes. With the emerging market of South Asian men's fashions, planning wardrobes is no longer limited to females, although more females than males mentioned fashions and wardrobes. This emphasis on ethnic attire leads to the development of a "South Asian" fashion norm. Those who do not follow the trend often feel left out of the group. Alka typified their sentiments: "I felt very segregated because I didn't come to the meeting in ethnic wear. The girls were all dolled up." Irrespective of the type of event, wearing "South Asian" fashions is a growing trend. Namrata described a South Asian conference she attended, where several social events were categorized in ways such that she and her friends knew when to wear ethnic clothes and when to wear other types of formal attire.

The new ways of using fashions to indicate distinctiveness was exemplified in a college-based show that I attended. A group of ten performed a "Pakistani wedding fashion show." The females wore a variety of *salwar-kameezes* (a two piece long shirt-like top over loose-fitting pants, usually with an additional piece for covering the upper body and /or head) *ghararas, lehengas* (variations on blouses and long, floor-length skirts), and saris.[4] The men wore *sherwanis* (attire typically worn by Muslim men in Pakistan and northern India for formal occasions), but with a great deal of variety of cuts, colors, and embellishments to reflect current fashions. A variety of "remixed" music framed their walking and posing on stage. The show concluded with the men dancing a version of *bhangra* (a dance and music form from northwestern India and Pakistan that is discussed later in this chapter). The event was choreographed with fashions, music, and dancing, and reflected the increasing openness in colleges and universities to foster multiculturalism through student group performances. This show was repeated within a few months when a college administrator organized a multicultural event in her hometown, illustrating the "fit" of the program to mainstream expectations.

Colleges are not the only sites to gather in the company of desi youth. On weekends, clubs organize "parties" for desi youth, complete with South Asian DJs (Maira 2002). South Asian Americans often travel as groups to these events to be with "a whole bunch of people who look like us." However, there is a shift of emphasis about the purpose of the gathering that is reflected in the clothes. Meena, who was in New York City, described how males and females changed clothes to suit different arenas.

The guys all conform to baggy pants or really preppy looks. Either very ghetto or preppy. Girls are long-haired, definitely greasy, highlighted, dark eyeliner, lipstick, greasy, high heels. When you are in college, there's the club scene the girls wear tank tops and pants, some girls go showing really, really a lot of stuff, very anti-Indian culture, not like cover yourself up, they're like out there. Then they go home and put on their salwar kurtas [synonymous with salwar kameez]. Its funny when you see these Indian girls in fashion shows and saris and they look so pretty . . . then they change into their tank tops and they are showing skin. At other times you are a good Indian girl, at clubs, you're like the opposite.

Shaheen, who grew up in suburban Connecticut, described the club scene in
Boston, but emphasized the fusion aspect of the fashions and music.

> [A]ll these Indian girls with long hair, it's amazing, it's fusion, some wear
> fusion American and Indian clothing . . . it's Indian music dancing. It's the
> hip-hop. If you listen to Bhangra music, the beat it's similar to reggae
> music. So that's what they take out and mix it. . . . [The dancing] it
> depends it's literally on the floor; if it were techno music it would be a
> certain kind of dancing, but with hip-hop it's the beat of it that's getting
> you going. Most of the time people aren't paying attention to the music.
> It's the excitement of being there, seeing Indian people interacting with
> them in this manner where it is acceptable to do so and living off that.

These statements suggest a clear separation, in these participants' minds,
between what is South Asian American, and what is American. Yet, as Alka—
who had felt out of place for not being "dolled up"—pointed out, this emphasis in college on *ethnic* fashions bears little resemblance to what is in vogue
among college students, of comparable background, in India. She pointed out
that while she was in Delhi, she attended college events: she argued that girls
did not go to events dressed in the kind of clothes adopted by the South Asian
Americans. In her opinion, the United States–based South Asian college culture was clearly behind the times. Although Delhi does not represent the
norm of what college students wear to different occasions in South Asian
countries, it is important to note the social meanings attached to these clothes
and fashions. The hybrid ethnicness is not a simple fusion of what exists in
South Asian countries along with what exists in the United States. Rather, it
is a melding of what is interpreted as South Asianness in the United States
along with what is considered as non-ethnic American.

The rapid growth in the number of such college events encourages South
Asian Americans to acquire ethnic clothes and ties them into a transnational
industry of fashion production.[5] Many of the ethnic fashions are ordered
through buyers with links to the South Asian countries, or through relatives.
Rehana, whose parents are from Bangladesh, described a more "traditional"
way of acquiring clothes. She told me that her mother knew a woman in
Canada, who traveled several times a year to the United States and brought
over salwar-kameezes which were custom-made *in India.* Clearly the ethno-
national boundaries are not as relevant in matters of consumption: both in
terms of the transnational purchasing strategies and in terms of the transnational mixing of ethnic styles. South Asian American participants in this study
often described how they acquired clothes from several countries when their
friends or relatives traveled.[6] Every time someone visited one of the South
Asian countries or *England,* they were asked to bring back specific kinds of
embroidered, painted, woven or block printed clothes in cotton and silk. Thus

5.1. Indian clothes for a Diwali event at a college. Photo by
Amrita Purkayastha.

lehengas with silver *zardosi* (raised embroidery work), kurtas with Lucknow
chikan (eyelet work), Nepalese "Tibetan" jewelry, and Bangladeshi *tants* (woven
cottons) were some items mentioned by South Asian Americans females, along
with the names of some British and Indian designers of "Indian" clothes.

The growth of fashion designers who have "boutiques" and who "show"
their collections is a newer phenomenon on the subcontinent. It is driven by

global trends in business organization. For this research, I was particularly interested in getting more information on the designers that some participants mentioned and to get a sense of where these designers are located and what markets they appear to target. In other words, were these fashions regular attire in South Asian countries or were they marketed specifically with an emphasis on cultural image? A search through the web confirmed the growth of fashion designers who sell these "cultural" images and cater to the relatively affluent immigrants and their children in North America and Western Europe.[7] Most of the clothes are described as Indian, and sometimes as Pakistani or Bangladeshi. Nepal was rarely mentioned in these descriptions. These designer "Indian" clothes are increasingly available from many countries around the world. Some of the fashion houses are based in India, Pakistan, or Bangladesh, with India dominating the designer market: the participants mentioned Ritu Kumar and Bibi Russell, but designers are also promoted through mainstream outlets such as Lord and Taylor (*The New York Times,* April 27, 2003).[8]

Several participants who attended weddings in the United States, in Europe, or in India or Pakistan, acquired designer clothes for the occasion. One female mentioned that she attended a "fairy tale" wedding that was held in a castle rented in western India and that it gave her cousins and her an opportunity to acquire a collection of designer clothes. The top United Kingdom–based boutiques like *Khubsoorat* (a mother and second generation daughter enterprise), *The Rang Collection, Aahrouge, Urban Turban,* and *One BC for Asians* are increasingly advertising through Zee TV (a South Asian channel) and the internet to South Asian consumers in the United States. Fashion journal/websites such as Bibi's published from Houston, Texas, contribute to this trend as well. Here, "collections" are introduced based on subcontinental festivals and modeled by South Asian celebrities (Melwani 2001). A transnational beauty pageant market, which features many recent winners from the subcontinent contributes further toward the creation of a *South Asian* consumer market for clothes and fashions (Prashad 2000b). This nexus of the Bollywood movie industry and the designer clothes market was featured in a recent issue of the ethnic newspaper *India Abroad.* The Bollywood Fashion Awards were held at Trump Taj Mahal in Atlantic City, New Jersey, and several film stars from Bollywood (Mumbai) presented awards to fashion designers whose work, according to a journalist, "represent(s) a harmonious blend of Western style and Indian elegance" (Lakshman 2003, 36).

With a relatively affluent market segment, stitched clothes which command high prices and profit have begun to dominate this fashion scene. Thus the emerging "South Asian" attire is not the sari which continues to dominate in the subcontinent (as a whole), but it emphasizes stitched clothing with ethnic accents, that is, embellished with a variety of regional embroideries, mir-

5.2. A South Asian American modeling a sari at a multicultural event at a suburban library. Photo by Bandana Purkayastha.

ror work, and paint work. The second generation South Asian Americans appear to wear saris only to weddings or multicultural fashion shows.

In her study on the consumption patterns among British South Asian women, Parminder Bacchu (1995) has argued that, depending on their class position, young British Asian women actively negotiate and transform the meaning and content of "traditional" cultural practices. Punjabi women with disposable incomes frequently use cultural frameworks like the *daaj* (obligatory dowry-like gifts given during weddings) to acquire a range of consumer items *in their own interest* which represent their class and subcultural positions. "Their patterns of consumption and cultural styles grow out of the specificities of their . . . [middle-class] locations . . . [and the] translation of their earnings into a cultural trait—thus commoditizing 'traditional' patterns" (Bacchu

1995, 238). A similar pattern appears to be emerging among these South Asian Americans. Their consumption of ethnic fashions is not a simple reflection of strict adherence to (unchanging) tradition. For many, consumption of designer apparel is a way of constructing identity that is similar to that of their mainstream peers: in their minds their consumer choices make them nontraditional. But such choices provide the additional advantage of conforming to some aspects of ethno-nationality: looking Indian or Nepali or Pakistani or Bangladeshi for ethnic community and other events, or sharing conversations about fashions with cousins in other countries. More importantly, this recreation of pan-ethnic fashions does not, as yet, reflect any strict social norms of who—Hindus, Muslims, Sikhs, Christians, or people of specific nationalities or language groups—wears particular kinds of clothes. Instead, it represents an emerging homogenized South Asianness: a South Asian image that can be adopted by the second generation of different national origins and religious identities. Thus, South Asian Americans negotiate the content, meaning, and direction of ethnicity through their consumption practices, creating pan–South Asian American tastes and consumer identities. In doing so, they are able to breach some, but not all, of the boundaries that constrain their lives. At the same time, though most of these participants, who come from middle-class backgrounds, seemed to take the ability to buy these types of clothes for granted, their emphasis on designer fashions introduces a very definite class-based notion of expressing "South Asian American" ethnicity.

Bhangra and Remixed Music

Like the fashions, the music that is popular among South Asian Americans illustrates fusion and emerging pan–South Asianness. Their preference for certain types of music transcends specific ethno-national roots and ties them into an emerging global production network of new South Asian music. A broad genre of remixed music—music from Bollywood movies or bhangra mixed with popular American music, including hip-hop and reggae—was mentioned by most of the South Asian Americans, male and female, of varying religions and national origins as "our music." Sumaira, a female of Pakistani origin, who actively identifies with her culture explained,

> I watch so many movies, and sometimes people are like "Oh my God, you know every song there is. But what they do here now, and even in Pakistan and India, they mix it with the American music. And sometimes it sounds so awful because you have like this cultural music that the verse finishes and you have this hip-hop and reggae going on . . . [at the clubs] they have to get a different beat going because a lot of American people, a lot of Indian and Pakistani Americans, don't really know how to dance to like the cultural music, and they can only dance with the American

beat in the back, so they have to do that, and that's what gets the crowd going. Sometimes it just annoys me, because sometimes it's just awful, like I don't wanna hear the American in it, I just wanna hear the original. And so I get regular tapes that are just regular Indian.

Maya, who is Indian American, explained another facet of the music. She discussed how two traditions—Indian and American—were brought together. "Because Bhangra has its roots in India, we bring hip-hop to the Indian culture . . . maybe we are not secure enough or comfortable enough to do it through other organizations. Maybe some people would be that's so cool and others would be that's so weird. Maybe it brings out the Indian and American things strongly and gives people a chance to say that's my culture and feel some pride. This defines us and we are Americanized Indians and it's so cool. You take what you see and create what you like."

Clearly the emerging "rhythm-nation," to borrow Sunita Mukhi's (2000) term, has fluid boundaries. Even though this music is frequently described as "Indian," bhangra is a music and dance tradition from rural Punjab, a state that is now partitioned between India and Pakistan. This genre grew out of a harvest festival tradition: the beat and rhythm are vigorous and the music and dance emphasize a robust masculinity. Bhangra went through changes in its encounter with hip-hop and reggae in the Southall section of London (Banerji and Bauman 1990). In communities composed of Indians and Pakistanis from the subcontinent and East Africa, hip-hop bhangra and rock bhangra emerged as the new "Asian" sounds. This music paved the way for (South) Asian youth in London to dance to an energetic beat while they claimed they were maintaining tradition. However, the exact responses to the music varied in the United Kingdom: some interpreted it as a way of creating a collective "black" identity in opposition to white racism in the United Kingdom, while others continued to frame it as a unique "Asian" tradition (Bennett 1997). Certainly when bhangra is played at Punjabi weddings, it means something different in terms of cultural signification, than when it is played in clubs. The music moved from the United Kingdom to the United States where it now represents a South Asian genre. It is played in clubs in large cities in the United States and has developed a subculture of aficionados, who call this British Asian music instead of Indian music (Wartofsky 2001). And, increasingly, much of this music is being re-mixed with other kinds to create new fusion genres. Remixed music, which was first created by South Asian American DJs in clubs, is becoming more mainstream since musicians like Jay-Z mixed Punjabi lyrics on female modesty with sections from Knight Rider, and made it to the top charts in Europe and the United States (Sanneh 2003). Remixed music is also played by airlines such as Virgin Air on board some of its flights from New York to London.

Many South Asian Americans find this prominence of bhangra and remixed music exciting even if they, personally, do not understand the lyrics or the language. In fact, like Arya, who was part of the *Bend It Like Beckham* discussion, many South Asian Americans do not speak Punjabi or Hindi, so they just respond to the essence of the music. Sumi, who was born in England, and has parents who were born in Kenya and India, said, "Often we'll remix it with rap and with Hindi songs. We appreciate that. A bhangra song will be mixed in with a rap song . . . [Interviewer: What kind of songs are those?] I think they are guy meets girls kind of music, but I don't really know Hindi that well. I don't even understand most of it so I want to cut a lot of it and I can't even be affected."

Since linguistic proficiency or long years of training in the "grammar" of the music is not a precondition for enjoying this music, bhangra has become the symbolic expression of "our music" among the youth in the diaspora. Sharma quotes Neiyyer's description of this music/dance form in the United Kingdom: "Bhangra . . . The music, clothes, dances are the medium through which otherness of British/South Asian experience is articulated . . . it is both a form of cultural resistance and the affirmation of lives we lead . . . it is perceived as something distinct belonging to us. . . . It is definitely a break with tradition. . . . The Bhangra beat is a pulse, a soundtrack, and a distinct manifestation of the South Asian urban experience" (1996, 35).

Most of the South Asian Americans I interviewed also perceive bhangra in a similar way: it is *their* medium for expressing their distinctiveness. It is different from their parents' forms of doing ethnicity. It represents their agency in creating a type of social identity that affirms their South Asianness, and expresses *their* construction of their difference from whites. In addition, for the more politically conscious South Asian Americans, the fusion of bhangra and hip-hop indicates potentially permeable boundaries with blacks.

The popularity of bhangra "traditions" is fostered by a variety of events in the United States. "Bhangra competitions" are becoming very popular events at universities. For instance, Somini Sengupta describes a major "bhangra-blowout" competition at Georgetown university where groups come from all over the United States to compete, as "a rite of spring for the growing legions of South Asian American college students . . . akin to spring break pilgrimages . . . to Fort Lauderdale, FL to the streets of Atlanta, where black students gather for Freaknik" (Sengupta 1999, 2). Several South Asian Americans who participated in this research had gone to these bhangra competitions, and many practiced assiduously for them throughout the year. Similarly, the program from the South Asian Student Alliance (SASA) conference in San Francisco, in 2001, which was given to me by a participant in this study, showcased this emerging fusion genre. Among other groups were NYC Masti and NYC Nasha, which had been mentioned by one of the participants who went to

New York University. NYC Masti performed "a mix of techno, R & B, classical beats, Hindi, and Malayalam songs." while NYC Nasha performed a mix of classical, contemporary Indian, and hip-hop dances.

Despite the hybridity of this music, underlying racial structures continue to attribute different labels and social meanings to this genre depending on the context. It is labeled Asian in the United Kingdom and South Asian in the United States. In *Disorienting Rhythms,* Sharma, Hutnyk, and Sharma (1996) discuss the hierarchies embedded in the process of creating this diasporic genre. First, as I pointed out earlier, this genre is not purely subcontinental in origin, yet it is marketed in this way while making the other music traditions invisible. So although this music is marketed primarily as "Asian" music, it co-opts black music. The fusion of Asian and black music in this way does not necessarily create permeable race boundaries between these groups; in fact, a whole range of new hierarchies are introduced. Apart from downplaying the black contributions to this Asian music, the marketing strategy emphasizes these essential cultural identities of the "South Asian" musicians. "In World Music marketing practices, a pervasive strategy has been to promote specific artists as representations of authentic ethnic national musical cultures" (Sharma 1996, 23). Bally Saggoo's albums are good examples of this phenomenon. Saggoo has long been an important figure in the British bhangra scene, and Sharma (1996) discuss how Sony markets Saggoo globally as an "authentic Indian" to capture the global market for such music. Saggoo's Britishness is made invisible in these cultural marketing strategies. The widespread nature of such labeling practices was also brought to my attention by one participant in this study who was trying to break into the music market in the United States. She explained the positive side of her liminality: "My business partner says that the biggest strength you have going for you in the music world is that you fit in with everyone. People think I'm part black, I am Brazilian, very Island Caribbean, South American, Indian. . . . The record companies will go which shelf should we put you on? And I can name a variety of shelves."

But she then went on to describe how she was not able to break into the mainstream music scene, despite her formal training as an opera singer, because she had to be marketed as ethnic. Even the hybrid genre she was developing, combining opera and other forms had to be marketed as "ethnic music."

A second aspect of how this music promotes hierarchies is that it erodes the influence of the music of the home countries. Artists and musicians who were born and brought up in the United Kingdom or the United States become representatives of "Indian" or "Pakistani" music because of the assumptions about their essential cultural identities. Since they are better positioned to sign up with multinational companies that control significant global markets: their music defines South Asian music for the South Asian Americans.

Musicians from India, Pakistan, Bangladesh, and Nepal are not as well positioned to capture these segmented markets. Overall, like the fashions, the consumption and performance of this music/dance form provides new cultural tools for South Asian Americans. Bhangra and remixed music help to build bridges *among* South Asian Americans who collectively enjoy this genre. But as "South Asian" music, it also contributes to the creation and sustenance of new and old boundaries.

Movies

Movies, especially those made by Bollywood, form the bridge between music and fashions. Based on her work on Indian youth in the United Kingdom, Gillespie (1995) has demonstrated how the ubiquity of VCR and DVD players has created a global market for Bollywood movies. She has argued that second generation youth in London sort out their ethnic identity in relation to these movies. Many of her conclusions apply to South Asian Americans as well. Since Hindi is the language of a large proportion of the South Asians in the United States, these films have been widely available through various commercial outlets. With the increasing popularity of DVDs, which come with English subtitles, these movies are poised to reach even larger audiences. In addition, a new genre of movies in English like *Bend It Like Beckham* and *American Desi,* which was mentioned by Pranata, are being made as well.

Since these movies are produced for widespread consumption in India, enjoying them does not require "deep" knowledge of any regional culture or history. Most of the South Asian Americans (of Indian, Pakistani, Nepali, *and* Bangladeshi origin) I spoke to, watch and enjoy Bollywood movies. Most of the non-Hindi speakers were comfortable following the theme via English subtitles. In this way, South Asian Americans are able to become part of a collective, transcending, at least at this level of practice, many national, regional, religious, and cultural boundaries. Even more than music, most of the South Asian Americans, whether they were Nepalese, Bangladeshi, Indian, or Pakistani, talked about enjoying Hindi films.

Suhani's case is instructive. She saw possibilities of building pan–ethnic networks with other Indians through shared enjoyment of movies. She explained the similarities in terms of a Bollywood movie: "[J]ust the way we speak, what we listen to. My parents listen to Bengali music, they watch Indian movies, for example Devdas [a Hindi movie] it was written by a Bengali writer, we watched that."

Saira's statement at the beginning of the chapter reflects a similar sentiment, about a shared consumption of Indian movies, which leads to the acknowledgment of a common language among "Indians" and "Pakistanis." India's hegemonic position in the production of these cultural messages did not seem to matter to the participants who enjoyed Hindi movies. Suhita,

5.3. Nepalese American females perform a dance from a Hindi movie for Dashain. Photo by Bidya Ranjeet.

whose parents are from Nepal, explained that they watched Hindi movies throughout the year. Then, during Dashein, a religio-cultural celebration of Nepal, which is as important as Diwali in India, she and her cousins performed some Hindi film dances that they picked up from these videos. Later, as Fig. 5.3 shows, they performed this at an international function in college.

Movies certainly offer the vast majority of South Asian Americans a common theme for conversations with parents and relatives. Pranata, who is of Indian origin, and whose parents come from a cultural and class background where Hindi films are considered to be un-intellectual, tried to explain the role of Bollywood movies in her life:

> I think it did help me feel more comfortable with my ethnicity, also seeing people who were South Asian on the screen, you know who were adored ... my parents ... now they're really proud of the fact that I watch Hindi movies ... for them it reaffirms my Indianness and makes them feel more comfortable or makes them think "oh she's more comfortable." ... We were talking about this yesterday, the way Hindi films are looked at by people, especially in our economic class, but they're happy in some way that I've become part of that hype or whatever.

Another female described how studying Hindi movies in college affirmed her hitherto nascent interest in things that were Indian. From her perspective, she was making a choice to connect with her parents' experiences of childhood. Both she and her parents were developing a common set of ethnic practices based on their interest in Bollywood movies. This female comes from a family that is very progressive in terms of how they see their "ethnic culture": race and religious boundaries are not impediments to how family members construct their lives in the United States. So her attempts to build her ethnic life are not attended by the rigid boundaries imposed on the second generation from more conservative families that make up the hegemonic group. For those who come from families that are more conservative (those in the "essential-ethnicity" and "bounded-ethnicity" groups described in the last chapter), their growing interest in Bollywood movies can provide ways of sharing interests with parents *and* offer ways of subverting some of the extra surveillance on them. Taking advantage of some of their parents dichotomization of "South Asian" and "American" behaviors, they often told their parents they were hanging out with friends of specific ethno-nationalities and watching movies, while the opportunities to "hang out" were frequently occasions to explore relationships that went beyond "just friendship."

These movies offer them many ways of constructing their ethnicity. Like the females in the *Bend It Like Beckham* discussion, "seeing people who are South Asian on the screen" appears to make up for some of their continuing invisibility in mainstream media. More importantly, like the music, even if they do not or only partially, understand the language, these movies provide ways of asserting some versions of ethnicity. Thus Bollywood movies become wider symbols of South Asianness that transcend the specific national boundaries.

These movies facilitate ways of networking with other South Asian Americans. As college curricula begin to accommodate a variety of Asian, Asian American, or even specifically South Asian or Indian studies, a new range of books and research on popular culture also bring South Asian Americans in contact with such movies. One participant who had taken a course on "Indian movies" in a liberal arts college, explained how this course affected her identity. "I think [this class on Hindi movies] helped me become more comfortable with my ethnicity because so many people in the class were also South Asian . . . the women in this class, they were so nice. In some ways just talking to them, not even about stuff related to the class, but about other things just made me feel more in touch with my ethnicity . . . definitely I think that has made me comfortable with my ethnicity and I as I've gotten older, I find I like Indian clothes, I mean I don't wear them all the time but it is nice to get them."

The discussion about the movie *Bend It Like Beckham* that I narrated at the beginning of this book, also seemed to elicit similar responses. The three South Asian Americans seemed to relate viscerally to this movie, despite their age differences and diverse religious, national, and cultural backgrounds. Their discussion emphasized their commonalities in terms of structural locations, family structures, experiences of racialization.

However, it is important to note that there is no simple correlation between liking movies and transcending ethno-national boundaries. In Saira and Suhani's descriptions above, they both seemed to indicate that *Indian* movies provided a neutral space. But for Saira it was couched in terms of understanding Urdu, while in Suhani's case it was the Bengali story. When there are other entrenched reasons for rejecting people of selected ethno-nationalities, a shared interest in movies may create some possibilities for coming together, but it need not promote a total commitment to a South Asian American pan-ethnicity that includes these "'others." Suhani, who is of Bangladeshi origin, had passionately described the genocide (described in chapter 3) and how people mobilized to create a nation-state—Bangladesh—that was based on their language and culture. As I will discuss later, for South Asian Americans like her, who construct their identity in terms of specific socio-historical linguistic associations, the enjoyment of some Bollywood Hindi movies does not wipe out the other differences. This group of South Asian Americans is most apt to reject the desi identity which they associate with these movies, music, and fashions.

Like the fashions and bhangra, Bollywood movies gloss over gender, class, regional culture, and other distinctions. These movies present one version of India as "the Indian culture," wiping out cultural and regional specificities that are of central importance in all the South Asian American countries. In a critical essay, Aparna Sen (2003), a director of progressive women-centered films in India, and who had taught a film course in a well-known women's college on the east coast of the United States, emphasized this point. She points out that Bollywood movies are ahistorical and homogenized. The fantasies they produce represent no specific people. More importantly, there is little representation of vast swaths of India in these movies, since they ignore caste, class, religious, linguistic, political, and cultural diversities. She expressed serious reservations about "the India" the South Asian Americans were internalizing through the consumption of Bollywood fare.[9] In fact, these movies have been criticized for repackaging nationalisms in ways that fragment religious and other aspects of social identities in South Asia, and for upholding conservative perspectives on gender distinctions (Uberoi 1999). Some South Asian Americans of the pervious-ethnicity group rejected the movies as a building block of a shared identity for similar reasons.

Art and Books

South Asian Americans also mentioned buying art for their apartments or looking for Indian art posters.[10] Two South Asian American amateur painters— a female and a male—discovered the subcontinent's heritage of paintings during the interview period and began enthusiastically to weave these artistic motifs into their work arenas (graphic design) and marketing. Some other South Asian Americans had begun to sell Indian art posters at events to raise money for other performances. Like the fashions and movies, Indian products appear to be widely available and distributed, and their framing as Indian or South Asian depends on the particular circumstances of the groups which use these items to build their ethnic identity.

"South Asian" books are also very popular. The participants in this study described reading books written by South Asian and South Asian American authors as an important way of understanding their ethnic background. A significant number, especially the "older" participants, mentioned the books they had begun to acquire from South Asian countries. One Indian Muslim participant mentioned how she came back from a family vacation in India laden with books on Islamic history, architecture, and painting. Since India forms a segmented market for many major publishers, some of these books are published for Indian markets alone. Others mentioned going to England or India to buy literature in English (written by authors of various nationalities) before "South Asian" literature became a hit in the American market and the internet made it easier for them to hear about books from multiple countries.

The emerging market of South Asian literature in English, especially those books written by authors based in the United States, is very attractive to the South Asian Americans. Rehana, who is of Bangladeshi origin, said, "I read a lot of Indian and South Asian authors. I love Chitra Banerjee Divakaruni. I have all her books and I find her short stories fascinating. There was this story . . . when I read it, it was just as if I was reading about my father. I told my father about it and he was touched that I took the time to read something like that. And each story captures something of my experience and something of my parents' experience, at least what they have told me."

Chitra Banerjee Divakaruni, whose stories feature Bengalis in West Bengal and South Asians in the United States, is one of the earliest authors, along with Bharati Mukherjee, to be marketed widely in the mainstream. The number of "South Asian" authors are growing rapidly and several—like Jhumpa Lahiri, who is a second generation South Asian American and the author of *Interpreter of Maladies*—have won major prizes in the United States. Like the music, these books are now marketed globally.

Nonetheless, like the fashions and music and movies the *marketing* of these books draws on essentialized identities. Packaged as "South Asian" or multiethnic literature instead of American literature, the books emphasize the underlying assumptions about the boundaries between American and ethnic literature. Even though these books best reflect the political, social, and economic structures within which these authors and their subjects are positioned, the market labels and the South Asian American consumers categorize these books in ways that emphasize their difference from the category "American." The South Asian Americans are steered toward buying and reading this literature because it is about "them," and they end up describing their world in terms of what they read, often accepting the literature as insights about the whole society, or the ethnic community, instead of parts of it.

Overall, the consumption patterns of these books—like the fashions, movies, and music—show new possibilities of doing culture that have been made possible by the current phase of globalization. The ability to consume these products allows South Asian Americans to practice a form of ethnicity, which, on the surface, appears to resemble symbolic ethnicity. However, as these discussions illustrate, the embedded and emerging hierarchies that are an intrinsic part of such consumption, do not let the South Asian Americans become just American. They are, however, able to transcend some of the boundaries the hegemonic groups within the ethnic communities are presently trying to build.

CULTURE AND ETHNIC BOUNDARIES

The South Asian American emphasis on constructing an identity through consumption practices, is similar, at a general level, to practices of other middle-class groups in the United States (or in other Euro-American countries). Yet a number of embedded restrictions—on what they can express publicly, or the meanings assigned to these practices—maintain ethno-racial distinctions. Reflecting on the experiences of blacks, Willis (1990) and Gilroy (1993) point to ways in which these groups create alternative meanings through their consumption of selected commodified cultural items. As a racial minority group, South Asian Americans exhibit a similar pattern. In this section, I discuss the extent to which the South Asian Americans are able to breach some of the restrictions they encounter.

The previous section indicated several potential advantages of adopting this form of doing ethnicity. First, the restrictions on practicing many aspects of ethnic cultures (as we saw in the discussion of transnational weddings), coupled with the ready availability of commercially packaged items that are already labeled as "ethnic," allow South Asian Americans to fashion their ethnicity, as Namrata described, as a fusion of "Indian" and "American." As opposed to learning the language or regular attendance at religious establishments, ethnic consumption is a more neutral form of doing ethnicity. And, such consumption practices also allow them to build bridges with their parents' versions of doing ethnicity: while the first generation attempts to emphasize their versions of *South Asian* cultures, these ideas are adopted, transformed, and reinvented by the second generation to create the South Asian American form.

Second, the discussion in the previous section also showed how this form of doing ethnicity allows South Asian Americans to build bridges among the second generation of Bangladeshi, Indian, Nepali, and Pakistani origin and create South Asian American networks. The consumption of similar items across these nation-based groups helps to build a level of pan-ethnic South Asian Americanness, which conforms to the racial boundary imposed upon them. By emphasizing homogeneity, style, and fun, such consumption provides South Asian Americans an opportunity to try on ethnicity at a time when they are in contact with other South Asian Americans, and in turn helps to build bridges among them. While these practices may not represent "deep" versions of ethnicity—practice of languages, immersions in history through family socialization—but this form helps them to avoid some of the religious, nationality, and gender boundaries constructed through families and communities. Therefore, this form is particularly amenable to building more pan-ethnic bonds among people who do not share common languages. In this way they are more similar to other Asian Americans than Latinos (who share a common language) in how this higher-level ethnic layer is being formed.

Third, such consumption practices, to the extent these appear to overlap with mainstream economic interests, also allow South Asian Americans to feel more included in the mainstream. As celebrities like Madonna started consuming *mehendi* and *bindis* and mainstream fashion houses have started adopting "Indian" silks and motifs, the boundaries between "ethnic" and mainstream fashions have appeared to fade. The South Asian American way of "doing culture" appears to be no different, to some extent, from the culture of "the mainstream."

However, the introduction of homogenous "South Asian" cultural consumption patterns that are mobilized through the creation of new consumer markets, introduces within-group and between-group boundaries. First, the creation of such cultures is dependent on homogenizing and simplifying what makes up the universe of ethnic practices. As South Asian Americans exercise their choice in reinterpreting "traditions" in ways that these can be commoditized, they end up drawing most heavily on materials that are easily accessible (that is, widely marketed) and suitable for leisure time activities. Given the numerical dominance of people from northern and western India in this segmented market, the consumer items that are most widely available reflect the cultures of those regions, along with the cultures of Urdu-speaking, geographically contiguous parts of Pakistan. South Asian Americans who are not part of this culture are either forced to adopt it, or to choose their way of expressing their particular culture. In other words they can attempt to insert some of their cultural items into the mix, and thus negotiate the meaning of desiness or they can disengage from the desi culture and form sub-cultures of their own. For instance, along with some Indian Americans, many Bangladeshi Americans expressed their alienation from the desi culture because of the cultural and linguistic hegemony embedded in the consumption forms that are emphasized. In addition, a few South Asian Americans, usually from the bounded-ethnicity or pervious-ethnicity groups, mentioned in the last chapter, voiced reservations about the need to mark off a hybrid version as "Indian."

PRANATA: [P]eople, in some ways, try to reclaim something that is of their ethnicity. But, it's kind of hard at this point in time to even isolate anything that's Indian, you know like bhangra music. Like people, that may be a way for the second generation here to be like oh, I like Indian music, I like bhangra music. But it's such a fusion of different things that I think when you hold onto something that's purely Indian, you can't cause, it's almost like dragging other influences there too. That's definitely interesting I think just with trying to identify with being a certain minority when you can't really because it's very diverse.

A few others said they were disengaged from the emerging desi cultures because of the emphasis on consumption. They felt that South Asian Americanness should be based on building blocks that include and acknowledge class, religious, and national-origin diversity. They felt the significant emphasis on consumption simply created new class-based hierarchies among South Asian Americans. Instead of using cultural tools to avoid the differences, they advocate focusing on tools that work through the differences to create a more meaningful South Asian Americanness. These critics of the emerging desi culture said, however, that they were very committed to building *South Asian American* networks. They argued that "the desi culture" did not challenge the mainstream "multicultural" boundaries sufficiently.

Thus, for those South Asian Americans who do not associate with the consumerist recreations, or who consider their regional cultures important, or who attempt to weave more inclusive dimensions to construct their identities, such consumption-dependent forms of ethnicity are problematic.

Second, such consumer practices foster covert gender distinctions. For instance, several South Asian Americans (especially of the essential-ethnicity and bounded-ethnicity groups) had mentioned gender norms within their families as a significant way in which they were different from the mainstream. Their peers stigmatized all of them as un-American because of enforced female subordination, and, indeed, some of their families tried to construct "superior" ethnic identities by imposing extra scrutiny of females. For these females, this form of doing ethnicity allowed them to subvert "traditional South Asian" ideas and become "more empowered." Yet to what extent these practices lead to greater gender equality is debatable. In discussing how corporate marketing policies have co-opted feminist ideas about empowering women through sports, Dworkin and Messner argue that because of successful marketing of their products, "displaying the Nike swoosh on one's body becomes a statement to the world that one is independent, empowered and individual—a successful young woman in the nineties" (1999, 349). In a similar way, for many South Asian Americans, making consumer choices becomes a sign of modernity and gender equality, where equality is regarded as being synonymous with becoming autonomous consumers. But dissenters, like Pratibha, a Nepalese American, who was very active in women's empowerment issues, said that this "ultra-consumerist" form of practice only exaggerates ultra-femininities. Females have to look good in certain ways to fit these norms. Describing the pin-ups of several Indian filmstars in the rooms of several South Asian American male students, Alka said that most of the consumption patterns were simply new ways of conforming to an older idea—that women should appear pleasing to men, which is a form of co-optation instead of real independence. Many critics of the bhangra lyrics and the female templates in Hindi movies also pointed to how these products limited the range of how an individual might enact and challenge gender distinctions.

Third, who has the authority to define what represents a "cultural" rather than mainstream practice is often hidden by such consumption patterns. Since the aim of mass produced products is to maintain market loyalty, the ethnic consumers are drawn into a transnational ethnic field in ways that ensure commercial producers the "authority" and "expertise" to choose what represents a culture. As the discussion about music clearly indicates, the labor of the artists in South Asian countries as well as black artists in the United States or United Kingdom is co-opted in the production of these "South Asian" items of consumption.

Several politically conscious South Asian Americans offered critical insights into who the emerging experts are and who reaps benefits from culture. Highly critical of mainstream outlets which profit from selling body arts and other "exotic motifs" from South Asia, they honed in on yoga as an example of the new forms of structural inequality in the marketing and selling of "cultural" items. The co-optation of this cultural practice by the American mainstream illustrates the ways in which the profits and authority are taken over by commercial interests. This thousands-of-years-old practice of mental and physical discipline from the subcontinent, according to Malhotra and Joshi (2002) now generates about 27 billion dollars per year to mainstream American businesses. Yoga in the United States is reorganized as time-delimited physical activity (sometimes with meditation), in ways that detach the practice completely from the holistic life philosophy that is the basis of the South Asian practice. Individuals join yoga classes, buy yoga outfits and equipment, or buy yoga videos (which are patented to protect the producers from *intellectual piracy*), and perform the exercises under structural conditions that are profitable to mainstream entrepreneurs. These South Asian Americans pointed out that they do not benefit from the association of their ethnic cultures and such knowledge systems; they continue to be framed by the imagery of lack of empowerment, of subordination, and traditionalism, while others set themselves up as experts.

Another overlapping issue is how essential identities are created in order to create new identity markets. The need to have new ways to conduct identity-marketing each season often leads to emphases on aspects of identity that may not have been salient among the second generation (or even among segments of the first generation) earlier. For instance, fashions that hark back to a Muslim identity or extol the virtues of a Hindu musician often emphasize distinctions based on religious identities that may not have been as relevant before. Yet, these identity-marketing tropes often fit neatly with the attempts by more conservative first generation groups to assert fundamentalist identities based on exactly the same divisions. Thus "modernity" and "fundamentalism" both develop essential identities that complement each other. But they work against the South Asian Americans' initiatives to develop bridges across nations.

The development of these tropes about essential identities also creates differences between different racial minority groups. As one South Asian American explained her reason for not being Asian American, she pointed to segmented marketing boundaries. She said, "No I don't [identify as Asian American]. If I'm on the phone they'll think the Far East and then go into oriental type questions." In her work on the Chinese American and Korean American second generation, Kibria has argued that mass culture and consumption industries play a major role in the racialization of ethnic traditions. Asian Americans are presented only in terms of "filial piety, sukiyaki, Confucianism, Kung Fu, flower arrangement, pigtails and kimonos" (Kibria 2000, 82). Since different sets of images are evoked to market to South Asian Americans, and they construct their ethnicity based on shared consumption of these "essentialized ethnic" items, many of the South Asian Americans in this study internalize these racial frames, and do not identify with other Asian Americans.

CONCLUSION

Overall, this chapter illustrates that it is important to consider the influence of ethnic consumption in examining contemporary ethnicity. The influence of market-driven ethnicity opens up some possibilities of breaching ethnic boundaries within communities that are divided by language, religion, nation of origin, and other social markers. For groups like South Asian Americans, ready availability of ethnic consumption items allows them to construct repertoires of shared practice. It allows them a certain degree of autonomy because what they choose is not mostly mediated by their families. The forms of desi culture that are developing through shared consumption patterns emphasize practices that are closest to the practices of other ethnic Americans: the emphasis on music, dancing, movies, literature, and arts as a way of expressing ethnic identity.

But these processes introduce new hierarchies, and strengthen existing ones. New chasms develop within ethnic communities as music or fashions begin to be marketed on the basis of religious identity or some other social marker that was not salient before. More importantly, the need to market "ethnic" and "cultural" products means that groups such as South Asian Americans are ascribed essential cultural identities that they can rarely transcend to become "just American." The next chapter shows how organized groups of South Asian Americans try to mediate and challenge these different axes as ways of constructing their ethnicity.

As the literature on globalization predicted, understanding cultural practices of ethnic groups cannot be confined to models that only consider the family and the nation-state alone. Clearly, the transnational production processes are important influences on South Asian Americans. But, this chapter has illustrated the continuing salience of local structures. Even though shared consumption of movies might facilitate bonding with cousins across the globe, this overwhelming emphasis on cultural consumption is based on the structural circumstances of the South Asian Americans as middle-class consumers in the United States. The local structures encapsulate global influences, and this group is not free to construct their ethnicity in a neutral transnational space. They are not free to be "American consumer citizens" since they have to constantly deal with the many implications of their supposed essential cultural traits.

Thus, despite the "ethnic options" that they exercise through consumption and performances, racial boundaries continue to shape the meanings and implications of their choices. How these boundaries are addressed collectively is discussed in the next chapter.

CHAPTER 6

Sifting Through "Traditions"

Akash [describing a Diwali event in a college]: We'd start with a Brahmin priest explaining the traditions of Diwali, but then we'd have a party so there was something for the Muslim students as well. You can't have firecrackers, but you can include everyone in parties.

Namrata: Definitely because of our parents but also what we do. Actually, my cousin in England said they don't talk to Pakistanis at all. They just separate. I was completely shocked. Like why? We just hang out with each other all the time. We're friends.

Kader, who is of Bangladeshi Muslim origin: What I found is that Pakistanis and Indians have a lot in common and I found that Bengalis have always been the oddballs, at least Bangladesh has always been an oddball. And West Bengal [in India] too . . . Bengalis are not part of the subcontinent. Indians and Pakistanis are into Punjabi and Hindi or Urdu. They find it easy to understand each other. But Bengali, it does not easily lead to those. Culturally we are a bit different too. Pakistanis are, how should I put it, they define themselves very rigorously as Muslim. And Indians [from] Gujarat and other states identify themselves as strongly in terms of being Hindu. But the whole Bengali region is one region. It is one place where the two groups are almost equal in terms of culture, and there is a lot of assimilation. It is a lot more diverse than India and Pakistan and a lot more syncretic.

IN THE EARLIER CHAPTERS I focused on how individuals negotiate ethnicity and looked for recurrent patterns to delineate the group experiences of South Asian Americans. In this chapter I focus on second generation organizations and their role in creating collective identities. These organizations develop and promote sets of affirming representations and relations; they develop a sense of shared "we" through interaction (see, for exam-

ple, Gamson 1996 or Taylor and Whittier 1992 for descriptions of the construction of gay and lesbian identities). The statements in the chapter's epi-
graph and the evidence in the earlier chapters indicate that positioned at the
nexus of interacting local, national, and transnational structural relations,
South Asian Americans vary in how they think of their ethnic identities. While
individual South Asian Americans challenge, subvert, and negotiate multiple
boundaries, they also attempt to develop ethnic repertoires—constellations of
shared understandings and practices—that facilitate the process of negotiating
ethnicity. These organizations are group-level expressions of how South Asian
Americans negotiate their structural location by shaping the content, understanding, and boundaries of ethnicity.

This focus on organizations reiterates the non-essential, dynamic character
of ethnicity. Organizations sift through "traditions" to pick and construct particular repertoires. While this chapter is entitled "Sifting Through Traditions," I
do not use the term in the sense assimilation scholars or the media use it to
refer to deeply rooted cultural practices of groups.[1] Here I reinforce the argument, evident through the previous chapters, that ethnicity is forged through
social relations. The word "tradition" refers to the discourse these organizations
often use to mobilize individuals and establish their own legitimacy as a group.
Organizations sift through cultural practices and pick "tools" to develop ethnic
repertoires that are likely to promote certain kinds of belonging. Organizations
claim that *their* representation of ethnicity is most salient because it ties individuals with particular sets of established practices, whether these are arts and
music, histories, or certain kinds of knowledge.[2] Which version gains the most
widespread recognition is an outcome of the power of organizations to assert
their version as "normal" blueprints of social life. The representations and relations that develop through organizations encapsulate how they challenge and
negotiate the boundaries that structure and limit their lives. Since different
"traditions" are developed and deployed, there are ongoing struggles within
and between organized groups to define and demarcate ethno-national and/or
South Asian American ethnicity. These different versions of ethnicity *together*
contribute to the vitality of South Asian Americanness.

The chapter is divided into two parts. It begins with a description of the
organizations. I describe the context in which the organizations operate, who
becomes "members" of such organizations, the ethnic repertoires they
develop, display and assert, and some of their challenges. In the second section,
I discuss the boundaries these organizations create and the implication of
these boundaries.

ORGANIZING ETHNICITY

There are a large number of organizations to which South Asian Americans devote their time and energy. Recent issues of the *Amerasia Journal* and

Samar magazine focused on these groups' activism (for example, *Amerasia Journal* volume 2000/2001; *Colorlines* 2003; *Samar* 2001). These journals and magazines feature organizations that focus on redressing a variety of inequalities: gender, sexuality, class, labor, racism, as well as immigration and racism.[3] Many of the organizations emphasize their ethno-national "Indian" or "Pakistani" identities, others their "South Asian" or even "Third World" character. In the following paragraphs I describe three of the organizations (in which the participants in this study were involved) as a way of illustrating three very different ways of negotiating ethnicity.

Each of these second generation organizations plays a crucial role in promoting ethnicity in four overlapping ways. First, they facilitate ways for individuals to *try on* ethnicity. While their families (sometimes along with their ethnic communities) promote particular versions of essentialized-, bounded- or pervious-ethnicity, the organizations allow individuals opportunities to experience other ethnic repertoires. Equally important, they provide the formal and symbolic *public* space—away from family and the first generation organizations—for developing ethnic repertoires with their ethnic peers. Second, they create affirming narratives of belonging that valorize versions of ethnic identities. These narratives help individuals to disengage from some of the ideological frames—the controlling imageries in the mainstream and/or those promoted by the hegemonic section of the ethnic communities—that marginalize them. Instead, they attempt to control at least some of the social symbols that constrain their lives. Third, the organizations act as nodes of *networks*. Virtual networks complement face-to-face meetings in most of these organizations and increase the intensity of within-group interactions. The increased interaction promotes the sense of belonging to "the group." During their college years when individuals have a greater choice of becoming members of a variety of ethnic and non-ethnic organizations, these second generation organizations often act as conduits for participation in selected ethnic and other organizations with similar agendas. The more individuals are enmeshed in a range of organizations with similar interpretive frameworks—for instance, racial ethnic coalitions—the deeper their involvement in particular versions of ethnicity. Fourth, these ethnic organizations emphasize *boundaries*— who is part of the group and who is not. While the criteria for the boundaries vary, these organizations enhance the consciousness of who belongs within the boundaries and who does not. Organizations are able to breach some of the boundaries imposed upon them, but they often create others in order to remain different from other similar organizations. Race, gender, religion, nationality, and other social hierarchies are brought into play in negotiating externally imposed *and* internally created boundaries. Demarcation of these boundaries leads to conflicts among the organizations, but these conflicts can enhance group loyalty and help to keep individuals committed to particular repertoires. Thus conflicts and coalitions, bridges and chasms, keep South Asian American ethnicity dynamic, multilayered, and fragmented.

Even though the presence of several ethnic organizations provides ethnic choices, these choices operate within the rules and norms of the mainstream. These organizations reflect the structural demands of the context in which they operate. For instance, in order to justify membership, obtain grants, or formalize their status, student organizations have to demonstrate that they have a sufficient number of members. While the exact definition of "sufficient" varies by colleges, Indian- and Pakistani-origin groups are far more likely to find the minimum number of students required to form a substantial group on a college campus. The smaller groups of Bangladeshi and Nepalese origin do not always have this option on campuses, so they often have to "find their place" within existing organizations and/or set up more informal networks of their own. Organizations that are not located on college campuses also have to resolve their own institutional challenges. They have to cater to their audience, and follow the rules of the "space" in which they assert their ethnicity. Groups that are more dependent on virtual networks face different opportunities and constraints than those that are dependent on rented auditoriums to promote their version of ethnicity. How they balance these institutional demands with the aspirations of their members leads to the organizational shaping of collective identity (Gamson 1996).

The three South Asian American organizations presented here illustrate some of the more visible ways of doing South Asian American ethnicity. The first is a college-based organization which I will refer to as "Students of Indian Origin" (SIO). This organization typifies the organizations that exist in major universities with "large" South Asian student populations. As other examples of the same type of organization, I also present a "desi group," DG, which focuses more specifically on transcending Indian/Pakistani/Bangladeshi boundaries, along with an "Indian Foreign Students Organization" (IFSO) to illustrate some of the differences among the three college-based groups. The second organization, which I refer to as Young Indians Association (YIA), draws on college students and young professionals but organizes its events in settings outside colleges. This group comes together to stage public events to mark Indian celebrations. The third organization—which I will refer to as South Asian American Social Change Association (SASCA)—focuses on education, political consciousness-raising, and empowerment among second generation South Asian Americans.[4] This third organization is more like a "camp" or "conference" and often meets on college campuses. These do not exhaust the range of organizations that exist but represent the three "types" most often mentioned by participants in this study as "their" organizations. The organizations are structurally quite dissimilar both in their formal presence and nature of membership. Although the leaders are often more middle class, the memberships of these organizations are not confined to the children of middle-class migrants exclusively. The groups are not solely run by the second generation South Asian Americans. Both SIO and DG are run by second generation undergraduate students, while YIA and SASCA combine second generation individuals and a few younger members of the first generation who are, in age and experience, closer to the South Asian Americans than their parents. Together, these groups create competing ethnic repertoires and networks that structure South Asian American ethnicity.

The organizational context of the groups, their members, the ethnic repertoires they develop—the cultural tools they use, the understanding and sense of belonging they promote—their networks, as well as the boundaries they create, are the subject of the following section.

The College Groups: Students of Indian Origin and its Variant the Desi Group

Students of Indian Origin is an undergraduate student organization at a large public university. As I discussed earlier, since these South Asian Americans do not live in ethnic neighborhoods, the first time they encounter many others like themselves is at college. The relative openness of post–Civil Rights era colleges in the United States facilitates the ability of students to create a variety of organizations, including ethnic organizations, in college. They are now able to develop ethnic networks of their own as they attempt to show-case their culture. The SIO is located on a campus with a visible Asian American Center, as well as a variety of ethnic-racial and women's centers and studies programs. Thus, along with the funds that are available through their student activity fees, SIO operates in an environment where there is formal recognition of their presence as ethnic Americans.

MEMBERSHIP. Despite the name, members of SIO are of different South Asian national origins. Given the usual demographics, students of Indian origin predominate. While there is a formal membership process to meet the requirements of the college—a minimum of eight members—the actual participation pattern varies. Usually a smaller group is in charge of the events and a larger number of participants "drop-in" depending on their inclinations.

Exactly who joins these groups is influenced by the content of ethnicity (a topic that is discussed next) and by the presence of other similar ethnic organizations. The campus where SIO is located also has a Pakistani Students' Organization (PSO). This organization has a more conscious emphasis on a religious identity, since it provides, among other facilities, a place for Muslim students to gather for their evening meal during the month-long fasting during Ramadan.[5] While SIO does not consciously promote a religious identity, the existence of PSO on campus means that SIO gets identified as the organization for students who do not actively practice particular versions of Islam.

One of the recent presidents of SIO was Christian, and under her leadership SIO organized a comprehensive series of events including week-long India Awareness events featuring contemporary artists, politics, foods, and fashion accessories. Several Nepalese, Bangladeshi, and Pakistani origin participants said they went to SIO events when their friends were involved. Sometimes SIO and PSO formally collaborate on events, but they usually co-exist as separate entities. Namrata, who promoted a conscious ethos of South Asian Americanness in SIO during her presidency, said that having two organizations allowed "the group" to get extra funding from the university.

ETHNIC REPERTOIRES. Despite its name, it was evident, at least during the two years when I gathered information, that SIO tried to remain inclusive. The core group was aware of the boundaries built up by families and attempted to transcend it. As Namrata, who was quoted at the beginning of this chapter explained, these students of different national origins hung out all the time, building interactional "South Asian" bridges. Since Namrata came from a family that actively promotes pervious-ethnicity, her view about the role of the first generation is influenced by her family socialization. Many other SIO members, who are drawn from the essentialized- or bounded-ethnicity group described in chapter 4, did not think their parents promoted such openness. For them, SIO represented the first space where they could subvert and negotiate the religious, nationality, and gender boundaries that their families tried to inculcate in them. Indeed, the ability of SIO to act as a node of these networks contributes to building a form of South Asian Americanness.

The Students of Indian Origin organizes several events per year: there are balls, *garba* dances, Diwali celebrations, and, occasionally, an India Awareness week. The cultural tools they use emphasize fun in a "desi style." The "traditions" that are emphasized are fashions, music/performances, and movies. The typical SIO events represent an attempt to find frames that resonate with the maximum potential of group members. Working with students who are from multiple linguistic and religious backgrounds, the organization tries to find common symbols that will keep it open to a number of participants. Diwali is a case in point. Shorn of its religious underpinnings in the college context, a Diwali cultural event becomes a salad bowl of different dances, songs (often Hindi film songs and dances which have been remixed with western beats), plays, and other performances, along with an "Indian" dinner.[6] What is presented as "Indian" is an ongoing balance of the orientation of the leaders and what the members like to do. Shanthi, who was also an SIO president, said, "The first year I was involved it was a really well-run organization. For Diwali we'd plan to promote ourselves, and we would plan like Hindi movie nights to get everyone together. By my junior year the officers had changed, they were younger, and all they wanted was a semi-formal. They'd hire a couple of

DJs, the usual party scene, get drunk and dance. The only thing that made it cultural was there was a mix of Indian music."

Despite Shanthi's misgivings about the content of culture, this version of Diwali—little formal knowledge of any cultural practice is required and anyone can join—resembles how the event was described by the focus group of Indian foreign students in the last chapter. They described it as a more public event for entire neighborhoods to join in, rather than a closed, Hindu event. In fact, whenever the college groups focus on dances or music that require more training in these genres, a large group of participants are unable to participate. Meena, who was quoted in the last chapter for saying she was not at all "Indianized" till she became friends with another Indian girl in tenth grade, expressed a sense of regret that her parents had not "forced her" to learn traditional dances. So she had to find new ways of joining into these ways of doing culture. She said,

> We have a South Asian organization. It's huge and they throw parties. They do Indian dances Bharat Natyam and Kathak and stuff. They choreograph fashion shows. They do things like . . . you know, the things [performances] that uncles and aunts put you in and you did not want to be in when you were 10? Like the [first generation] Indian Association, when they say, oh you have to do it [you listen to them]. Now it [the second generation organization] has become like oh you can dance, so you have to [dance] for us. We have a dance troupe called ___ that competes all over the country. Or the all male Hindi singing cappella group out of UPENN, they are big! Anyway I was in the fall cultural show, and it was fun.

There are many South Asian American students like Meena who are not particularly versed in these ways of doing ethnicity, that is, they are not familiar with these specific types of dancing or music or movies. Their families may emphasize other regional cultures (like Kader) or they simply do not emphasize these vernacular forms of doing ethnicity. Namrata explained how even the leaders of SIO often had very different levels of familiarity with "South Asian" cultures. She said, "Like my co-president, she came here not knowing anything about [South Asian] culture. A lot of our South Asians are that way. I know a lot more since my father was so involved [in the ethnic community]. I remember when I became president my people were like how are you going to run the organization?"

Thus, these college groups use tools that encourage maximum participation, and draw upon the music and dancing and fashions that are easiest to access. At the same time, organizations like SIO also assign new meanings to these tools. Namrata, who has personally been immersed in "high Indian" culture (classical arts, music) because of her father's leadership in the Indian community and her own training in classical dancing, described the South Asian social events that she helped to organize in her college.

> [We play] mostly American music, with a little Indian music; they throw in some music to dance to. It's so like extensive, this culture we have created. . . . It's a fusion of everything—not just Gujarati, it is an Indian event. And I was leading the line of garbha people and they were like, "you are South Indian?" But it does not even matter anymore, we are here, its not so clear cut as it would be in India. Garba is an Indian event here . . . since the Pakistani Students Association is not too developed a lot of Pakistani students come too. Even for Diwali, two of our MCs were Pakistani. We don't see that as a problem. If we were one South Asian group we'd get less funding. The graduate student group, they would not have so much of the American culture, maybe like they'll have a garba strictly. Like in our garba, we played American music at the end.

Thus garba and bhangra become "Indian" *and* desi cultural forms. As Akash's statement at the beginning of the chapter indicates, using such fusion forms is the way in which most of the college groups try to balance religion, nationality, and greater openness among South Asian American students.

In contrast to SIO, which maintains the Indian label but tries to remain open to students of different national origins, the Desi Group (DG) was set up to formally promote a collective "Indian/Pakistani/Bengali" tradition. These students got together because they felt that Indian and Pakistani students shared more similarities than differences. They organized desi cultural events and later started reaching out to the Bangladeshi origin students as well. (They did not mention Nepalese students in their conversations.) The Desi Group's line-up of events typically includes dance sequences based on Indian *and* Pakistani films, a fashion show highlighting clothes from different countries, a skit on the cultural clashes between different generations as well as among the younger folk. Conflicts between the FOBs (first generation, young, fresh off the boats) and ABCDs (second generation American-born confused desis) are narrated through skits. Thus, though they share many of the same cultural tools with SIO, the "tradition" they emphasize is what is common to all "desis."

Both SIO and DG act as a node for particular networks. For individual students—usually from the bounded-ethnicity group whose parents are closer to the essential-ethnicity end of the continuum—who are trying to appear as though they conform to parental strictures, their participation in SIO keeps their parents happy. (As I described in chapter 4, these parents often operate on the basis of a dichotomized perspective: they think their children are primarily hanging out with a South Asian American crowd, they "did not do drinks, drugs and sex.")[7] And they develop their own wider network of friends. Both SIO and DG provide opportunities to meet South Asian Amer-

The Desi Students Association

The DSA needs your help to plan and carry out both Indian as well as Pakistani events, performances and much more.
Sound Interesting? Join us at the very first meeting to see for yourself what it's all about. The meeting will be held on Thursday October 4th at 12:15 in room 330.
Can't make it, but still want to know more? No problem, just contact either of the following:

6.1. A "desi club" flyer. Photo by Sabihah Dode.

icans in other colleges as well. Several SIO and DG members went to the bhangra competitions I described in the last chapter. They practiced together, and built up deeper friendship networks through these interactions. Attending the college festivals meant they also began to extend their networks nationally. While I was gathering data, a couple of the SIO organizers attended the national South Asian Students Association (SASA) conference in San Francisco, where they "picked up" new ideas of emerging cultural forms, along with knowledge about social and political issues concerning South Asian Americans (see Kukke and Shah 1999/2000). Amidst the parties (with the emphasis on the consumption of clothes and music) they also created more nationally dispersed networks. These e-lists then become the conduits for the circulation of certain sets of ethnic information and activist causes that linked these South Asian Americans to a more global set of networks.

In addition to these college networks, SIO members worked with non-college-based groups. They were occasionally invited to perform in events organized by YIA or first generation ethnic organizations. Some SIO members networked with SASCA-type groups as well. The Desi Group was not invited *as a group* by the hegemonic first generation organizations, although individuals might be invited to join in some event. Both SIO and DG are often asked to join in multicultural celebrations in the mainstream.

The limits of SIO's Indianness are most evident when we examine its relationship to the Indian foreign graduate students' organization (IFSO) on campus. Some IFSO organizers argued that the fare offered by SIO had little to do with India and IFSO organized its own "Indian" events that presented

6.2. Students performing at a "desi" event at a college. Photo by Sabihah Dode.

a "purer form of Indian culture." They often invite performing artists from the Indian subcontinent. Since their emphasis is on artists who command considerable respect for their skills in the subcontinent, their events attract significant first generation immigrant participation. Many of the SIO members are not as proficient in these genres or as familiar with these artists, and are left out of these assertions of Indianness. Another activity that IFSO organizes is getting together for cricket—either to play the game, or more frequently, to watch the test matches on large-screen televisions—but this activity is also foreign to the South Asian Americans. When there are any university-wide Indian events, IFSO members are usually asked to join planing groups first. Although SIO has also organized India Awareness Days, they have done this separately from IFSO. Occasionally, SIO and IFSO have collaborated on "social causes." Both raised money to help the victims of the Gujarat earthquake a couple of years ago. Most South Asian Americans referred to the IFSO students with a certain degree of awe, as holders of "real culture," thus reaffirming their own understanding of themselves as not being Indian (or Bangladeshi or Nepalese or Pakistani), but as Americans with hyphenated identities.

Overall, SIO's ethnic repertoire is more American than Indian, it is, as Namrata said in the last chapter, "our own Indian culture, it's a fusion, it's like American culture with an Indian theme to it." Desi Group's version is simply seen as American desi.

BOUNDARIES AND CHALLENGES. A closer look at SIO and DG shows how such collective construction of ethnic identity produces or minimizes gender, religious, nationality, and race distinctions.

Both SIO and DG promoted equal participation of males and females; in fact most of the leaders of both the organizations were female. Such participation is widely interpreted by many of the South Asian Americans as a sign of their confidence, capability, and outspokenness as *American* females. Although their activities are similar to other South Asian women (and women of color in general) in building and sustaining more open communities (Abraham 2000; Baca Zinn 1994; Kumar 1993), the majority of the SIO participants do not see any connections. Despite individual assertions that they were marginalized by over-generalized stereotypes about South Asian women in the mainstream, there is, till now, little widespread understanding or effort by SIO-like organizations to combat these controlling symbols.

Unlike SIO, which is called Indian, which organizes Diwali, and tries to remain open to all students, DG consciously avoids all references to religion. The Desi Group's events are organized without any associated ideas about religious celebrations. The organizers try to consciously keep all talk about religion and politics out of their events. However, since DG's events include the "different cultures," there is a recognition of embedded ethno-national identities within their version of desiness.

In SIO, while there is no overt religious tone there is a general Indian and Hindu emphasis, and specifically a north and west Indian emphasis that was the basis of Kader's complaint at the beginning of the chapter. While many people do not see religion as an issue, as the following statement illustrates, the many versions of "India" SIO tries to manage inevitably leaves many potential members feeling the organization was not for them. A Christian participant said, "I don't feel it [what SIO presents] as a problem, but I also try to learn a lot about the other cultures. People tell me I am a lot more Hindu than their Hindu friends. Since I make such an attempt to learn it's fine with me. But maybe my Hindu friend? Because she knows less she would feel more out of it because of cultural traditions. I personally don't."

Her reference to her Hindu friend who might not be comfortable was in fact reflected in the complaints of some other participants in this study who were in the same college. Some thought SIO was "too ethnic, the same crowds, same fights each year"; others thought it was not sufficiently "cultural." One student of Indian origin said, "I shun them. . . . They have a couple of Pakistani people in there but it is an Indian thing. Like the recent Diwali show, okay, all the songs were Indian, like recent Hindi movies. It's not like they put their culture in there."

There are similar levels of ambivalence and conflicts over religious identities within such organizations. The Nepalese students did not find a space within the Indian organization during SIO's major Diwali event because they celebrate Dashian (a Nepalese festival featuring Goddess Durga) at that time. Suhani complained that she had been accosted by some males at an SIO event and asked to explain the killing of Hindus by Muslims in Gujarat, India. Suhani, who is of *Bangladeshi* origin, said she told them to manage "their own house," but also decided not to go to SIO events again.

The relationships of SIO and DG with other groups partly reflect their institutional contexts and partly their own interests in creating some versions of ethnicity. Both were set up in order to create their space apart from their white peers, so there is a shared emphasis on developing cultural "nationalism." However, despite DG's openness to various South Asian origin groups, it did not have any formal interactions with any other group of color on campus. On the other hand, SIO often used the Asian American Center, and sometimes joined in events like the "Asian-nite." Members of SIO who joined pan–Asian American events were more aware of their Asian Americanism and often spoke about this layer as something that was important. As I mentioned earlier, individual SIO members also joined with other students of color to protest racism. While some individuals appeared to develop an awareness of their Asian American ties, they did not appear to be formally invested, *as a group,* in developing this layer. At the campus where the Desi Group is located there were no other "multicultural units" and the group leaders were convinced they had nothing in common with "Asians." While they deplored racism against any group, they had no formal mechanisms to build bridges with any other group. Thus DG was invested in the more pan-ethnic desiness but not any other broader racialized identity.

"Depoliticized" Community Group: YIA

The second organization, the Young Indo-American Association (YIA), organizes one main event and some supplementary events during the year—either in a school or a corporate setting—in a suburban location. The YIA's events focus primarily on performances and the audience for these performances is the first generation immigrants: the parents of the performers and their local networks. The YIA sells tickets for these events and the performances are usually sold out in advance. It also depends on corporate and ethnic-business sponsorship for these events.

MEMBERSHIP. According to one organizer, this group grew out of a need to address issues of the younger generation that were not adequately met by the generic "Indian" ethnic organizations (that is, first generation organizations). However, this organizer also felt members of student organizations like SIO needed to learn about Indian culture. The main organizers were mostly born in India though they came to the United States when they were young:

most came before they were twelve years old, a couple came during their late teens. Thus the lines between the South Asian Americans and South Asians are blurred among these leaders. The "membership" of the group is mixed: some are in college, often recruited through SIO-type organizations, while others are in the labor force. Like SIO, there is a small core group of members, and the rest of the "members" are recruited to perform some dances they prepared for other organizations or events. The YIA does not have a fixed place to meet. The group gets together in people's homes, or sometimes in local libraries or college classrooms to plan and practice their events. They depend on e-mail to maintain contact the rest of the year.

ETHNIC REPERTOIRE. Young Indo-American Association's cultural tools are similar to SIO or DG because the emphasis is on performance. However, YIA tries to impart its vision of "Indian" culture and a clear message of a version of Indianness is evident through their events. Examining which ethnic repertoires YIA promotes and displays illustrates how similar cultural tools can be used to produce very different narratives of belonging.

The celebration of India's independence day is YIA's major event, although selections from the performances are repeated on other occasions. The typical fare is a mix of items: plays that emphasize patriotism as well as more "neutral" songs and dances. One year, YIA presented a mix of plays on the Indian independence movement along with documentaries on India's recent military engagements with Pakistan. Gandhi is always mentioned during the performance, but the plays emphasize an overt and assertive form of nationalism, which is very different from the "feminine" nationalism of Gandhi (Nandy 1994). The other items on the program are dances that mix classical and vernacular forms, music and skits on arranged marriages, and the encounters of FOBS and ABCDs. These aspects of the performance are very similar to SIO or DG events. Despite the discourse about cultural traditions and authenticity, many of YIA's events are more similar to SIO and DG, than to IFSO's offerings.

Young Indo-American Association's assertion of ethno-national identity, which attempts to link the second generation of Indian origin with "their" history, not only conveys a message of disengagement from the more diffuse desi or South Asian *American* identity, it creates religious and gender distinctions of Indianness through selective erasure and emphasis. The content of one event—the celebration of India's independence—is instructive. While the event naturally focused on India alone, its paean on loyalty to family and motherland was cast in a way that leaves out references to multiple religions and histories of the subcontinent. Kader's insight about the invisibility of the Bengali culture within "Indian" (and "Pakistani") versions of culture was clearly reflected in this presentation: it only emphasized the hegemonic version of northern and western Indian history, with occasional representations of the south. The erasure is significant because the *syncretic* Hindu and Muslim history of Bengal (the pre-independence Bengal which is now split into Bangladesh and the Indian state of West Bengal) was central to the history of independence of India. Both the selective regional history, as well as absence of reference to most religious groups in India—whether they were part of Muslim, Christian, Zoroastrian, Buddhist, syncretic and indigenous traditions—sent very clear messages about who belongs in this ethno-national collective identity.

Even though females participated in equal numbers in this event, this nationalistic imagery also symbolically relegated them to subordinate positions within the families and homes. For instance, a major attraction was a play on Bhagat Singh, who was part of the armed uprising against the British. He was presented as an icon of the young male who sacrificed his life for his beloved Mother India.[8] The central importance of the mother in many South Asian families clearly resonated with many in the audience, but this skit also emphasized the subtext of the *helpless* mother who awaited the masculine protection of her loyal sons. Ironically, this "motherland" imagery was developed (in Bengal initially) and widely used during the nationalist uprising to challenge the masculinist colonial British power. This imagery represented, during that period of history, a way to challenge the racialized gendered British ideologies—about effeminate and predatory males and helpless suffering females—that were used to justify the civilizing role of the British on the subcontinent (Kumar 1993). Indian nationalist leaders used the motherland imagery to indicate freeing the "homes" from the chains of "public" imperialism (Ratte 1995).[9] When the Bhagat Singh episode took place in 1931, several Indian women had acquired prominent political leadership positions; one had been elected as the president of the Congress Party, the main nationalist party of the country, and there were a number of prominent women's organizations. Gandhi had begun to organize the non-violent movement that drew on feminine principles in the construction of this motherland (Nandy 1994), and thousands of ordinary women were very active in the nationalist uprising. Thus the representation of this particular episode as an example of the brave son and helpless mother is an overt reconstruction of a historical event.

Since few South Asian Americans are very familiar with the history of India's independence movement, however, the accuracy problem with this imagery is not usually apparent to them. Young Indo-American Association's stated objective of glorifying the strength and power of the "cultural tradition of India," and to show how sons revere mothers makes its exclusions less visible. This message has a subtle implication that a similar relationship is not widespread among "non-Indians" (whether these are Muslims, Christians, or other excluded Indians or simply other Americans). More important, given the stark absence of strong women in non-family roles in the event—such as female political leaders or female goddesses as symbols of strength or even the myriad androgynous cultural images that continue to be used in India—the helpless mother–strong son image becomes "the gender frame" for all "Indians."[10] This imagery is potent because individuals in essentialized-ethnicity and bounded-ethnicity groups also internalize similar messages from the hegemonic community about the roles and status of Indian females. In addition, YIA's depiction of helpless females overlaps with mainstream ideology about South Asian females. As I described in chapter 2, South Asian/South Asian American males are weak and effeminate, yet dominating toward "their" females, the females are supposed to be docile and helpless and subordinated; their acculturation into western values is supposed to be empowering for both sexes. While YIA attempts to change one part of the gendered ideology— where *strong* males sacrifice their lives to protect their beloved helpless mothers— the gender symbolism about the helpless female remains untouched. Thus, in its attempt to create affirming versions of masculinity (and counter the mainstream ideological constructions of males as weak and effeminate) it re-inscribes "traditional" gender symbolism within the ethnic community, and helps to maintain the racialized boundary that constructs them as people with non-American cultural values.

BOUNDARIES AND CHALLENGES. As with SIO and DG, the emphasis on performance means that the level of rootedness of individual members in this organization varies a great deal. A few of the participants in the YIA program revealed a great deal of ambivalence about their association with YIA. They joined in performances but did not feel "especially close to" what was being offered on the whole. For them, this event remained an episodic, public assertion of ethnicity. Like the student who said SIO offered her a way to reassure her parents about her essential Indianness, the YIA participants expressed a similar sentiment. Other people (like the DG members) avoided these events because of the religious and nationality boundaries. For the core members, the organization provided multiple opportunities to gather and network.

Young Indo-American Association's message of ethno-nationalism is based on presenting culture as separate from politics, which is very like the mainstream multicultural model. Indeed, YIA's ability to gather corporate sponsorship reflects how well it fits the mainstream institutional context. But its message also makes it easy for this organization to link up with the hegemonic first generation groups. Young Indo-American Association's message resonates with first generation immigrants who seek to inculcate similar messages of gendered ethno-nationalism among their children. These first generation immigrants then support and legitimate YIA as "the youth voice" of the second generation Indians.

However, emphasizing this version of nation-of-origin ethnicity through performance means that unlike SIO (with its casual openness to different groups) or DG (with its conscious openness to students of all South Asian nationalities), *South Asian* Americanness has no place in YIA's display and promotion of ethnicity.

Creating a Political Community: SASCA

CONTEXT AND MEMBERSHIP. The third group, South Asian American Social Change Association, is different from the two other groups in form and focus. This group conducts workshops and intensive training for groups of South Asian Americans during selected times of the year. The training is conducted in mainstream institutional spaces that the organizers can readily access. The South Asian American Social Change Association uses its member networks and web-based information to bring together a variety of South Asian Americans to disseminate its overtly politicized collective identity. The organizers are usually academics and community activists, while the participants are typically students of various ages (high school and beyond). The South Asian American Social Change Association encourages participation irrespective of gender, religion, sexuality, class, and other social markers. It offers financial aid to facilitate the participation of a variety of people. A participant said that she shared her "desi common-ness . . . but also . . . radical liberal views . . . [with] a gay male student who shared with us his struggle to not lose his Indianness as a queer, [and] a female labor union organizer." While the group comes together at certain times of the year, ongoing e-dialogue helps to maintain and expand networks around the nation.

ETHNIC REPERTOIRE. The South Asian American Social Change Association focuses on histories of popular struggles in North America *and* South Asia, and promotes the understanding of race, religion, gender, sexuality, and class as relations of domination and oppression. The objective is to use cultural tools—histories, arts (including performances), and literature—for mobilizing a version of South Asian Americanism with pervious boundaries. The South Asian American Social Change Association's focus on United States leads the organization to frame "community traditions" in terms of the racialized position of South Asians in the United States. Emphasizing the racialized history of immigration that paved the way for the arrival of the post-1965 groups (that I described in the introductory chapter), this organization highlights the similarities of the South Asians (of all classes) with African Americans, other Asian Americans, Native Americans, and Latinos in the United States. The South Asian American Social Change Association also highlights the less visible post-1980 immigrants and their struggles in the non-white-collar labor markets of the United States, constructing a history of class relations that relate middle-class South Asian Americans to more blue-collar ethnic group members. Instead of promoting the idea of solidarity through deep-rooted cultural traditions or imagined ties to single nation-states, it presents this "ethnic" history in terms of domination and subordination between groups.

The SASCA participants explore how racialized ethnicity is constructed and how ethno-racial boundaries emerge. It emphasizes ethnic dynamism and diversity and uses this framework for challenging the emerging hegemonic discourse about "one authentic" tradition among different groups of South Asians. Its objective is to help participants consciously think about imagined traditions and social structural relations, and to help them use their knowledge effectively for creating social change. One participant in this study remarked how she had always been liberal, but now she had developed a consciousness of the political dimensions of ethnicity. She described her "new" perspective on the mass killings of Muslims (and Hindus) in Gujarat and how she saw this violence in relation to the construction, political mobilization, and financing of certain religious identities within a transnational context.[11]

The South Asian American Social Change Association sets itself up to oppose the hegemonic versions of ethnicity and its messages are often diametrically opposite to YIA's messages. While YIA emphasized the Bhagat Singh episode in India, SASCA emphasizes the roles played by South Asians *in the United States.* For instance, SASCA teaches about Bhagat Singh Thind who, in 1922, challenged the legalized notion of whiteness that prevented Indian immigrants from becoming citizens of the United States. When SASCA focuses on the Indian independence movement, it emphasizes transnational connections and the history of Indian organizing in the United States. The history of the Ghadr party, which was formed in the United States, primarily by Sikh immigrants, to help liberate the subcontinent from British colonialism, is part of the SASCA repertoire. It teaches its members that the activism of the Indian immigrants during that period allowed the United States to justify including the Indians in the Asian Migration Ban of 1917. Overall, this recounting of history is inclusive of South Asian Americans of different religions and national origins and helps participants to situate their lives within a longer history in the United States.

South Asian American Social Change Association's presentation of women as active participants in the public sphere is another arena of difference from YIA. The association also discusses sexual citizenship and offers a space for the full participation of gay and lesbian South Asian Americans within its ethnic repertoire. Similarly, the relatively submerged history of cooperation between blacks and Asians both transnationally and in the United States, as well as the collective histories of the South Asians and Latinos, like the Punjabi Mexican communities described by Leonard (1992), are among the "traditions" presented to South Asian Americans.[12] In focusing on these versions of ethnic history SASCA encourages its participants to question the construction of whiteness and the role minorities can play, if inadvertently, in supporting racial hierarchies, along with their roles in the production of class, gender, and other social relations.

Just as SASCA's version of ethnicity is overtly political, so are its networks. Members frequently forge relations with other activists who are engaged in a variety of social-change campaigns in the United States. One organizer described how they used performances (drawing on a Brazilian tradition) as a way to initiate self-discovery and social change among activists in different organizations. Unlike cultural parades or the celebration of multiculturalism, the SASCA networks weave the youth into festivals like Desh Pardesh that focuses on progressive causes. The organizers make the participants aware of anti-domestic violence groups (like Manavi and Sakhi), gay and lesbian groups (like the South Asian Lesbian and Gay Association), workers' rights groups (like the Taxi Workers' Alliance or Worker's Awaaz), and anti-racism groups (like Desis Rising Up and Moving Against Racism). And, given its emphasis on the construction and control of knowledge, SASCA links its members to the rapidly growing scholarly world of research and writings on Asian Americans and a variety of other marginalized populations (often around the world).

BOUNDARIES AND CHALLENGES. Unlike YIA, SASCA's success is not dependent on ticket sales or accolades within the hegemonic community and it uses this "outsider" position to expand the meanings of South Asian Americanness. It challenges both the mainstream and the hegemonic community constructions of "ethnic boundaries," and builds trans-ethnic and multiracial coalitions to achieve its objective. These views lead to ongoing conflicts. Maira (1999/2000) and Melwani (2001b) have described the encounters between progressive youth in groups like SASCA and fundamentalist youth (who are socialized through the efforts of the more extreme sections of the hegemonic groups) during the India Day Parade in August in New York City. These groups exhibit two different ideologies of ethnicness and the boundaries they create between them are, at least, as relevant to their version of ethnicity as are the boundaries between them and the mainstream.

The South Asian American Social Change Association, like SIO, ends up creating new boundaries, in spite of the intentions of some of the organizers. Middle-class South Asian Americans have to see *themselves* as part of the privileged and powerful (in some aspects of their lives) in SASCA's narrative of relations of domination and subordination between different classes (also see Maira 1999/2000). Also, SASCA's emphasis on challenging boundaries means that South Asian Americans seeking affirmation of some aspects of their ethnic identity—alternative religious traditions, or more recognition of a hitherto marginalized regional culture—are less likely to find these types of content being developed through SASCA-type organizations. In fact, SASCA's version of ethnicness promotes the individual's ability to transcend it at some level. At the same time, SASCA's version of ethnicity requires deeper commitment in terms of time and effort, than joining in performances with SIO or YIA. So its message is less appealing for individuals who are looking for periodic opportunities to "put on ethnicity." Thus, SASCA's specific challenge is to remain inclusive but be able to reach out to a variety of groups that are not *already* seeking ways of challenging ethnic boundaries.

Negotiating Ethnicity

Even these brief descriptions of the three organizations presented here indicate the range of ethnic repertoires—shared understandings and practices— that are available to the South Asian Americans. As these organizations sift through traditions to create ethnic repertoires, they create differences and distinctions within and between groups. All the groups draw on transnational cultural tools and networks; all three develop some versions of hybrid cultures. Instead of promoting similarities and homogeneities, their activities lead to differences and conflicts. In this section, I focus on the boundaries they challenge and the kinds of ethnicity they negotiate.

Ethno-national or Pan-ethnic Organizations?

While both SIO and YIA share the "Indian" label, we saw that these organizations develop very different ethnic repertoires. The Students of Indian Origin, despite its name, is interested in building networks among "desi" students and maintains a level of interactional openness among these students. Since SIO's ethnic repertoire emphasizes "fun"—through music, dancing, fashions, and movies—its boundaries with other groups remain pervious.

While SIO and DG share in creating versions of desiness, there are some important qualitative differences between these organizations. The Desi Group tries to avoid such explicit Indianness. Its performances are explicitly labeled "Pakistani," "Indian," or "Bangladeshi." Students of Indian Origin's desiness signals an *Indian* character; since Indianness is the hegemonic frame, SIO members are often able to claim "South Asianness" without substantially altering their ethnic-repertoire. For members of organizations like SIO, Indian American ethno-national identities and pan-ethnic desi identities meet and *merge* over a continuum (instead of being separable layers). The Desi Group, in contrast, emphasizes its collective identity, in a way that acknowledges diverse ethno-national identities as part of this desiness. Both groups use "fun and culture" to promote their versions of collective identity. These different ways of trying to accommodate ethno-national and pan-ethnic layers imply that the Bangladeshi and Nepalese Americans have more opportunities to be accommodated by DG than by SIO. At the same time, by emphasizing the fun and culture framework, both groups give the impression, often inadvertently, that in their minds, ethnicity is synonymous with culture. So these groups challenge some racial boundaries by claiming their own space and right to organize, but they also conform to the institutional demands of setting themselves up as "multicultural" groups, that is, groups which are identifiable by their deep-rooted cultures. Overall, then, these two groups are able to negotiate some of the family, ethnic community, and mainstream boundaries imposed upon them. They do so by disengaging from some of the underlying ideologies and creating their own space and own affirming cultures and networks. But they do not directly challenge any extant social boundaries through their public presentations of their ethnicity.

In contrast to the college-based groups, YIA works within the racialized mainstream boundaries by promoting the idea of the essential Indian. The YIA intensifies the emphasis on a specific version of ethnic identity by promoting distinctions on the basis of national origin, religion, gender, and race distinctions. Young Indo-American Association's focus on one version of Hindu India to promote an ethno-national identity means that this group's members disengage from all opportunities to build pan-ethnic group ties within the United States. The Young Indo-American Association remains apart from other South Asian and South Asian American groups that challenge racial boundaries in the United States.

The South Asian American Social Change Association's collective identity is South Asian American, but their networks and coalitions with like-minded groups in the mainstream *and* ethnic community mean that their ethnic repertoires do not conform to any pre-set notion of South Asian Americanness. Unlike SIO and DG which attempt to develop desi versions of ethnic identities that draw on cultural tools that are already being marketed as Indian or Pakistani or South Asian, SASCA attempts to dilute such attachments. The main characteristic of their repertoire is anti-essentialism; the cultural tools they pick are consciously hybrid in character. Their pan-ethnicity is defined by how they challenge the multiple marginalities rather than how they promote certain cultural practices. Thus SASCA's collective identity is multi-layered and multifaceted. It promotes construction of a variety of layers of identity, including an Asian American identity, by channeling participants into a variety of activist networks.

Ethnic Repertoires and Transnational Networks

All these organizations are also linked to transnational networks directly or indirectly. The ethnic repertoires of SIO and DG that are primarily based on performances and consumption do not explicitly tie them to other formal organizational networks. Members maintain a range of informal ties with family members in other countries and these networks serve as conduits for information on what is popular in other places or discussions about who is seen as part of their ethnic groups. Namrata's realization that in England sections of Indians and Pakistanis do not talk to each other led her to make sure when she was the leader of SIO it was an inclusive organization. And, discussions about movies like *Bend It Like Beckham* can draw people into local and virtual networks as they discuss meanings of terms like "Paki."

Because SIO and DG are not already enmeshed in too many formal organizational networks, both YIA- and SASCA-type organizations often target them to draw SIO and DG members into their own—SASCA- or YIA-type—ethnic repertoires. The South Asian American Social Change Association links participants with networks of transnational activists who focus on global issues such as labor rights, anti-racism movements and human rights issues (Gandhi 2001; also see Cohen 1998, or Vireswaran and Mir 1999/2000). These transnational networks are not "ethnic" in their primary identification—for example, they could be anti-racist movements, labor, environmental, or feminist movements. However, they allow SASCA network members to challenge and subvert some social boundaries imposed upon them in their families and communities as they challenge boundaries at the national or international level. The YIA featured in this book did not directly channel its participants to transnational networks. However, the links of this and other YIA-type organizations with the first generation hegemonic community organizations creates an indirect link. For instance, South Asian Americans in SIO, who occasionally participate in YIA events, are solicited to participate in the activities of first generation organizations that are attempting to construct essentialized ethno-national collective identities.[13] These hegemonic first generation organizations which promote exclusionary ethno-nationalisms are setting up camps and conferences, much like the SASCA model, to teach about "Hindu" identities (Khandelwal 2001). Even though there is a growing similarity of the tools that these non-college-based organizations use, their very distinctive sets of discourses and local and transnational networks contribute to very different versions of ethnicity.

These differences between the collective identities that organizations promote generate conflicts: the confrontations between SASCA-type groups and YIA-type groups are increasingly becoming more visible.[14] Nonetheless, these conflicts have to be seen as an intrinsic part of constructing ethnicity. Such conflicts serve to keep the members more firmly entrenched within their own groups (Coser 1956). Equally important, such conflicts work to keep the content of ethnicity diverse and dynamic.[15]

In sum, such conflicts and differences over collective identity formation and dissemination, and the internal and external boundaries that are challenged or sustained, testify to the dynamic, fragmented, and multilayered character of ethnicity.

CONCLUSION

This discussion of the role of ethnic organizations indicates the diversity and dynamism of ethnic practices among the second generation South Asian Americans. The variety and dynamism of ethnic repertoires described here clearly indicate that South Asian Americans do not draw on similar cultural templates. These organizations delineate the contours of South Asian American ethnicity as they struggle to control "the social myths, language, and symbols—to shape how people define their concerns and options" (Katzenstein 1995, 49). Thus, the organizations provide ways of reconstructing within-group ethnic options as well as enhancing within-group differences.

While these organizations use transnational symbolism and networks, they provide several blueprints for negotiating the South Asian American position in the United States. Young Indo-American Association's version—which is clearly demarcated on the basis of religion and nationality—leads members to fit in with external racial and gender boundaries, including the contemporary mainstream discourses about deep-rooted cultures. The SIO version is American in its form: it focuses on consumption and performances like many other ethnic groups in America. South Asian American Social Change Association's primary focus is to challenge social boundaries in the United States; while it links its members to transnational social justice causes its focus remains at the node, changing some of the race, class, religion, nationality, and gender boundaries like many other change-oriented groups in the United States. Thus all three groups contribute to the formation of multiple layers of ethnicity that coalesce or fragment and play a crucial role in shaping and re-shaping South Asian American collective identities.

While much of the ethnicity literature continues to focus on the shifts and changes that occur as individuals encounter external social influences, that is, whether individuals acculturate or integrate, this chapter illustrates the importance of also looking at organizations. This group-level focus shows that organizations play active roles in sifting through cultural practices to create ethnic repertoires that become part of shared social understandings that define any individual's notion of what is ethnic about her/him. My argument about cultures in situated contexts is evident in this chapter as we find organized groups respond to multiple levels of structures and their potential members and pick cultural tools to promote their specific agenda. Thus the picture of ethnicity that emerges through this focus on collective identity is the interplay of structures and culture, of individuals, organized groups, and larger social structural relations that together contribute to the formation of ethnicity. Transnational, national, and local social relations are drawn into these collective displays and promotions of ethnicity which remain fragmented, diverse, multilayered, and above all, dynamic.

CHAPTER 7

Bridges and Chasms

MUCH OF THE WORK on children of immigrants examines to what extent they become "American," that is, whether they come to reside in mostly white suburbs and whether their educational and occupational achievements are similar to middle-class whites. This book has focused on the children of highly educated, non-white immigrants, who already meet this criteria and asked whether and how they remain ethnic. Focusing on South Asian Americans who grew up in mostly white suburbs, who have or are acquiring advanced degrees, and who expect to be in white-collar professions, I examined why they describe themselves with hyphenated labels, as well as the meanings, practices, and boundaries associated with these labels. The data presented in this book indicate that South Asian Americans actively negotiate ethnicity, maintaining multiple layers in response to the variety of structural constraints they encounter.

Since the South Asian Americans in this study grew up in mostly white suburbs and are integrated into the mainstream through their education and occupations, I began by asking whether, like middle-class white-ethnics, the ethnicity of South Asian Americans was symbolic. The evidence in this study indicates exactly the opposite. Ongoing racialization continues to constrain their lives as Americans in multiple ways, and the forms of racialization they encounter because of their integration in mainstream institutions shapes the contours of their ethnicity. Their ability to maintain transnational family networks, and the efforts of their nuclear families to help them disengage from the racial ideological framework of the United States leads them to situate their lives within a context that extends far beyond the boundaries of the nation-state. The rapid growth of the global industry for selling cultures facilitates their engagement with a global arena: they are able to use a variety of cultural tools that are produced in multiple countries, by mainstream industries, to assert their ethnicity. In spite of their ability to draw on a transnational context to negotiate their ethnicity, we also saw that this field is not a neutral cultural space. As the South Asian Americans use the opportunities available in this field, they also have to negotiate the complex web of social relations, including race, gender, nationality, and religion, at different levels—transnational,

national, and local. As individuals *and* as members of organized groups, they have begun to negotiate and weave ethnicities that respond to these complex structural forces, which often fragment their ethnic identities in significant ways. The efforts of organizations to create collective identities, in turn, draw them into transnational networks that support different versions of ethnicity. Overall, many of these South Asian Americans are engaged in creating ways to "collect" these ethnic layers into more pan-ethnic forms.

The theoretical implications of these experiences shared by the study participants are the subject of this concluding chapter. Although their South Asian American identities have more salience than their Asian American identity, I begin by discussing the potential and limits to such racial integration in the United States. Then I review the major bridges and chasms that constitute South Asianness among these participants and consider some possible future directions. I conclude with a discussion about increasingly fragmented and fluid identities in a globalized world.

ASSESSING ASIAN AMERICANNESS

The long-standing debates about assimilation of immigrants have recently been recast to analyze the impact of racialization of ethnicity. The immigration and ethnicity literature, such as the segmented assimilation perspective I described in chapter 1, has begun to recognize different routes that groups take to adjust in the United States. The segmented assimilation perspective focuses on a white-black framework of integration, and considers whether groups become upwardly mobile by integrating with middle-class whites or downwardly mobile because they integrate with inner city blacks. I considered the "other route" suggested by Kibria (2002), that groups become racialized because they are integrated with middle-class whites. Like Kibria (2002), I assumed that becoming middle class is a starting point, not the end point, for understanding the ethnicity of children of highly educated immigrants who are treated as non-whites. In this section, I consider to what extent the South Asian Americans are becoming Asian American.

A number of scholars such as Espiritu (1992) and Wei (1993) have described how racial lumping—on the basis of supposed similarities of "Asian" phenotypes and cultures—of groups that saw themselves as dissimilar, created the structural conditions for the development of racial ethnogenesis. The efforts of organized groups to build networks and cultures of solidarity to resist such racialization have led to the development of a pan-ethnic Asian American identity. On the other hand, much of the recent work on the post-immigrant generation among various Asian American groups—Chinese, Korean, Filipino, Vietnamese Americans—suggests that "Asian American" is just one layer among the many ethnic layers these groups maintain (Kibria

2000; Min 2002; Min and Kim 1999). To what extent are the South Asian Americans following a similar path?

The South Asian Americans are marginalized through a process of racialization similar, in a general way, to that of other Asian American groups: they are also designated as foreign, and they have been subject to the same Asian migration ban. However, the specific form of racialization constructs differences between these groups. As the dominant society assigns social meanings to broad sets of physical appearances, Asian American is constructed, despite official classifications, as "oriental," and, as this study illustrated, South Asian Americans are treated as black, Latino, or "Muslim," but rarely Asian American. In addition, other Asian Americans are racialized through meanings ascribed to their "traditional cultures"—stereotypically symbolized in terms of Confucianism, dim-sum, or sushi—while South Asian Americans' racialization draws on a different "culture set" based on arranged marriages and distinct religious practices, and a range of non-American values. The increasing use of religion as a marker of difference, either through discourses about incommensurable civilizations or through policies, further contributes to this divergence. And, the "common-sense" understanding of their difference is most apparent when Asian Americans and South Asian Americans are targeted as different identity markets for ethnic consumption. Thus, the structural, interactional, and symbolic processes racialize them as different groups.

Scholars are beginning to document the role of organizations to develop the cultures that create pan-ethnicity within racial boundaries that mark groups off from the mainstream—the development of Native American and Latino pan-ethnicities illustrates how specific types of *American* identities can be used for challenging racial hierarchies. However, such identities are dependent on the development of such larger-scale affiliative networks. Indeed, the extent to which the other Asian American groups feel "Asian American," is an outcome of an interactional process. The evidence that other Asian Americans also maintain ethno-national identities points to the possibility that many more South Asian Americans may add an Asian American layer to their ethnic identity in the future. The evidence in this study indicates that several contradictory efforts, spearheaded by different organized groups, are underway to add and inhibit the formation of this pan-ethnic layer.

Clearly, according to the participants in this study, most of the first generation community efforts are not focused on this form of integration; instead the first generation groups are building institutions and organizations that reflect their—often fragmented—ethno-national identities. Some of the second generation's groups like YIA also promote ethno-nationalism. In contrast, there are groups like SIO that leave the question of Asian Americanness open to individual preferences. Overall, this study has indicated that Asian American racial ethno-genesis remains fragile and fragmentary among this second generation group, *at present*. Among the individuals and groups I studied, dealing with the specific barriers they face seems to push them toward privileging their ethno-national *and* South Asian American identities rather than the broader Asian Americanness. In the presence of others like themselves in colleges, they develop nation/religion-based identities and/or South Asian American ties; they discover an opportunity to become South Asian American, just when they have an opportunity to become Asian American, and most do not work actively to develop both layers.

Maintaining the South Asian American layer is a response to the specific kinds of racialization these Bangladeshi, Indian, Nepalese, and Pakistani Americans encounter. Networks and affirming cultures of solidarity that they develop with other South Asian Americans help them to disengage, to a certain extent, from the dominant society's definitions of who they are and what the boundaries of their lives need to be. And the building blocks they use to build South Asian Americanness also allow many of them to negotiate some of the boundaries produced through their families and communities. But as Anthias (2001a) predicted, their involvement with the transnational layer often means they are less focused on their local context. Unable to practice specific aspects of their cultures in multicultural America, where they have grown up expecting to be able to exercise such freedoms, they use their class privileges to practice these aspects of their culture within a wider geographic context. This larger horizon (and the mediating efforts of the South Asian organizations) acts as a deterrent (in terms of time investment in developing and maintaining meaningful ties) to developing *Asian Americanness.* The sphere of focus and action is shifted away from the political sphere in the United States, to what many see as a "private" transnational sphere of family. Only the more consciously politicized South Asian Americans weave and balance the Asian American layer with their South Asian, ethno-national, and other relevant layers of identity. So Asian American racial ethno-genesis, which provides a path for challenging racial hierarchies in the United States, remains fragile and incomplete.

Yet, as this study also indicates, there are an increasing number of pan-Asian organizations including various Asian American cultural centers in colleges, and community-based activist organizations that promote Asian American pan-ethnicity among the second generation South Asian Americans (and other Asian American post-immigrant generation groups). These efforts are paralleled by South Asian groups such as SASCA that work to "raise consciousness" and weave individuals into a series of networks that make the Asian American layer more salient. Depending on which groups are better able to promote their versions of collective identities—YIA and community organizations with their restricted ethno-nationalism or SASCA and Asian

American organizations with their pan-ethnic versions—will decide the outcome of this question in the future.

A growing number of Asian American Studies programs, since the 1990s, which include scholars of South Asian and other Asian origins, have been constructing the social imaginaries—the histories, literatures, sociologies, politics—of Asian Americanness (Min 2002). In this study we saw that when South Asian Americans were involved in some direct way with organizations that promote pan–Asian Americanness, they develop an awareness of their affiliation with other Asian-origin groups in the United States. Their increasing familiarity with bodies of knowledge that emphasize their common experiences, whether this is promoted through SASCA-type organizations, or through studies programs and formal courses at colleges, appears to increase their awareness of the relevance of Asian Americanness to their multilayered identity. At present this Asian American layer has remained an instrumental political layer among a subset of this study's participants: as a way to get together with other Asian Americans on *some* racial issues. They have come together episodically, on issues such as protesting the imprisonment of Wen Ho Lee as a Chinese spy (see <http://www.asianam.org>), while the rest of the time they are mired in "South Asian" battles. After the terrorist attacks in September 2001, a large number of scholars and activists and scholars of color (Asian American, black, and Latino) spoke out individually and collectively about the renewed harassment of Muslims and all those who "resembled" them. Many Asian American authors linked the internment of Japanese Americans during World War II to the extra scrutiny of "Muslims" at the present time (see *Amerasia Journal* 2001/2002). To the extent South Asian Americans adopt these frames for understanding their racialized structural location in the United States, it may lead to the development of more salient "cultures of solidarity" with other Asian Americans.

However, at present, the process is incomplete.

BUT WHAT ABOUT SOUTH ASIANNESS . . . ?

If their links with others in their official race group is weak, what are the emerging dimensions of South Asian Americanness? This study shows that both ethno-national identity layers and more pan-ethnic South Asian American/desi layers are relevant to most of these participants. However, given the different entities that are engaged in influencing the direction of ethnicity—their nuclear and transnational families, multiple ethnic community organizations, mainstream economic and political interests in the United States, as well as a range of other globalized forces—South Asian Americans have to negotiate multilayered identities to balance these sets of opportunities and constraints. Their hyphenated identities are not made up of two internally homogenous, clearly separable sides that reflect their American and non-American roots. Instead, these sides are composed of multiple layers; the meanings and boundaries of these layers diverge, intersect, coalesce, and clash. Therefore the emergence of the South Asian American layer—whether it is a desi "cultural" layer or a more generic South Asian American layer to which some participants were strongly committed—remains fluid and context-sensitive. The description of the family networks and internal family dynamics showed how very different sets of networks can sustain or impede the formation of this layer. The description of the organizations also showed how significantly these entities influence and impede the shape and content of this layer. Despite the variegated forms, this layer serves as a way to balance some of the contradictions of their multiple situated contexts. It also encapsulates the non-essential, dynamic, and diverse nature of such ethnicities.

While the emerging South Asian Americanness allows this group to negotiate many of the constraints they encounter, there are at least two aspects of this layer that need to be discussed further. I first discuss the probability that a "South Asian" transnational identity will form across some second generation members in the United Kingdom and in the United States. Then I discuss the impact of increased scrutiny of religions on ethno-national and pan-ethnic identities.

Although the data from this study, which focuses on a segment of the second generation South Asian Americans, cannot be directly compared to most of the studies on South Asian origin populations because those are not similarly stratified, it is possible to comment on some general patterns. There are clearly many similarities among the "British Asians" and South Asian Americans. British Asians are composed of people of Indian, Pakistani, and Bangladeshi origin much like the South Asian Americans, although the British Asians are more likely to have a larger proportion of people who migrated from Africa. The groups are racial minorities in both countries. And, among the second generation, we saw how the global circulation of cultural products leads to similar patterns of cultural consumption. The work on British Asians (for example, Back 1993; Gillespie 1995; Modood et al. 1997) indicates that this group also maintains a range of formal and informal networks with people in other places. Indeed, participants in this study mentioned a number of family connections between British Asians and South Asian Americans, including the discussants in the *Bend It Like Beckham* vignette at the beginning of this book. So, at one level, British Asians are woven into a transnational context similar to the South Asian Americans. However, I would argue that despite this similarity the "South Asian American" layer and the British Asian layer are unlikely to coalesce into a transnational pan-ethnic layer. (In fact, none of the participants in this study described their ethnicity in terms of a *multi-country* context.) There are differences of class and migration histories that make these ethnic populations different. But the main underlying factor is that "pan-ethnic" layers, by their very nature, contain a very local, "reactive" component (Anthias 2001a; Olzak 1992). The South Asian American layer is forged in relation to whites and Asian Americans along with blacks and Latinos. The British Asian layer is forged in relation to whites and Afro-Caribbeans primarily (see Sudbury 2001). The content, boundaries, and meanings of these layers are consequently not the same in these two countries. Ethnicity, even at the transnational level, is not a matter of cultural commonality alone; it is forged out of shared structural position. Aspects of cultures are always mobilized within situated contexts to create new ethnicities, as Barth (1969) and others have pointed out; but it is easier to create discourses about more widely recognized tropes such as common origins or religious identities and then draw on selective histories to promote these versions of transnational identity. Such movements, emphasizing the development of ethno-national or ethno-religious transnational solidarities, appear to be underway at present (see Khandelwal 2001). In comparison, the larger scale identities that include multinational, multireligious formations (which are characteristic of pan-ethnic identities) are more likely to get included in larger "people of color," "interfaith," "Third World," "feminism," or "peace and non-violence" type collective identities (for example, see Gandhi 2001). Overall, the node-and-field-type transnational context in which various South Asian origin groups organize their lives at the present time makes it less likely that South Asian will become a very significant transnational ethnic identity in the near future.

Second, how religious identities are going to affect the ethno-national and South Asian Americanness remains an open question. Currently, multi-level boundaries, which are developing on the basis of religion, are opening up new chasms within the group. I have already described how religion is increasingly being used as a formal marker of difference, both in the mainstream and within the ethnic groups. The use of religions as markers of racialization is not new to the American social landscape. The earlier experiences of Jews and Catholics provide ample testimony to this form of racialization. However, there are some crucial differences that influence divergent outcomes among South Asian Americans. The Jewish groups arrived as exiles, fleeing traumatic experiences in their countries of origin, and experienced a great deal of discrimination in accessing education and jobs. However, despite a great deal of anti-Semetism at the everyday level, Jewish populations have not also been subject to the additional symbolic burden of being "from an enemy country." Similarly, even during the height of the Second World War, "Catholic" Italian Americans who were "the enemy" were not confined to internment camps like the Japanese Americans. For South Asian Americans, the uneasy relationship between United States and all the South Asian countries, which changes in response to other geopolitical forces, has led to the development of a whole range of laws that I described in chapters 2 and 3. The convergence of the religio-nationality-based political sanctions and the hate crimes they encounter for looking "like the enemy," affect the South Asian Americans negatively at present.

While the convergence of these policies with discrimination and hate-incidents in everyday situations make some of the contemporary religio-national boundaries more potent, increasing globalization of security arrangements substantially extends the area in which such identities remain "marked." For instance, the United States is not the only country currently subjecting Muslims to extra scrutiny: several European countries and India are doing so as well. (And extra scrutiny of a number of other groups such as Sikhs, Christians, and Buddhists depending on geopolitical conditions in different parts of the world complicate these influences further.) As various nation-states attempt to extend their spheres of influence globally in terms of cooperating on security arrangements, and exchanging information on "marked" individuals, these policies often coalesce and create broader zones within which groups may be defined as security risks. Thus, if various countries' national security risks continue to be defined in terms of broad religious (or religious/nationality) identities, then the ability of South Asian Americans to travel, maintain meaningful connections, and manage multi-country families will become much more complicated. More importantly, whether or not their religion is the primary frame of their identity—irrespective of the depth of their affiliation with types of religious practices—their increased need to manage their religious identity will make their "foreign religion" in the United States centrally relevant to their everyday lives.

These processes of religion-based categorization work directly against the efforts of South Asian Americans trying to form bridges between South Asians of all religions and nationalities. Their ability to claim "common experiences of racialization" as a reason for building solidarity (which is common among most pan-ethnic movements) is on increasingly questionable grounds. Whether they are able to stay together as a group, understanding the relational nature of these complex racialization processes, needs to be systematically studied at another point in time. If Muslim identities continue to be marked, and other South Asian identities appear to be safer, it remains an open question whether more South Asian Americans will resort to their religious identities under situations of confrontation and marginalization. The terse conversations about the roles of Muslims in the Gujarat riots or the emphasis on Hindu Indian identities, when individuals were accused of resembling "Osama bin Laden's sister" may be the tragic repetition of disavowal of members of a group during times of trouble. Historians have documented how many Asian Americans distanced themselves from the Japanese Americans as they were being subjected to extra scrutiny during World War II. In addition, the data in chapter 4 and 6 showed how there are organized efforts to equate ethno-national identities with selected religious groups. The macro-structural conditions may continue to converge with processes of religious fragmentation within the communities, and create deeper chasms to fragment South Asian Americanness.

Thus the content of the South Asian American layer is tied to emerging and ongoing contemporary national, local, and transnational structures. The hyphenated identities that South Asian Americans picked to define themselves, and the other less-visible layers they described, reflect contemporary realities. Their ethnicity remains fluid and fractured, multilayered and dynamic, shaped by opportunities and constraints within multiple-structural circumstances.

CONTEMPORARY ETHNICITY

The theoretical framework of this book has been based on the idea that ethnicity is forged through socioeconomic-political relations. Until recently, this relationship has been conceptualized in terms of nation-states and ethnic groups alone. Globalization, new migration, and concomitant economic and political changes continue to shape the context in which contemporary ethnicities are created. In this book I argued that the structures within the nation-state—the node and the field—remain relevant for understanding ethnicity.

Multiculturalism at the node—in its economic and political dimensions—has a significant impact on contemporary ethnicities. It opens up spaces for ethnic groups to practice "cultures," and the intersections of the political freedoms to practice culture with the commercial interests in selling cultures influences the content of many of their ethnic practices. But we need to think of multiculturalism as it develops through multiple nation-states. The availability of a variety of "South Asian" cultural products and cultural packages in South Asian and other countries shapes how ethnicity is configured in the United States. At one level, the wide-ranging availability of these products introduces a sameness to cultural practices across immigrant communities in many countries. But, there are multiple global entities, nation-states, multinational corporations, organized ethnic groups, social movements, and family networks that are cumulatively shaping the structure of multicultural spaces in Euro-American societies. Contemporary groups pick and choose "elements of particular cultures . . . drawn from a global array, [which are] mixed and matched differently [to fit the structural circumstances] in each setting" (Cohen 1997, 174). In other words, multiculturalism is a very important contemporary influence on how expressions of ethnicity are facilitated *and* impeded in Euro-American societies.

Almost a decade ago, Appadurai had argued that "the formula of hyphenation . . . is reaching the point of saturation in the United States, and the right side of the hyphen can barely contain the unruliness of the left side" (1993, 808). For South Asian Americans, developing the left—South Asian—side has been based on a range of formal and informal relationships across countries. However, I would also argue that the South Asian American experience shows that the right side of the label can no longer be thought of as a unified identity contained within geographical walls. Instead of thinking about a unified politico-cultural Americanness that is bound by the nation-state, against which the integration of ethnic minorities is conceptualized, we also need to think of how Americanism develops through transnational relations. The South Asian Americans' construction as *American* in South Asia is an experience that is different from what their Americanness means "at home." Yet both these forms of Americanness are important to how they configure their identities. For racial minorities, who continue to be marginalized, and who actively seek transnational resources and relationships to mitigate the effects of such marginalization, multiple structural constraints in transnational spaces influence both sides of their identities. Thus, instead of thinking of how their ethnic side alone is affected by the interpenetration of local, national, and transnational processes, we need to systematically study how both sides of hyphenated identities are affected as multiple nation-states and "ethnic" groups adjust to globalization processes.

This idea about not thinking of "the host country" as a geographical container also implies that we may have to rethink what we theoretically mean by assimilation in contemporary times. If we mean that immigrants and their children try to integrate by following the educational, occupational, residential patterns of the white middle class, then we also have to consider the possibility that this is one of many processes of integration underway. The transnational literature, in many ways, has started to document this process. Or if assimilation is conceptualized in terms of adopting the values and cultures of the mainstream America (in terms of "work ethic," linguistic proficiency, religious practices, or consumption), then we may need to rethink what exactly constitutes Americanness at present. The current debate on whether transnationalism is a new way of assimilating into Euro-American countries has focused, thus far, on ethnic groups and their adaptations alone. But ethnicity expresses a relationship between marked groups and a larger social entity such as a state or a larger entity. We need to develop historically nuanced accounts of how other nation-states are extending their range of influence beyond their geographical territories and to what extent these zones of influence of many countries converge or diverge. In other words, a more systematic examination of the altered context needs to be part of our discussions on contemporary ethnicity. Concepts like assimilation reflect a historically contingent relationship. We need to find new language to describe the relationship between the node, the transnational context, and ethnic groups in the contemporary world.

The main layers I discussed in this chapter—the Asian American, South

Asian, and ethno-national layers—are each being shaped by the structures in which they are embedded. They are also outcomes of the sub-layers and boundaries that constitute each of them. Apart from thinking about multilayered ethnic identities that are fluid and fragmented, the lesson that seems to be most salient from this study is the co-existence of these layers. The extent to which these co-existing attachments, some of which transcend national boundaries, represent an "ethnic problem" in any nation-state, will remain a major contributory factor in how such ethnicity continues to develop and change. And groups such as the South Asian Americans will continue to negotiate some of the constraints they encounter in building their lives. Thus, ongoing intersections of structure and agency will shape contemporary ethnicity.

Appendix: Methodological Notes

INTERVIEWS

Gathering the Data

The participants for this study are children of migrants who arrived from South Asian countries between 1965 and 1985. They make up a purposive sample of South Asian Americans who grew up in Connecticut and New York. In order to ensure variety among the participants, I contacted them from different starting points, through college-based networks, and community groups. Participants would often refer to others, although I never used more than five participants based on one starting point. I only included participants who were born or came to the United States before they were twelve years of age, that is, they spent their formative teen years in the United States. There were three exceptions to this rule. One participant was born and brought up in England, the other lived in Saudi Arabia for four years; both arrived in the United States just before their high school years. The third person was born and brought up in Canada and went back and forth between United States and Canada several times. Since their insights provided a counterpoint to the views of those raised in the United States, I used their information in the chapter on racialization. All the interviews were conducted in English, and ranged from an hour to an hour-and-a-half on average. Interviews were semi-structured, based on twelve themes (details attached later). I spoke to one-third of the participants more than once, when they contacted me to share more information that they thought was important. All the interviews were completed between fall 2000 and 2002. (Some of the supporting archival data were gathered till spring 2003.) Their experiences after September 11 prompted several participants to contact me again to tell me about some incidents that they encountered. Since I had already completed two-thirds of the interviews, and I had no way of assessing how widespread these incidents were among this population, I only used the experiences of participants who also described earlier episodes of discrimination (in other words, these incidents further confirmed what they had experienced earlier) to illustrate the ways in which these individuals were affected. A full-scale analysis of the after-effects of September 11 on South Asian Americans is likely to reveal widespread and more varied ways in which people were negatively affected.

Although I use the term "middle class" in the book, I do not refer to a particular income bracket. Instead, this term refers to South Asian immigrants who arrived with high educational credentials and who settled in mostly white suburbs between 1965 and 1985. I used two strategies to create a sample of participants who would approximate the first group described in the segmented assimilation model. Instead of asking participants about their parents' income to decide whether they were of middle-class background, I used the 1965–1985 period of immigrant arrival as a first level filter, then I checked during the conversation to see if the participants had grown up in middle-class suburbs. All the participants knew when their parents arrived or could work it out based on their ages or years in the United States. I expected that due to the structure of the immigration laws, at least one member of the family would have arrived as a highly skilled migrant, although, by the early 1980s, some would have arrived under the family reunification scheme as well. Indeed, five families were sponsored by relatives, including the three who arrived later. All the rest had at least one parent who came as a primary economic migrant. Maintaining the mid-1980s cut-off was particularly important because of the new immigration laws that were initiated from 1986 that changed the condition under which spouses of migrants could get permanent residency status. From 1986, they were required to wait for two years, and prove non-fraudulent marriages after that time. Diversity visas and temporary work permits (which had been on the books) began to be used more widely by the end of the 1980s. Using the mid-1980s cut-off also allowed me to separate the Bangladeshi participants whose parents came as professionals from those who arrived later on diversity visas, and Indians who may have arrived on H1B visas. However, despite the general middle-class background of the parents, there is variability in this group. While many of the parents had white-collar, upper-tier professional/managerial occupations, some worked in the "second-tier" white-collar occupations. Some were very affluent, while others were more average middle class. This ensured some variety among the participants in terms of where they grew up: mostly white suburbs ranged from being the only minorities in town to having some more diversity. While most participants went to overwhelmingly white schools, at least nine went to schools that were mostly white but included some blacks and Latino students as well. Thus they are all part of middle-class white America, but with some variability of what that denotes.

The Participants in this Study

I interviewed forty-eight individuals. Most were born in the United States. Thirty-four were of Indian origin, four were of Pakistani origin. Two others had one Indian parent and one Pakistani parent. Of these two, one identified as Indo-Pak, and the other as Indian. Three were of Nepalese origin, five of Bangladeshi origin; although one of these five had an Indian parent. Thirty-two were females and sixteen were male. Thirty were Hindus, eleven were Muslims, three were Sikhs, two were Jains, and two were Christians. Twelve had lived in other countries, for three months and beyond. Ten of the participants were employed in full-time jobs when I interviewed them, while another four were students during the interviews, but contacted me after they found jobs with other snippets of information. The other thirty-four were full-time students. Two were interviewed in their senior years in high school, and then again later while they were in college. Five of the participants went to private high schools, others went to public schools.

ALL THE NAMES of the participants have been altered to maintain confidentiality. In addition I have occasionally withheld names to make sure that unusual identifying characteristics (which their peers may be able to identify) cannot be related to what these persons may have said on other topics. I made up an additional set of names for the *Bend It Like Beckham* discussion to ensure these three participants could not identify each other in the book.

A Note on Generalizing this Data

This study focused on middle-class participants and should not be used as a generalization for all South Asian Americans. Five crucial distinctions are likely to make the experiences of South Asian Americans in other class groups different. First, the neighborhoods and schools in which other groups may have grown up may be different. Living in more enclave-type situations would alter many of the experiences, including the ability to draw on geographically proximate ethnic networks and resources. For instance, with whom they can celebrate religious events may strongly influence the content of these practices. Second, the processes of racialization are relational. How individuals of South Asian ancestry may be viewed in schools with larger proportions of racial minorities is likely to be different, just as who make up their friends networks is also likely to be influenced by this process. Here the South Asian Americans were building multiracial networks in college; the earlier development of these networks could promote greater racial ethno-genesis than is evident among this group. Third, the relative degree to which they are targeted as ethnic consumers is increasingly a function of how companies track by zip codes. This does not suggest that other South Asian Americans do not consume ethnic products, but who they buy from, what are the choices, what are the meanings associated with the items can vary. Fourth, there may be a great deal of variability on their ability to access multinational work, leisure, and family gathering fields (as opposed to keeping in touch with family) based on

TABLE 1

Selected Characteristics of Participants

Name	Sex	Age	Other characteristics:
			Birth/years in the United States, Religion, Occupational status, Identification
1. ABHA	F	Late teens	Born in the United States. Hindu. Student. "Half and half, Indian and American."
2. ABBAS	M	Early 20s	Arrived at age 12. Muslim. Student. "Asian male in an American environment, or a Pakistani living in America."
3. AISHWARYA	F	Late 20s	Arrived at age 8. Hindu. Working (Administrative service). "Nepalese American."
4. AKASH	M	Early 20s	Born in the United States. Jain. Student. "Indian American."
5. AKSHAY	M	Early 20s	Born in the United States. Hindu. Student. "Indian American."
6. ALKA	F	Late teens	Born in the United States. Hindu. Student. "Depends on the context. On the phone I'll say I'm American, or I'll mark other and I'll put down Indian born in the United States."
7. AMIT	M	Early 20s	Born in the United States. Christian. Student. "Asian Indian male."
8. ANITA	F	Late 20s	Arrived at age 2. Hindu. Student/working (film-maker).★ "Indian American."
9. ANJALI	F	Late teens	Born in the United States. Hindu. Student. "Indian American."
10. ARJUN	M	Late teens	Born in the United States. Hindu. Student. "American of Indian descent."
11. ARVIND	M	Mid 20s	Arrived at age 10. Hindu. Working (Insurance). "Indian American."
12. DEEPA	F	Late teens	Born in the United States. Hindu. Student. "South Asian though I like Asian Indian best."
13. FAIZ	M	Late 20s	Born in the United States. Muslim. Working (Social work). "Many labels are appropriate, Pakistani American . . . South Asian . . . Asian American."
14. HEMA	F	Early 30s	Arrived at age 8. Hindu. Working (Social work). "South Asian."
15. KADER	M	Late teens	Arrived at age 9. Muslim. Student. "American of Bengali origin."
16. KHALIDA	F	Late teens	Arrived at age 5. Muslim. Student. "Bangladeshi American."
17. LEELA	F	Early 20s	Arrived at age 6. Sikh. Student. "100% Indian."

TABLE I *(continued)*

Name	Sex	Age	Other characteristics:
18. MALA	F	Early 20s	Born in the United States. Sikh. Student. "Indian American."
19. MALLIKA	F	Late 20s	Arrived at age 8. Jain. Student/working (social work).★ "Indo-American."
20. MAYA	F	Early 20s	Born in the United States. Hindu. Student. "American with Indian background."
21. MEENA	F	Late teens	Born in the United States. Hindu. Student. "American Indian."
22. NAMRATA	F	Early 20s	Born in the United States. Christian. Student. "Indian American, or American of Indian origin."
23. NAVEEN	M	Early 20s	Born in the United States. Hindu. Student. "Indian American."
24. NUTAN	M	Early 30s	Arrived at age 11. Hindu. Working (engineer). "Indian American or American of Indian descent."
25. PRAKRIT	M	Late 20s	Born in the United States. Hindu. Working (engineer). "Depends on the circumstances . . . at work and around non-Indians I am an American of Indian descent."
26. PARTHA	M	Late 20s	Born in the United States. Hindu. Working (graphics design). "Indian American."
27. PRANATA	F	Early 20s	Born in the United States. Hindu. Student. "Indian-American."
28. PRATIBHA	F	Early 20s	Arrived at age 2. Hindu. Student. "I'm from Nepal but I'm also American."
29. PAYAL	F	Late teens	Born in the United States. Hindu. Student. "Asian Indian."
30. RANJEET	M	Late teens	Arrived at age 9. United States. Sikh. Student. "I'm first Indian, then I am American."
31. RAJEEV	M	Late teens	Born in the United States. Hindu. Student. "American male of Indian origin."
32. REHANA	F	Early 20s	Born in the United States. Muslim. Student. "Bengali American."
33. RUBINA	F	Late teens	Born in the United States. Muslim. Student. "desi or Pakistani American."
34. SAMINA	F	Late 20s	Born in the United States. Muslim. Student/working (Social work).★ "Indian Pakistani."
35. SATYAKAM	M	Late 20s	Arrived at age 10. Hindu. Working (insurance). "Indian."
36. SELINA	F	Late 20s	Born in the United States. Muslim. Working (Research/advocacy). "South Asian and Bangladeshi American."

TABLE 1 (*continued*)

Name	Sex	Age	Other characteristics:
37. SUHANI	F	Early 20s	Born in the United States. Muslim. Student. "Bengali American."
38. SHAHEEN	F	Early 20s	Arrived at age 15. Muslim. Student. "Indian Muslim woman."
39. SHANTHI	F	Early 20s	Arrived at age 10. Hindu. Student. "Indian."
40. SOMA	F	Late 20s	Born in the United States. Hindu. Student/Working (physician).★ "Indian American."
41. SONI	F	Early 20s	Born in the United States. Hindu. Student. "Asian Indian female."
42. SUMI	F	Early 20s	Arrived at age 13. Hindu. Student. "British Indian first. I'm Indian and my British is merging with American a little."
43. SUHITA	F	Late teens	Born in the United States. Hindu. Student. "Nepalese and American."
44. SUMAIRA	F	Early 20s	Born in the United States. Muslim. Student. "Pakistani American by birth, Indian by parent's experience."
45. TULI	F	Early 20s	Arrived at age 3 months. Hindu. Student. "Asian Indian and American."
46. VARSHA	F	Late teens	Born in the United States. Hindu. Student. "I am Indian. I'm kind of American Indian. I fall in between."
47. VANI	F	Late 20s	First arrived at age 12. Hindu. Working (artist). "Indian Canadian, American."
48. VARUN	M	Early 20s	Arrived at age 6. Hindu. Student. "Indian American."

★changed status after initial interview.

the financial status of the family. For instance, if family members in other countries do not have access to computers or e-mail, then using this form of technology is not likely to be widely popular. Fifth, it is important to keep in mind that where their parents fall on the ethnic continuum—how radical or conservative they are—needs to be studied on the basis of empirical data. There is no reason to assume that there is a positive relationship between class background and being liberal.

Insider/outsider Issues

As a first generation immigrant from India my status as a researcher needs to be clarified. Being an "insider" allowed me to use community networks among Indians, Nepalese, Bangladeshis, and Pakistanis to contact the initial participants. However, insiders can face problems because participants assume the interviewer shares their knowledge framework. I was able to mostly avoid this problem because I have an ambiguous last name and most participants were unable to identify my regional affiliation, though they guessed I was of South Asian origin. I would always ask them to further explain any Hindi/Urdu term, and any reference to Bollywood or *bhangra*. In addition, two graduate research assistants (who are white) conducted eight of the earlier interviews to ensure that we were getting data that were not driven solely by demand characteristics. These graduate students also conducted three of the four interviews with people who solely traced their roots to Pakistan, to ensure these participants did not feel uncomfortable about expressing any view about India. The participants of Bangladeshi origin usually did not know I was a Bengali (from India), so they explained anything they felt strongly about, on the assumption that I did not know about the history or major personalities of Bangladesh.

OTHER DATA

1. I picked the three second generation organizations because these participants were connected with these organizations, and more than one mentioned these during their interviews. I used their descriptions as well as additional archival and ethnographic data I gathered. However, I have altered some of the specifics of these organizations to present them as generic types.

2. I gathered the ethnographic data on events with the assistance of two graduate students. We attended a number of events, although I attended more "community events" while they attended more "on campus" events to make ourselves less conspicuous. In addition, one undergraduate student, who attended the 2001 SASA conference in San Francisco, brought me back elaborate notes on that conference, after I explained to her how she could keep notes of the events. The information on some consumption practices and events organized by groups is derived from these notes.

3. Four South Asian Americans got married during the course of the research. I normally spend several weeks in Kolkata, India, each summer and I was able to attend Anita's wedding there. I later attended her receptions in the United States. I also watched several wedding and reception videos of other weddings that were shared by the participants.

4. I conducted two focus group discussions. Both of these were designed after a number of South Asian Americans would mention a theme that required further elaboration. The first group consisted of six foreign Indian graduate students; in a semi-structured two-hour discussion, they discussed their version of doing culture, their similarities and differences with the South Asian Americans, and their cultural practices. Several of these students mentioned how alienated they also felt from the first generation immigrant

cultures in the United States; the comments on Diwali, Hinduism in the United States, and Indian weddings are derived from this discussion. The second focus group discussion was with three members of a women's group to discuss cultural practices. This information was used to supplement archival material on alternative repertoires.

5. I also collected archival data to supplement some of the ethnographic data.

INTERVIEW FORMAT: SECOND GENERATION

1. Tell me a little about yourself: your background, family background, your interests, and your affiliations. (Probe for migration history.)

2. When you think about yourself, do you usually think of yourself as an/ a . . . ?

    a. American female

    b. Bangladeshi/Indian/Pakistani/Nepalese female

    c. Female American of Bangladeshi/Indian/Pakistani/Nepalese origin

    d. American male

    e. Bangladeshi/Indian/Pakistani/Nepalese male

    f. Male American of Bangladeshi/Indian/Pakistani/Nepalese origin

    g. OTHER . . . .

3. Why did you choose this label . . . ?

(Probe: If you chose b, c, e, or f above, can you recount specific incidents that made you realize your "difference/distinctiveness" from other "Americans"? [Probe whiteness, blackness, Asian Americanness.])

4. On gender differences: In your opinion are there differences in being an American female vs. a Bangladeshi/Indian/Pakistani/Nepalese female/ American male vs. Bangladeshi/Indian/Pakistani/Nepalese male?

(Probe: What does being male or female mean? What standards are you held to? What are the empowering possibilities or restrictions associated with any of these male or female roles? Probe on families. What about gender in schools and workplaces—how are you positioned in those places?)

5. Does the label South Asian mean anything to you? Why/why not?

(Probe: On the relationship/position of Bangladeshi/Indian/Pakistani/ Nepalese. Points of similarity or conflict.)

6. Do you have any connections with family in other parts of the world? (Name the countries around the world where your family stay . . .) How do you stay connected? Why are these connections important or unimportant? What kind of opportunities/impediments do you encounter in maintaining such ties? Do you think some of these ties will wither away with time?

(Probe: Extent of knowledge of relationships and who is significant.)

7. Has being a member of an ethnic community helped or hindered you?

(Probe: What are some of the advantages and disadvantages of your parent's [or your own ethnic community] social networks?)

8. If it were up to you, do you think it is important to maintain ties with people in your ethnic community? Why/why not?
(Probe: What kind of ties do *you* maintain?)

9. Do you practice Bangladeshi/Indian/Pakistani/Nepalese culture? In what way? What is most important to you? Which events or practices hold most meaning? (Probe: on "consumption" of music, movies, fashions, tourism, or other things.) Do you experience any contradictions between practicing your family's specific Bangladeshi/Indian/Pakistani/Nepaleseness vs. a more general Bangladeshi/Indian/Pakistani/Nepalese culture?

10. Do you see Bangladeshi/Indian/Pakistani/Nepalese/South Asian culture being practiced in the US/Canada? What are the most visible symbols of Bangladeshi/Indian/Pakistani/Nepalese culture? Which aspects are emphasized most?

11. What role do the organizations play? Are you a part of any Bangladeshi/Indian/Pakistani/Nepalese organization? Is there a difference between the Bangladeshi/Indian/Pakistani/Nepalese/South Asian youth culture (in the United States) and the Bangladeshi/Indian/Pakistani/Nepalese/South Asian culture of your parent's generation? What about non-ethnic organizational affiliations?

12. In your opinion how do you see your generation positioned politically—in North America or elsewhere?

13. What part does religion play, if at all, in terms of your everyday life?

14. Tell me about some of the people you would turn to if you needed some help (Probe 1: Advice, support, financial help, other; Probe 2: Who are these people, including ethnic racial background of friends and family members.)

15. Tell me about any other issue that is important to you (that we may not have discussed at all) that will help me understand your perspective better.

Notes

1. While this idea of a primary migrant coming to America along with his family is embedded in the popular imagination, a series of laws, from the 1880s, aimed at restricting the migration of females from Asian countries, ensured that very few Asian origin groups could form families here. As Leonard (1992) explains, the early Sikh (Indian) migrants, who arrived at the turn of the twentieth century, were not allowed to bring their wives even though many of them were already married. The only group they were allowed to marry in the United States at that time was women of Mexican origin. Given these constraints they formed scattered Punjabi Mexican communities. Later, in 1917, the Asian migration ban stopped all Asian migration to the United States. Thus the relative *newness* of these South Asian groups, and their "new" ability to form families in the United States is a function of the earlier racialized restrictions.

2. When migrants from the subcontinent began arriving in the 1960s, their official classification was white. Khandelwal (2002), among others, discusses how Indian organizations such as the Association of Indians in America lobbied the Department of Commerce to be moved to the Asian American category in the 1980 Census, with Asian Indian as a choice of "race" under this category. Their actions were prompted by a growing realization that Asian Indians were victims of discrimination and required reclassification of minority status in order to protest discrimination. These South Asian American groups argued that, regardless of official classification, they were rarely considered as "white" in their everyday lives.

3. Several terms are used to describe groups within more global contexts. Diaspora refers to connections between groups that are located in multiple nations whose commonality is based on the notion of a homeland (see Cohen 1998). In this book I avoid the term diaspora because of its association with ethnicities that privilege points of origin or cultures (see Anthias 2001b for a critique). I use the term "transnational" to indicate a context that develops through, and extends across two or more nation-states. I talk about transnational fields of networks to indicate an arena in which these networks exist. Transnational influences refer to influences emanating from this space that develops between nations.

4. The term "pan-ethnic" refers to large-scale identities that emerge in response to racialization of groups of people. Typically the term is used to refer to Asian Americans (Espiritu 1992) and Hispanics (Padilla 1985). Since I show that a distinct form of racialization affects the South Asian American groups and marks them as different from other Asian Americans, I use the phrase "more pan-ethnic" to refer to the emerging South Asian American identity.

5. Sri Lankans and Bhutanese are also part of Southern Asia, but this study confines itself to migrants from the four largest countries. The Nepalese migrants rarely appear in any of the official statistics because of their relatively small numbers.

Nonetheless, as migrants from an officially Hindu country, the only one not officially colonized by Europeans, they offer an interesting counterpoint to the other South Asians. More importantly, like the Bangladeshis, they are always assumed to be "Indian" by outsiders. The other group not included in this study is the Indo-Caribbean. Officially the Indo-Caribbeans are not part of the South Asians, and most first generation South Asians do not consider them to be part of their community (Sengupta and Toy 1998).

6. As I explain in the Appendix, this study should not be taken as a representation of all South Asian Americans, since this study is based on a middle-class subset.

7. For instance, most of the Bangladeshis now present in the United States arrived on "diversity" visas instituted to correct the global imbalance of which countries were able to send migrants to the United States (Islam 1996). This "correction" meant that the earlier "high-skills" filter no longer applied to these later migrants. In addition, new restrictions on highly skilled workers, especially information technology workers, ensures that these temporary workers cannot easily become permanent residents of the United States. Family reunification rules have also changed the profile of the groups. Thus, a dichotomized profile, by achievement, is characteristic of all the groups, though the proportion of highly educated and those with less education varies among the nationalities. While an equally interesting study could be conducted within group and across group differences, that is not the subject of this study.

8. According to the U.S. Census Bureau (2000), the total proportionate breakdown of the foreign-born population is 92,294 Bangladeshis, 223,447 Pakistanis and 1,022,522 Indians. Figures for Nepalese were not reported separately. The numbers for the native-born children of the immigrants are not available separately.

9. Nepal was never a British colony but Nepalese Americans share the same formal history of migration restrictions against Asians in the United States. Like the other three groups, Nepalese Americans also have family members spread over multiple countries, including India and the United Kingdom; they too are Hindus like the majority of the Indian Americans.

10. There is a lively controversy in the immigration literature on whether economic immigrants, who may take their cultural backgrounds for granted, are fundamentally different from political refugees, who by definition suffered because of some aspect of their social identity (see Hein 1993 for a summary). The point I wish to emphasize here is that these histories of recently experienced political conflict tend to influence the first generation's ideas of who belongs to their group and who does not. These ideas are often at odds with whom the second generation see as in-group members. This theme is discussed further in chapters 2, 3, and 4.

11. The increasingly stringent immigration laws included the now infamous virginity tests. Females from the Indian subcontinent who migrated to join their fiancés were expected to prove the veracity of petitions to get married by proving that they had not been sexually associated with other men earlier. The assumption was that since female chastity before marriage is highly valued on the subcontinent, any female who was not a virgin was probably lying about her marriage intentions in order to migrate to the United Kingdom (Joseph 1999; Prashad 2000a).

12. In an interview with Kavaree Bamzai, in the news magazine *India Today*, the Kenyan-born British director Gurinder Chadha (who is a Sikh from Southall in London and is married to an American), said that she saw "*Bend it* . . . as being very specific to the East African Punjabi community in Britain" (Bamzai 2002, 36). So the discussion among the three is clearly a reflection of their racial understandings, which are an outcome of their experiences of never being "American."

CHAPTER 2   RACIAL BOUNDARIES AND ETHNIC BINDS

1. I use the term "liminal" in a very specific way to indicate a state of not quite fitting into any group. South Asian Americans are non-white, but they do not neatly fit their Asian American categorization, or claim to be black as groups have done in the United Kingdom. I use "liminal" to indicate an outsider position, where a group falls between established social categories, without the additional implication that the group is evolving into something else, as some critical theorists have argued (see Anthias 2001a for a brief discussion of this issue). I follow Homi Bhabha's (1994) analogy of a stairwell: a person in the stairwell is neither in the upper room, nor in the rooms below or outside the building. It is in this sense, as a descriptor of their current position, that I use the word liminal.

2. People from South Asia include a variety of phenotypes; some people from the eastern parts of India and Bangladesh resemble East Asians closely, while others resemble blacks, Latinos, and Southern Europeans (see Mampilly 2002). But racialization is based on over-generalizing and stereotyping the sameness of all race groups. The South Asian American experience shows the relational nature of this stigmatization. Without a clear fit with Asian Americans, they are ascribed other non-white identities depending on the local circumstances.

3. Recently, movies portraying Asian males as adept in martial arts have begun to reinvent them as powerful. However, not all powerful masculinities are ideologically depicted as equal. In fact, a whole series of cultural meanings designate which males are freedom loving and progressive, and which ones are animal-like, uncontrolled, or scheming. For the South Asian Americans, however, their lack of fit with any of these images constructs their marginality.

4. Lighter skin tones, especially among females, are also prized in many South Asian communities, so this attempt to be lighter skinned could reflect more complex reasons. According to Lury (1996), washing their skins in an attempt to lighten it is a widespread response to the internalization of racialized messages.

5. A defining symbol in the Asian American movement, which brought many groups together, was the murder of Vincent Chin, a Chinese American, by some white men. These males wanted to beat up a "Jap" for their supposed culpability in the relative economic success of Japan which led to the loss of jobs in the United States (Espiritu 1992). Such hate crimes, based on "lumping of phenotypes," mark the difference between people of East Asian origin and people of South Asian origin.

6. The perception of the "common person on the street" has a legal historical precedent. In 1922, a lawsuit brought by Bhagat Singh Thind challenged the exclusionary laws that were directed against Indians. Thind argued that since the courts had decreed that persons of Aryan origin should be considered white, Indians who were of Aryan origin, could not be brought under the purview of the exclusionary laws. Judge Sunderland ruled that irrespective of origins and roots, as long as the common person on the street saw Indians as non-white, they would be so categorized under the law.

7. Seven had studied abroad; four had completed internships, including working for non-governmental organizations. Another four had lived in other countries. The majority of the South Asian American youth had traveled for pleasure, most were aware of their liminality as American tourists as well.

8. Amit, a Christian male of Indian origin, explained that because of his family's minority status as Christians in India, it was the practice for the entire community to get involved in bringing males and females of a certain age together, to ensure the survival of their community. They would then meet and decide whether or not they would like to go ahead with the marriage. According to him, South Asian American

Christians emulate these Indian practices in the United States. He felt arranged marriages were not as socially limiting as the American mainstream might think. It made sense for the community to participate in the arrangement of marriages; it facilitated wider networking to find people who might suit each other, especially in a geographically large country like the United States where "Indians" (including Indian Christians) live geographically dispersed lives. Once the preliminary work was done by the community, the individuals meet and make their own decision about the marriage.

9. Sinha (2000) and Oldenburg (2002) describe how some of the most persistent images of sati (burning of widows), notions of depraved men preying on infantile women, and dowry deaths, were constructed both to justify the presence of the British in the colonies, and to explain the broad immigration exclusions against South Asians in the United States.

10. Mallika was referring to Bangladesh, Pakistan, and India, the three countries that have elected female heads of states several times. India, the largest country, has had a comprehensive set of rights for women since the constitution was written after independence in 1947. (According to historians like Kumar [1993], demands for such legislation were made to the British early in the twentieth century). In 1993, India passed a "positive discrimination" legislation that reserves 33 percent of the seats at the *panchayat* (village) level. Forty percent of these seats are now held by women (Purushothaman et al. 2004).

11. Several second generation males and females of Bangladeshi origin expressed dissatisfaction about the hijab-wearing female stereotype used to represent all Muslim women. They pointed out that Bangladesh is unique in the world for electing two female prime ministers, both of whom were elected more than once, as heads of state. Most women in Bangladesh still did not wear the hijab, especially the middle-class women of their families. Each of them emphatically pointed out that the image of the veiled subjugated woman might be true of other Muslim countries but it was not true of Bengalis. Yet in the over-generalized images, Bangladesh's gender norms and women's achievement are usually invisible. As children of middle-class, educated immigrants who came from a non-hijab wearing, democratic nation, they felt particularly angry about the "ignorance" of the media and all the people who just accepted whatever information the media provided.

12. Hate crimes against South Asians following the terrorist attacks on September 11, 2001, as individuals wanted to take revenge on Muslim terrorists, illustrate this concept. Other groups have been similarly victimized. The Chinese Spy scandal surrounding Wen Ho Lee is one recent example.

13. Newspaper reports corroborated the fact that people of different classes and races were involved. For instance, Robin Clark (a Singaporean, whose parents are white and British) was stabbed in San Francisco because he was characterized as a white person who loved blacks, and his friend, an Anglo-Indian (Christian), who originated from Calcutta, as an Arab. The attackers "were guys and girls who looked like the type I would like to meet and hang out with in a club. They were well dressed and looked well educated. They were not drunk but were in total control of what they were doing" (Ibrahim, 2001, H2). The only help they received was from a homeless man, who stepped out to support Clark when he collapsed from his wounds. In another case, a university administrator in the Midwest used her university e-mail to spread false rumors about two young men who ran a local gas station (Dodge 2001). While many of the perpetrators were white, other Asian Americans (see Yoshino 2001) and blacks (Fulwood 2001) were occasionally involved. These racial incidents were not confined to the United States alone; Sikhs were harassed in other countries as well (Kelly 2001).

14. This registration, directed against people on visitors' visas that allow people to stay

for six months, required these males to register with the INS each month. This provision was withdrawn in December 2003. This has been supplemented by biometric profiling at the airports. However, the strictures against foreign students, which require them to report changes of courses, and any change in campus (or off-campus) addresses to the Citizenship and Immigration Service are still in place.

CHAPTER 3   MAINTAINING MEANINGFUL CONNECTIONS

1. The differences between the two generations in how they traverse these transnational terrains have to be understood in terms of the specific kinds of transnational activities in which the different generations are involved. This chapter clearly shows that maintaining family networks does not lead to a simple transmission of "family culture" that subsequently forms the basis of a shared ethnic culture. Family relationships do influence how groups view the world. Certainly the South Asian Americans' insistence upon the "unique" closeness of family members is a shared trait among all four groups. But it is the shared experience of these South Asian American groups within their specific structural context in the U.S. that makes it a basis for developing ethnic commonalities, rather than the culture itself. This chapter shows how different sets of structures interact to influence what South Asian Americans choose to emphasize as their ethnicity.

2. Visitors' visas were normally granted for six months. If an applicant from South Asia fits the profile of someone who might want to migrate (that is, overstay their visitor's visa) he or she has to prove their connection to the home country. (Most educated middle-class individuals who have been employed in the South Asian countries fit this profile.) Such evidence includes property documents, employment certificates (and prospects of employment), certificates of marriage, proof of dependent children and relatives, and a variety of related material. The sponsoring individuals in the United States have to prove—by submitting their Internal Revenue Service tax records—their current ability to support their visitors.

3. This provision was rescinded in December 2003.

4. For sections of this group increasing property and expanding businesses internationally also forms a significant part of these connections (Tatla 1999).

5. Another interesting addition to their description of families was their inclusion of fictive kin in the United States. They generally added a few people, friends of their parents, who they addressed according to family relationships, and felt they could call up for various kinds of support and advice, even if they did not see them regularly. This is similar to family forms among blacks, Latinos, and other Asian Americans who have also been affected by restrictive laws from forming their "ideal" families (see Dill 1994; Espiritu 1997, Renteria 1992).

6. Leonard (1997) has argued that the belief among South Asian Americans that their families exemplify greater closeness and bonds than families of their white peers is not justified because "in the United States too, families still emphasize love and support, although they may show this differently than South Asian families do" (1997, 149–150). I would argue that these are indeed different levels of commitment because in the United States, for natives who have full access to citizenship privileges, a range of social welfare benefits bolster the individualism and independence of family members. South Asians are used to structurally relying on their family for care (of all individuals) in South Asia. Since family members are unlikely to be together in the United States, and even if they are, their access to social security, Medicare, and unemployment benefits are contingent upon their immigration and naturalization status, South Asian Americans are not structurally positioned to exercise their independence in the ways Leonard describes. Thus their socialization about degrees of love and obligation are different as well. The different access to

structural benefits means that within South Asian American families, cultures of mutual obligation and duty have to be nurtured constantly through a variety of cultural routines, to inculcate the closeness that motivates family members to help and support each other rather than putting greater emphasis on their individual interests. Thus, the nature of this family closeness is qualitatively different from the love and closeness among American natives who are structurally positioned differently vis-à-vis the welfare state and can act more often on individual interests while maintaining bonds of love. The structures that undergird these social constructions of love differ among the groups.

7. One participant who was married to an African American had told me that she could never take her partner to her "South Asian" home country because the extended family would never accept a person who was black. Yet she also said that she wanted to take her child over for extended periods of time so that the child could benefit from the loving family relationships. So how much of the family closeness is a constructed ideal may be a question for future research. However, what is relevant for this discussion is that this real or ideal image of the extended family was being used by these South Asian Americans to distance themselves from the racial discourse in the United States.

8. In the previous chapter, I featured Dworkin and Messner's (1999) argument about how contemporary masculinities and feminities are being co-opted and reconfigured, not in terms of an increasing structural equality, but as freedom to consume. Their argument touches on a larger scholarly debate about the extent to which the relationships between individuals and society are being structured through their ability to consume. While I discuss the notion of "consumer citizens" in chapter 5 in greater detail, it is important to note here that their extended family experiences led this subset of South Asian Americans toward adopting the view that life can be lived richly with fewer material things. This view, they felt, set them apart from their peers.

9. Two South Asian American participants described how they volunteered in India and one described how she set up a medical rotation in Delhi. While these activities are not systematically described in this book, some South Asian Americans see the South Asian countries as the larger context within which they organize their work/volunteering lives. A number of foundations and organizations have developed to facilitate this process. One participant made me aware of the American Indian Foundation, which works somewhat like the Peace Corps and offers similar opportunities.

10. While the first participant did not encounter similar incidents, there is a theoretical commonality among their stories. Those who are singled out as "Muslims" in the United States, and those who have to hide their religious identity (irrespective of whether it is Muslim or Hindu) during political tensions in Pakistan, India, or Bangladesh, are subject to multiple sets of structural constraints. (New South Asian feminist histories have begun to document how similar strategies were adopted by women of different religions to avoid being conspicuous during the post-partition riots in 1948.)

11. The government subsidizes many of these educational institutions, so these colleges are cheaper than equivalent colleges in the United States. More importantly, many of these colleges are the alma mater of the first generation, and many have maintained active links through endowments and other donations. Some of these institutions, like the Indian Institutes of Technology (especially the one located in Kanpur) and the Indian Institutes of Management, are among the leading institutions *in the world.* Earlier, access to these educational institutions was restricted to citizens of the country. Now the PIO card allows people without citizenship new access to these institutions. Thus, the new access to these and other lower-tier insti-

tutions, opens up new prospects for South Asian Americans (provided they pass the qualifying examinations). For those who do not qualify for these top institutions other institutions supplement their educational choices.

12. This seemed to be especially characteristic of the groups that were usually present in large numbers within the South Asian American groups. Since their larger numbers meant they were able to meet many others of their specific backgrounds, it was easier for them to equate their culture with the culture of the nation-states in South Asia. However, which cultural practices become hegemonic is not a matter of numerical strength of the subgroups alone. I will discuss other factors that influence the emerging hegemonic versions of South Asian national cultures in the next few chapters. Here, my point is that South Asian-Americans who were numerical minorities *in the United States* were more apt to reflect on their fragmented Indianness (or other national identity).

13. Sanskrit is like Latin, most of the Indians and Nepalese do not understand it. Traditionally a language taught to Brahmin men, and in some enlightened Brahmin families to the women as well, it is not a language that has widespread use outside religious ceremonies. So it is possible for priests to intone the wrong prayers, without any of the participants realizing what is going on.

14. When I showed some of these wedding pictures to some colleagues in the United States one of them was surprised to see the sign of the swastika at the wedding site. This is a traditional symbol of goodwill and blessing in Hindu practice. However, the adoption of this symbol by the Nazis has imbued this symbol with very different meanings in the United States and in Europe. Hindu families from India and Nepal rarely use the symbol publicly in the United States.

15. These venues increasingly allow ethnic hor d'ouevres; still, the dinner is catered by the hotels and clubs. The exceptions are when a South Asian owns the facility.

16. See, for example, <http://www.hrhindia.com/day1.html> or <http://www.royalrajasthantour.com> to get an idea of this phenomenon.

17. The rapid growth of the heritage tourism is part of the post-industrial transformation that is described by Zukin (1995). Buildings and other sites are marketed for the consumption experience they provide—a sense of being a part of history and tradition that can be bought by anyone who can afford to pay the entrance prices. There is significant literature on this subject, which I discuss further in chapter 5. It is important to remember, for purposes of this discussion, that every country on the subcontinent is full of historic buildings, which can be transformed into sites of consumption. The castles that sell wedding packages now may be the forerunners of this trend.

CHAPTER 4   CONSTRUCTING ETHNIC BOUNDARIES

1. South Asian American parents often point to their superior levels of earnings from the "average" white person as a measure of achievement. A more appropriate measure would be a comparison with whites of similar levels of education and/or occupational concentration. An insidious dimension of culture and achievement argument is that some groups point to how United States businesses are increasingly moving to India, but not Bangladesh or Pakistan or Nepal, in search of trained workers.

2. This latter group, the newspaper kiosk owners, taxi drivers, small business owners has been growing since the 1990s, and is often caricatured in the media as "the" South Asians. Irrespective of whether families always intend to emphasize the difference between working class South Asian Americans and themselves, their "high achievement" discourse does, in fact, have this effect. If superior achievement

defines all South Asian Americans, all those who did not meet these criteria are marginalized through this discourse.

3. The schisms about racism run deep among the first generation since the women's group that had sponsored this panel soon split because one group was extremely uncomfortable with another group of first and second generation members' attempts to be racially inclusive and build coalitions with other Asian Americans, blacks, and Latinos.

4. Whether immigrant parents fully understand the complex dimensions of racialization, or know about racial histories of their group, is an issue that needs to be systematically studied. Such studies would be important because the composition of the group requires understanding the multiple fragmented processes of racialization. Recent writings about the South Asians mostly emphasize the hegemonic position (for example, Prashad 2000–2001, Maira 2002, Mukhi 2000). The point I want to emphasize here is that without explicit socialization that rejects mainstream characterization of minorities, even the South Asian Americans who grew up in families which were not distancing themselves from other minorities, ended up interpreting their experiences in terms of the mainstream framework which separated them, as a "cultural group," from other minorities.

5. There are a large number of temples in the United States. Without a systematic study of their organizations and initiatives, it would be methodologically unsound to conclude that *all* temples are controlled by hegemonic groups described here. This discussion is based on what the participants in this study described as "the" temple-based form, that is, what they see as the public face of the institutions they are familiar with.

6. None of the South Asian Americans I spoke with went to these camps. The few who mentioned that their parents wanted them to go also said that attendance at "achievement-oriented" camps got priority. Recent articles by the South Asian Americans in progressive journals have documented the sectarian character of many of these Hindu camps (for example, Khandelwal 2001).

7. During a focus group discussion with several Indian graduate students, they pointed out that private religious practices (which may be carried out in homes, temples, or by visiting with spiritual leaders) and public religio-social celebrations like Diwali or Holi (two Hindu celebrations) are organized differently in India. Diwali and Holi blur the private-public lines because people in the neighborhood (often of different religions) can participate in the fireworks or splashing of colors on *public streets.* In the United States, when the practice of Hinduism shifts to the temples in response to the policies and requirements in the United States, boundaries between who can join in and who cannot become more clearly marked.

8. Two-parent families can be composed in a variety of ways, but the specific form that is propagated here is based on a package of ideas: this is a heterosexual family where males are high achievers and primary bread-winners, females are achievers as well but with the primary responsibility of upholding "traditions" in the homes. They are responsible for keeping South Asian homes separate from the public world of America. Some scholars (Rudrappa 2002) have described the attempts of the hegemonic group to be similar to the attempts during the independence movement in India to create "uncolonized hearts." During the independence movement, Indians challenged British colonial imagery through cultural nationalism, along with disengaging structurally, which was the thrust of the Gandhian movement for economic self-sufficiency. The South Asians integrate educationally, occupationally, and politically, but attempt to maintain an arena of family life that reflects a "pristine culture." Unlike the attempts during the independence movement to reject British colonial structures by creating cultural nationalism, in the United States the effort involves merging structurally and creating and sustaining cultural differences according to racialized boundaries.

9. While this does not include all members of the hegemonic group, some members use their positions in temples to send written material describing how Hinduism is in crisis and requires Hindu males to become strong and assertive to let the world know about the glories of the community (indians of connecticut, December 28, 2002, letter on file). Nandy (2000, 2002) has written extensively about this re-created use of older British colonial imagery of Indian males as effeminate by groups in India which attempt to mobilize "strong males." They use the rhetoric that unless males stand up and become assertive, they conform to the stereotypes that are used against them. Nandy sees this as a way of purging Hinduism of its androgynous and feminine elements and politically organizing the boundaries between Hindus and Muslims. At the same time, the attempts to create strong males are reminiscent of the Promise Keepers–type movements in the mainstream (Messner 1997).

10. Maira's (2002) study on desi cultures, which focuses on New York City, reports that some second generation individuals are also involved in actively building these hegemonic communities. However, since her study was not limited to a class-based subset of this group, it is not clear whether there is a class-based association or simply a matter of family/community socialization; and whether her focus on New York, compared to the larger geographical swath of this study might contribute to these different findings. However, such a trend among the second generation to build more fundamentalist identities does exist, and like other religious fundamentalist movements in the United States and elsewhere, they are likely to claim more South Asian Americans as members in future.

11. I have a copy of this letter requesting a pleasant female icon. Ironically, Durga is rarely worshipped in temples in Bengal, a custom developed in the nineteenth century to challenge the power of Brahmin priests in temples. The goddess who is worshipped in temples in Bengal—Kali—appears without clothes, with a garland of skulls around her neck, and with her foot on the supreme male god Shiva (Saxena 2004). Internal discussions within the Bengali community had already led to the decision that proposing the installation of Kali would simply not be acceptable to "the public." Durga had been offered as a compromise.

12. The only group that did not mention any concern about emerging rigidities in their ethno-religious community were the Christian participants in this study. Their concern was to maintain their practices as different from that of mainstream Christian groups. Syrian Christians are among the oldest Christian communities in the world, since they were converted long before Christianity reached Europe. One participant explained how Easter was a day-long ceremony conducted in Malayalam, unlike the shorter ceremonies in the mainstream churches.

13. The politics of knowledge construction—who constructs it, who is recognized as an expert, which histories are available for "use" by activist groups to define their versions of communities—is an emerging area of study. For instance, for an essay on the politics of South Asian American Studies in the United States see Vireswaran and Mir (1999/2000). For "alternate" histories of the subcontinent see the subaltern study group's history of the marginalized (for example, Guha 1992), the work of Ashis Nandy, and the scholars at the Center for the Study of Developing Societies in Delhi (for example, Lal 2000). For a succinct history of women's activism on the subcontinent, see Kumar (1993).

14. A few of the males also explicitly mentioned these double standards. Four had been involved with groups that advocated against male violence toward women.

15. While the friendship networks of this group, like many in the bounded-ethnicity group, included whites, blacks, Hispanics, and other Asian Americans, only one was in a long-term relationship with a racial minority person. Whether or not this indicates openness to whites alone has to be systematically studied as more data becomes available for this group.

16. Some of the ethnicity literature operates on the assumption that ethnic identities are traditional whereas mainstream identities in Euro-American nation-states are modern, and these modern societies are the source of more universalistic values (see Okin 1999 for one such argument; Nandy 2000, Sheth 1999 for critiques). As I described in chapter 2, this view is also criticized by the scholars who study cultural racism. Here, if we do not hold on to assumptions about traditionalism and modernity in thinking about ethnic groups and the mainstream, it is difficult to differentiate whether this group is culturally ethnic or a part of the mainstream. In fact, this group's experiences illustrate how racialized structural positions, rather than any cultural differences, construct ethnicity.

CHAPTER 5   ETHNIC PRACTICES, CULTURAL CONSUMPTION

1. This emphasis on cultural consumption does not suggest that "real culture" transmitted through families is somehow natural and pristine, untouched by commerce. Nor does it suggest that such cultural consumption practices represent breaks from the "more traditional" forms of culture—for example, religion and histories—that ethnic groups impart to the next generations. This chapter emphasizes that their consumption of these material cultural items is inextricably linked to the diverse challenges that South Asian Americans face as they negotiate their ethnicity. Ethnic consumption allows them to address some of the tensions and contradictions that arise from their ethno-racial class identities in the mainstream *and* their membership in a globally dispersed family network. Consumption allows them a degree of autonomy in their choice of cultural items. They are able to balance, to a certain degree, a sense of individualism and a sense of community. Positioned as middle-class groups in post-industrial settings, consumption of material objects is the main way in which groups denote their distinctive lifestyles. They are American in following this choice, but without being able to wholly overcome their structural marginalization.
2. This is a rough translation of the title of a contemporary Hindi movie "Dil Hai Hindustani."
3. A quick search through the Internet revealed that almost every Indian student organization at colleges and universities in the United States organizes Diwali. Diwali, popularly referred to as the festival of lights, is a Hindu festival in the sense that the general stories that are associated with the celebration come from Hindu epics. However, what is most associated with Diwali are the fireworks which are lit on neighborhood streets and on rooftops. All Hindus in India do not celebrate Diwali, though it comes closest to a festival with a pan-Indian character. However, even when people do not celebrate Diwali, the fireworks remain a unifying theme. For instance, in Bengal, people worship the Goddess Kali within the same general time frame, and that event is also marked by noisy fireworks and illumination of homes and buildings with lamps, candles, and electric lights. Depending on the region of the country and the particular version of Hinduism practiced among a group, Diwali can also be marked by gambling among friends and family, and by drinking intoxicants.
4. While saris are primarily associated with India, they are worn in all four countries. The ratio of how many people wear saris compared to salwar kameezes (or other similar attire) increases toward the east of the subcontinent. The actual saris—their length, width, weave, material, designs, color, and social meanings—and ways of draping them express a variety of regional cultural forms. There are thousands of varieties of saris that are produced and worn in these countries.
5. None of the men described fashions in their descriptions of ethnic practices, although I have watched several performing on stage in ethnic clothes. Clearly there is some gender variation about how one describes "doing ethnicity."

6. When they described their visits to family, most South Asian American females talked about shopping. Part of this shopping is related to customary gift exchanges. Relatives took them shopping, or their parents went shopping for clothes, jewelry, etc. Given the continuing preference for saris and other South Asian attire for all social occasions, acquiring clothes is often an ongoing social ritual.

7. The marketing of khadi products, which are being marketed by sites such as <http://www.apparel.indiamart.com/lib/apparel/khadi10101998.html> or <http://www.hinduonnet.com/thehindu/mp/2002/08/15/stories/2002081500320300.htm> provides interesting information on the use of images. Khadi, a coarse cotton, became the symbol of the Gandhian non-violent resistance during the nationalist uprising against British colonial powers in India. It represented the conscious adoption of anti-consumerist attitudes as a form of political mobilization. The ability of the British to control the textile market was, at least symbolically, shaken. Khadi, therefore, has symbolic resonance as a piece of Indian history.

8. Bibi Russell, who is from Bangladesh, organizes shows in Europe, the United States, India, and Bangladesh. Since Bengali cottons were in vogue at that time, a couple of this study's participants had bought some "suits" from a show in London in 1998. This designer uses the weaves and motifs of the locally renowned Bangladeshi handloom saris to design her costumes (<http://www.bangladeshshowbix.com>). Coincidentally, Russell's show in Kolkata (Calcutta) earlier this year was featured in a Bengali magazine that is available in the United States, while I was conducting the interviews. During a discussion about fashions, I asked a Bangladeshi American female, Selina, who had lived in several countries, whether she had heard about Bibi Russell. Selina told me that while she was familiar with Russell's designs, and liked her ethos, she was personally not very attracted to the clothing because she was so used to associating these textile traditions with saris from different parts of Bangladesh. A few of the participants mentioned Ritu Kumar, who has several boutiques all over India and regularly shows her collections in Europe and North America.

9. However, parents vary in their reaction to Hindi movies. One participant, Anjali, said that her parents told her Bollywood movies were considered "trash" when they were growing up in India, and their perception was that only non-intellectual people watched them. In her household, the only Hindi movies were "art" movies, which often featured strong female characters in films with very strong messages about radical social change. The South Asian American who took the film class described how her instructor had shared a similar story of being directed to research "art Hindi films" by *her* family in India who also considered Bollywood movies to represent the tastes of the uneducated folk. Clearly, transnational family fields of comparison featured, even if unconsciously, in these discussions.

10. One South Asian American focused on artists from Bengal, the place of her parents origin. Many of these artists are now featured through galleries, which could be located in New York or in India. Most galleries such as Artsindia or Saffron Art have elaborate websites. While many of these artists are very affordable in the United States given the ratio of the dollar to the rupee, they are mostly out of the range of middle-class consumption in India. There, being able to buy art is a sign of real affluence.

CHAPTER 6   SIFTING THROUGH "TRADITIONS"

1. See, for instance, Susan Moller Okin's essay "Is Multiculturalism Bad for Women?" where she declares that most non-western cultural traditions are detrimental for women and therefore women of minority cultures should be rescued from such oppressive burdens of traditional practices by allowing the groups to become extinct (Okin 1999).

2. As I mentioned in chapter 4, these organizations can access different kinds of "mainstream," "alternative," or "subaltern" knowledge. Their relative power to emphasize any of these sets of knowledge is part of the process through which ethnic repertoires are created.

3. Some of the major groups are the gay and lesbian organizations such as the South Asian Lesbian and Gay Association, labor movement groups like Workers Awaaz, or New York Taxi Workers Alliance, anti-racism groups like Desis Rising Up and Moving (DRUM), and youth leadership organizations like South Asian Youth Action (SAYA!) The details of these groups are available elsewhere (see Malik and Ahmad 2001).

4. None of the groups cater exclusively to middle-class South Asian Americans. Because of its philosophy, SASCA makes the most conscious attempt among all the other groups to attract individuals of different class backgrounds. In this chapter I focus on the ethnic repertoires and then look at how the participants in this study viewed these organizations.

5. I did not formally gather ethnographic data on PSO. However some of the participants were members of PSO and their accounts indicated that PSO's members are not exclusively from Pakistan. For instance, the participant whose Indian parents were offended with her for hanging around with Pakistanis was a de facto member of this organization. Moreover, many of PSO's members were actively involved in other South Asian American and Asian American activities. As Saira, who is of Pakistani origin, participated in SIO, and was quoted in the last chapter, explained, there was a general sense that Indians and Pakistanis were desis. However, the Bangladeshi students felt that it did not advocate the version of Islam that they practiced: both the language and the cultural practices were different. With the increasing salience of religious identities in civic life after 2001, organizations like SIO are increasingly being described as "Hindu" organizations. However, when I was gathering this data the organizational identity was more diffuse.

6. Even though there is a widespread acceptance of Indian restaurant foods being representative of "the culture," many of the foods have been developed to suit the local context. Heritage cookbooks have also begun to document how much of the "Indian" food that is popular in Europe and America are actually cuisines developed in these countries. Interestingly, Nepalese businessmen own most of the better-known "Indian" restaurants in Connecticut. Islam (1996) points out that many Indian restaurants in Los Angeles and New York are owned by Bangladeshis. So when the South Asian Americans talk about Indian dinners, these should not be interpreted as foods that reflect deep cultural roots.

7. This participant did not claim that the South Asian Americans were not into drinks or drugs or sex. In fact she said that South Asian Americans did engage in these behaviors, but the parents thought that she and her friends were not part of the "American" youth scene.

8. There is a rapidly growing literature on the use of similar imagery in India by political parties like the RSS (for example, Kishwar 1998, Sarkar 1991). While the similarities between the theme in this performance and those described by authors in India may be entirely coincidental, nonetheless, it does indicate a certain convergence in how symbols of nationality-consciousness are deployed across countries.

9. The rise of the worship of Durga mentioned in chapter 3 was popularized during this period of cultural nationalism when female-icons and feminine power were evoked in order to disengage from masculinist British knowledge frames and challenge their power by emphasizing indigenous alternatives. While many of the people who were engaged in the nationalist struggles were males, the symbolism in many regional languages refers to mothers and *children,* not mothers and sons. The participation of thousands of women in violent and non-violent mobilizations, in

informal roles as community organizers and formal roles in insurgent armies, or as political leaders that are well documented (for example, Forbes 1996, Kumar 1993), also illustrate the reconstructed nature of this particular gender imagery.

10. While I do not discuss sexuality explicitly in this book, this imagery of the mother (and the absence of the father) reinforces the "chaste female" image that is promulgated by the hegemonic community.

11. This participant was referring to the same series of incidents that had led to the terse exchange between Suhani and some students of Indian origin that I described earlier in the chapter.

12. See, for instance, Sean Chabot's essay on the transnational diffusion of Gandhi's ideas on non-violence through the black organizers of the non-violent Civil Rights Movement (2002). Or see Gosine (1990).

13. While I did not gather data on any other religious group, some participants mentioned that a similar process was underway among "the Muslim" organizations.

14. See, for instance, the bitter struggles over the financial connections of the India Development Relief Fund (IDRF), a group that channels donations from South Asian Americans to India. While IDRF claims it is neutral and distributes money to impoverished villagers including those hurt by natural disasters, the opposition groups publicize its links to the RSS, an extremist Hindutva group, in India (available at <http://www.stopfundinghate.org>). The YIA's message fits the hegemonic community's discourse about culture as a separate sphere of action, separate from the political travails of the public world, along with its overt ethno-nationalism.

15. For instance, the nineteenth century conflicts between generations of Brahmos—a socio-religious reform group that was the source of female and male leadership in the Indian independence movement—became extremely bitter as they carved out the degree of their dis-identification with mainstream Hinduism (for example, Kopf 1979). Similar contemporary examples are available from the building of multiracial coalitions in the United Kingdom (Sudbury 2001) or the Caribbean (Gosine 1990, Kale 1995) as groups work out what it means to be black or Asian or East Indian in these different contexts.

References

Abelman, Nancy and John Lie. 1995. *Blue Dreams: Korean Americans and the Los Angeles Riots.* Cambridge, Mass.: Harvard University Press.

Abraham, Margaret. 2000. *Speaking the Unspeakable: Martial Violence and Activism in South Asian Communities.* New Brunswick: Rutgers University Press.

Alba, Richard and John Logan. 1993. Minority Proximity to Whites in Suburbs: An Individual Level Analysis of Segregation. *American Journal of Sociology,* 98:1388–1427.

Alba, Richard and Victor Nee. 1997. Rethinking Assimilation for a New Era of Immigration. *International Migration Review,* 31:826–874.

Amerasia Journal. 2000. *Across the Color Line.* Special Issue. Volume 26, Number 3.

———. 2001/2002. *War Justice and Peace.* Special Issue. Volume 27, Number 3 and Volume 28, Number 1.

Ancheta, Angelo. 1998. *Race, Rights, and the Asian American Experience.* New Brunswick: Rutgers University Press.

Andersen, Benedict. 1983. *Imagined Communities: Reflections on the Origin and Spread of Nationalism.* London: Verso.

Anthias, Floya. 1992. Connecting Race and Ethnic Phenomena. *Sociology,* 26:421–438.

———. 1998. Evaluating Diaspora: Beyond Ethnicity? *Sociology,* 32:557–580.

———. 2001a. New Hybridities, Old Concepts: The Limits of "Culture." *Ethnic and Racial Studies,* 24:619–641.

———. 2001b. The Concept of "Social Division" and Theorising Social Stratification: Looking at Ethnicity and Class. *Sociology,* 35:835–854.

Anthias, Floya and Nira Yuval-Davis. 1989. *Woman-Nation-State.* London: McMillan.

Appadurai, Arjun. 1993. The Heart of Whiteness: Pluralism, Diversity and Democracy in America. *Callalloo,* 16:796–808.

———. 1996. *Modernity At Large: Cultural Dimensions of Globalization.* Minneapolis: University of Minnesota Press.

Baca Zinn, Maxine and Bonnie Thornton Dill. 1994. *Women of Color in U.S. Society.* Philadelphia: Temple University Press.

Bacchu, Parminder. 1995. New Cultural Forms and Transnational South Asian Women: Culture, Class and Consumption among British South Asian Women in the Diaspora. In *Nation and Migration: The Politics of Space in the South Asian American Diaspora,* edited by Peter van der Veer, 222–244. Philadelphia: University of Pennsylvania Press.

Back, Les. 1993. Race, Identity and Nation within an Adolescent Community in South London. *New Community,* 19:217–233.

Bacon, Jean. 1996. *Life Lines: Community, Family and Assimilation among Asian Indian Immigrants.* New York: Oxford University Press.

Bald, Suresht. 1995. Coping With Marginality: South Asian Women Migrants in Britain.

In *Feminism, Postmodernism, Development,* edited by M. Marchand and Jane Parpart, 269–301. London: Routledge.

Balibar, Etienne. 1991. Is There a Neo-racism? In *Race, Nation, Class: Ambiguous Identities,* edited by Etienne Balibar and Immanuel Wallerstein, 17–28. London and New York: Verso.

Bamzai, Kavaree. 2002. Southall Shapes My Sensibility: An Interview with Gurinder Chada. *India Today.* The Global Indian Section. December 16.

Banerji, S. and G. Bauman. 1990. "Bhangra 1984–8: Fusion and Professionalization in a Genre of South Asian Dance Music." In *Black Music in Britain: Essays on Afro-Asian Contribution to Popular Music,* edited by P. Oliver, 9–22. Milton Keynes, U.K.: Open University Press.

Barringer, Herbert, Gardner Robert, and Michael Levin. 1995. *Asians and Pacific Islanders in the United States.* New York: Russell Sage Foundation.

Barth, Fredrich. 1969. *Ethnic Groups and Boundaries.* Boston: Littlefield and Brown.

Bennett, Andrew. 1997. Bhangra in New Castle: Music, Ethnic Identity and the Role of Local Knowledge. *Innovation,* 10:107–116.

Bhabha, Homi. 1994. *The Location of Culture.* London: Routledge.

Black Sisters of Southall. 1990. *Against the Grain.* London: Southall Black Sisters.

Bonilla-Silva, Eduardo. 1996. Rethinking Racism: Towards a Structural Interpretation. *American Sociological Review,* 62:465–480.

———. 2001. *White Supremacy and Racism in Post Civil Rights America.* Boulder, Colo.: Lynne Reinner.

Bose, Monika. 1999. Multiple Identities. In *Struggle for Ethnic Identity: Narratives by Asian American Professionals,* edited by Pyon Gap Min and Rose Kim, 120–129. Walnut Creek: Altamira Press.

Bourdieu, Pierre. 1984. *Distinction: A Social Critique of the Judgement of Taste.* London: Routledge and Kegan Paul.

Canclini, Nestor. 2001. *Consumers and Citizens: Globalization and Multicultural Conflicts.* Minneapolis: University of Minnesota Press.

Chabot, Sean. 2002. Transnational Diffusion and African American Reinvention of the Gandhian Repertoire. In *Globalization and Resistance,* edited by Jackie Smith and Hank Johnston, 97–114. New York: Rowman and Littlefield.

Chandrasekhar, Subramanium. 1982. *From India to America: Brief History of Immigration; Problems of Discrimination; Admission and Assimilation.* La Jolla, Calif.: A Population Review Book.

Chen, Hisian-Shui. 1992. *Chinatown No More: Taiwanese Immigrants in Contemporary New York.* Ithaca: Cornell University Press.

Clark, Colin, Ceri Peach, and Stephen Vertovec (eds.). 1990. *South Asians Overseas: Migration and Ethnicity.* Cambridge: Cambridge University Press.

Cohen, Robin. 1997. *Global Diasporas.* Seattle: University of Washington Press.

———. 1998. Transnational Social Movements: An Assessment. Available at <http://www.transcomm.ox.ac.uk/working%20papers>. Retrieved May 5, 2003.

Cohen, Steven. 1977. Socioeconomic Determinants of Intraethnic Marriage and Family. *Social Forces,* 55:997–1010.

Collins, Patricia Hill. 1991. *Black Feminist Thought.* New York: Routledge.

ColorLines. 2003. Enemies of the State. Summer, 2–27.

Connell, Robert. 1995. *Masculinities.* Berkeley: University of California Press.

Conzen, Kathleen, David Gerber, Ewa Morawska, George Pozetta, and Rudolph Veccoli. 1992. The Invention of Ethnicity: A Perspective from the U.S. *Journal of American Ethnic History,* 12:3–41.

Cose, Ellis. 1993. *The Rage of a Privileged Class.* New York: Harper Collins.

Coser, Lewis. 1956. *The Functions of Social Conflict.* New York: The Free Press.

Crowley, Daniel. 1990. The Remigration of Trinidadian East Indians. In *Caribbean Asians: Chinese, Indian and Japanese Experiences in Trinidad and the Dominican Republic,* edited by Roger Sanjek, 82–95. New York: The Asian/American Center at Queens College, CUNY.

Das Gupta, Monisha. 1997. What is Indian about You? A Gendered Transnational Approach to Ethnicity. *Gender and Society,* 11:572–596.

Dasgupta, Sayantani and Shamita Das Dasgupta. 1996. Women in Exile: Gender Relations in the Asian Indian Community in the U.S. In *Contours of the Heart,* edited by Sunaina Maira and Rajini Srikanth, 381–400. New York: Rutgers University Press.

———. 1997. Bringing Up Baby: Raising a "Third World" Daughter in the "First World." In *Dragon Ladies, Asian American Feminist Breathe Fire,* edited by Sonia Shah, 182–199. Boston: South End Press.

Dill, Bonnie Thornton. 1994. Fictive Kin, Paper Sons, and Compadrazgo: Women of Color and the Struggle for Family Survival. In *Women of Color in US Society,* edited by Maxine Baca Zinn and Bonnie Thornton Dill, 149–170. Philadelphia: Temple University Press.

Dodge, Susan. 2001. Racial Strain on Campus. *Chicago Sun Times.* News Special Edition, September 26, 15.

Dworkin, Sherrie and Michael Messner. 1999. Just Do . . . What? Sports, Bodies, Gender. In *Revisioning Gender,* edited by Myra Marx Ferree, Judith Lorber, and Beth Hess, 341–361. Thousand Oaks: Sage.

Eckstein, Susan and Lorena Barberia. 2002. Grounding Immigrant Generations in History: Cuban Americans and Their Transnational Ties. *International Migration Review,* 36:799–837.

Espiritu, Yen-Le. 1992. *Asian American Panethnicity.* Philadelphia: Temple University Press.

———. 1997. *Asian American Women and Men: Love Labor, Laws.* Thousand Oaks: Sage.

Essed, Philomena. 1991. *Understanding Everyday Racism: An Interdisciplinary Approach.* London: Sage Publications.

Falk, Richard. 2000. *Human Rights Horizons: Pursuit of Justice in a Globalizing World.* New York: Routledge.

Farley, Reynolds and Richard Alba. 2002. The New Second Generation in the United States. *International Migration Review,* 36:669–701.

Feagin, Joe and Melvin Sikes. 1994. *Living with Racism: The Black Middle Class Experience.* Boston: Beacon Press.

Felice, William. 2003. *Global New Deal: Economic and Social Human Rights.* Lanham, Md.: Rowman and Littlefield.

Fernandez-Kelly, Patricia and Richard Schauffler. 1996. Divided Fates: Immigrant Children and the New Assimilation. In *The New Second Generation,* edited by A. Portes, 30–53. New York: Russell Sage Foundation.

Ferree, Myra Marx. 1990. Beyond Separate Spheres. *Journal of Marriage and Family,* 56:816–839.

Fong, Timothy. 1994. *The First Suburban Chinatown. The Making of Monterey Park, California.* Philadelphia: Temple University Press.

———. 1998. *The Contemporary Asian American Experience: Beyond the Model Minority.* Englewood Cliffs: Prentice Hall.

Foner, Nancy 1997. What's New about Transnationalism: New York Immigrants Today and at the Turn of the Century. *Diaspora,* 6:355–376.

————— (ed.). 2001. *Islands in the Sun: West Indian Migration to New York.* Berkeley: University of California Press.

Forbes, Geraldine. 1996. *Women in Modern India.* Cambridge, U.K.: Cambridge University Press.

Frankenberg, Ruth. 1993. *White Women, Race Matters: The Social Construction of Whiteness.* Minneapolis: University of Minnesota Press.

Fulwood, Sam. 2001. Arab-Americans Unfairly Targeted. *The Plain Dealer,* Metro Section, September 19, B1.

Gamson, Joshua. 1996. The Organizational Shaping of Collective Identity. *Sociological Forum,* 11:231–261.

Gandhi, Ajay. 2001. An Activism of One's Own. *Samar,* 14:15–18.

Gans, Herbert. 1979. Symbolic Ethnicity: The Future of Ethnic Groups and Cultures in America. *Ethnic and Racial Studies,* 2:1–20.

Gibson, Margaret. 1988. *Accommodation without Assimilation: Sikh Immigrants in an American High School.* Ithaca: Cornell University Press.

Giddens, Anthony. 1999. *Runaway World: How Globalization is Reshaping Our Lives.* London: Profile Books.

Gillespie, Marie. 1995. *Television, Ethnicity and Cultural Change.* London: Routledge.

Gilroy, Paul. 1990. One Nation Under a Groove: The Cultural Politics of Race and Racism in Britain. In *Anatomy of Racism,* edited by David Theo Goldberg, 19–48. Minneapolis: University of Minnesota Press.

————— . 1993. *The Black Atlantic: Modernity and Double Consciousness.* London: Verso.

Glenn, Evelyn Nakano. 1999. The Social Construction and Institutionalization of Gender and Race: An Integrative Framework. In *Revisioning Gender,* edited by Myra Marx Ferree, Judith Lorber, and Beth Hess, 3–39. Thousand Oaks: Sage.

————— . 2004. *Unequal Freedom: How Race and Gender Shaped American Citizenship and Labor.* Cambridge, Mass.: Harvard University Press.

Glick-Schiller, Nina, Linda Basch, and Christina Blanc-Szanton. 1992. Transnationalism: A New Analytic Framework for Understanding Migration. In *Towards a Transnational Perspective on Migration,* edited by Nina Glick-Schiller, Linda Basch, and Christina Blanc-Szanton, 1–24. New York: New York Academy of Sciences.

Gonzalez, Juan. 1996. *Racial and Ethnic Groups in America.* Dubuque: Kendall Hunt Publishing.

Gosine, Mahin. 1990. Ethnic Participation in Black Power Movement in Trinidad: The Case of the East Indians. In *Caribbean Asians: Chinese, Indian and Japanese Experiences in Trinidad and the Dominican Republic,* edited by Roger Sanjek, 62–81. New York: The Asian/American Center at Queens College, CUNY.

Greeley, Andrew. 1971. *Why Can't They Be Like Us? America's White Ethnic Groups.* New York: E. P. Dutton.

Grillo, Ralph. 1998. *Pluralism and the Politics of Difference: State Culture and Ethnicity in Comparative Perspective.* Oxford: Clarendon.

Grillo, Thomas. 2001. Baptist Book Spurs March By Hindus. *The Boston Globe.* Third Edition, Magazine, November 22, 1999, B4.

Guha, Ranajit (ed.). 1992. *A Subaltern Studies Reader, 1986–1995.* Minneapolis: University of Minnesota Press.

Hall, Stuart. 1990. Cultural Identity and Diaspora. In *Identity, Community, Culture, Difference,* edited by James Rutherford, 222–237. London: Lawrence and Wishart.

Halter, Marilyn. 2000. *Shopping for Identity: The Marketing of Ethnicity.* New York: Schoken Books.

Hamamoto, D. 1994. *Monitored Peril: Asian Americans and the Politics of Representation.* Minneapolis: University of Minnesota Press.

Hebdige, D. 1977. *Subculture: The Meaning of Style*. London: Methuen.

Hein, Jeremy. 1993. Refugees, Immigrants, and the State. *Annual Review of Sociology*, 19:43–59.

Hirsch, F. 1977. *The Social Limits of Growth*. London: Routledge.

Hondagneu-Sotelo, Pierette. 1994. *Gendered Transitions: Mexican Experience of Immigration*. Berkeley: University of California Press.

Huntington, Samuel. 1996. *The Clash of Civilizations and the Remaking of World Order*. New York: Simon & Schuster.

Ibrahim, Zuraidah, 2001. Racial Attack Can't Keep Him Down. *The Straits Times* (Singapore). Home Section, October 4, H2.

Ignatiev, Noel. 1995. *How the Irish Became White*. New York: Routledge.

Islam, Naheed. 1996. Signs of Belonging. In *Contours of the Heart: South Asians Map America,* edited by Sunaina Maira and Rajini Srikanth, 85–90. New York: Asian American Writers' Workshop, distributed by Rutgers University Press.

Jensen, Jane. 1988. *Passage from India: Asian American Immigrants in North America*. New Haven, Conn.: Yale University Press.

Joseph, May. 1999. *Nomadic Identities: The Performance of Citizenship*. Minneapolis: University of Minnesota Press.

Kale, Madhavi. 1995. Projecting Identities: Empire and Indentured Labor Migration from India to Trinidad and British Guiana, 1836–1885. In *Nation and Migration: The Politics of Space in the South Asian American Diaspora,* edited by Peter van der Veer, 73–92. Philadelphia: University of Pennsylvania Press.

Katzenstein, Mary. 1995. Discursive Politics and Feminist Activism in the Catholic Church. In *Feminist Organizations: Harvest of the New Women's Movement,* edited by Myra Marx Ferree and Patricia Yancy Martin, 35–52. Philadelphia: Temple University Press.

Kelly, Jan. 2001. Indian Sikhs Appeal for Tolerance. *Herald Sun*. News, October 26, 31.

Khan, Nasima. 2003. Closer Home. *India Today*. May 19, 30.

Khandelwal, Anita. 2001. Long Distance Sectarianism. *Samar*, Fall/Winter, 14:23–25.

Khandelwal, Madhulika. 2002. *Becoming American, Becoming Indian: An Immigrant Community in New York City*. Ithaca: Cornell University Press.

Khanna, Simar. 2001. Fear at Home. *The San Francisco Chronicle*. Editorial, September 24, A15.

Kibria, Nazli. 1998. The Racial Gap: South Asian American Racial Identity and the Asian American Movement. In *A Part, Yet Apart: South Asians in Asian America,* edited by L. Shanker and R. Srikanth, 69–78. Philadelphia: Temple University Press.

———. 2000. Race, Ethnic Options, and Ethnic Binds: Identity Negotiations of Second Generation Chinese and Korean Americans. *Sociological Perspectives*, 43:77–93.

———. 2002. *Becoming Asian American: Second Generation Chinese and Korean Identities*. Baltimore: Johns Hopkins Press.

Kishwar, Madhu. 1998. *Religion at the Service of Nationalism*. New Delhi: Oxford University Press.

———. 2004. The Idea of India: Bollywood as India's Cultural Ambassador. *Manushi*, 139:4–14.

Kistivo, Peter. 2001. Theorizing Transnational Immigration: A Critical Review of Current Efforts. *Ethnic and Racial Studies*, 24:549–577.

Kitano, Harry and Roger Daniels. 1995. *Asian Americans: Emerging Minorities*. Englewood Cliffs: Prentice Hall.

Knuckolls, C. (ed.). 1993. *Siblings in South Asia: Brothers and Sisters in Cultural Context*. New York: Guilford.

Kofman, Eleanore, Annie Phizacklea, Parvati Raghuram, and Rosemary Sales. 2001. *Gender and International Migration in Europe*. London: Routledge.

Kopf, David. 1979. *Brahmo Samaj and the Shaping of the Modern Indian Mind*. Princeton: Princeton University Press.

Kukke, Surabhi and Svati Shah. 1999/2000. Reflections on Queer South Asian Progressive Activism in the United States. *Amerasia*, 25:129–137.

Kumar, Radha. 1993. *A History of Doing: An Illustrated Account of Movements for Women's Rights and Feminisms*. London: Verso.

Kurien, Prema. 1999. Gendered Ethnicity: Creating a Hindu Identity in the United States. *American Behavioral Scientist*, 47:648–670.

———. 2002. *Kaleidoscopic Ethnicity*. New Brunswick: Rutgers University Press.

Lakshman, Ganesh. 2003. Designers Beri, Lulla, Khan and Bowen at Bollywood Fashion Awards. *News India Times*. May 16, 36.

Lal, Vinay (ed.). 2000. *Dissenting Knowledge, Open Futures: The Multiple Selves and Strange Destinations of Ashis Nandy*. New Delhi: Oxford University Press.

Leonard, Karen. 1992. *Making Ethnic Choices: The Punjabi Mexican Americans*. Philadelphia: Temple University Press.

———. 1997. *The South Asian Americans*. Westport, Conn.: Greenwood Press.

Levitt, Peggy. 2001. *The Transnational Villagers*. Berkeley: University of California Press.

Lury, Celia. 1996. *Consumer Culture*. New Brunswick: Rutgers University Press.

Mahendru, Shivani. 2003. I Love The Stuff, But My Self Designed Limits. *News India Times*. May 9, 24.

Maira, Sunaina. 1999/2000. Ideologies of Authenticity: Youth, Politics, Diaspora. *Amerasia*, 25:139–149.

———. 2002. *Desis in the House: Indian American Youth Culture in New York City*. Philadelphia: Temple University Press.

Malhotra, Priya and Anuja Joshi. 2002. Americanization of Yoga. *The Indian American*. December 13, 22 and 24.

Malik, Badal and Shomial Ahmad. 2001. Youth on the Move. *Samar*, 14:5–10.

Mampilly, Zachariah. 2002. Black Like Me: On Being Post-South Asian. Available at http://www.Inthefray.com. Retrieved March 15, 2002.

Massey, Douglas and Nancy Denton. 1987. Trends in Residential Segregation of Blacks, Hispanics and Asians. *American Sociological Review*, 1:802–825.

———. 1994. *American Apartheid*. Cambridge, Mass.: Harvard University Press.

McLuhan, Marshall. 1964. *Understanding Media*. London: Routledge.

Mediratta, Kaveetha. 1999. How Do You Say Your Name? In *Struggle for Ethnic Identity: Narratives by Asian American Professionals*, edited by Pyon Gap Min and Rose Kim, 77–86. Walnut Creek: Altamira Press.

Melucci, Alberto. 1995. The Process of Collective Identity. In *Social Movements and Culture*, edited by H. Johnston and B. Klandermans, 41–63. Minneapolis: University of Minnesota Press.

Melwani, Lavina. 2001a. What's Hot! Summer of Fashion. *Little India*, June, 11:11–22.

———. 2001b. The Battle for the Indian Mind: The Left. *Little India*. January 15, 2001. Available at <http://www.littleindia.com/india/sept2k/mind.htm>. Retrieved April 25, 2003.

Merenstein, Beth. 2003. Racial Reproduction: The Development and Expression of Racial Knowledge Among Immigrants. Unpublished Ph.D. thesis. Department of Sociology, University of Connecticut.

Messner, Michael. 1992. *Power at Play: Sports and the Power of Masculinity*. Boston: Beacon Press.

————. 1997. *Politics of Masculinities: Men in Movements.* Thousand Oaks: Sage.

Min, Pyong Gap (ed.). 2002. *Second Generation: Ethnic Identity Among Asian Americans.* Walnut Creek, California: Altamira Press.

Min, Pyong Gap and Rose Kim (eds.). 1999. *Struggle for Ethnic Identity: Narratives by Asian American Professionals.* Walnut Creek, California: Altamira Press.

Modood, Tariq, Richard Berthoud, Jane Lakey, James Nazroo, Patten Smith, Satnam Virdee, and Sharon Beishon. 1997. *Ethnic Minorities in Britain: Diversity and Disadvantage.* London: Policy Studies Institute.

Moghadam, Valentine. 1994. *Identity Politics and Women: Cultural Reassertions and Feminisms from an International Perspective.* Boulder, Colo.: Westview Press.

Mohanty, Chandra. 1991. Under Western Eyes: Feminist Scholarship and Colonial Discourses. In *Third World Women and the Politics of Feminism,* edited by Chandra Mohanty, Anne Russo, and Lourdes Torres, 3–29. Bloomington, Ind.: Indiana University Press.

Mukhi, Sunita. 2000. *Doing the Desi Thing: Performing Indian-ness in New York City.* New York: Garland Publishing.

Mullings, Leith. 1994. Images, Ideology and Women of Color. In *Women of Color in US Society,* edited by Maxine Baca Zinn and Bonnie Thornton Dill, 265–290. Philadelphia: Temple University Press.

Murphy, Caryle, 2001. Muslims Debate Diverging Loyalties; Faith, Patriotism Sometimes At Odds. *The Washington Post.* Metro Section, November 19, B01.

Nagel, Joanne. 1994 Constructing Ethnicity: Creating and Recreating Ethnic Identity and Culture. *Social Problems,* 41:152–176.

————. 1996. *American Indian Ethnic Revival: Red Power and the Resurgence of Identity and Culture.* New York: Oxford University Press.

Nandy, Ashis. 1994. *The Illegitimacy of Nationalism.* New Delhi: Oxford University Press.

————. 2000. The Fantastic India-Pakistan Battle: Or the Future of the Past. In *Dissenting Knowledges, Open Futures: The Multiple Selves and Strange Destinations of Ashis Nandy,* edited by Vinay Lal, 186–200. New Delhi: Oxford University Press.

————. 2002. Telling the Story of Communal Conflicts in South Asia: Interim Report on a Personal Search for Defining Myths. *Ethnic and Racial Studies,* 25:1–19.

Naples, Nancy and Manisha Desai (eds.). 2002. *Women's Activism and Globalization: Linking Local Struggles and Transnational Politics.* New York: Routledge.

Narayan, Anjana. 2004. *Asian Americans in Connecticut.* Storrs: Asian American Studies Institute.

News India Times. 2002. WNEW Radio Relents, Airs Anti-bias Crime Spots. February 22, 10.

Okin, Susan Moller. 1999. Is Multiculturalism Bad for Women? In *Is Multiculturalism Bad for Women?* edited by Joshua Cohen, Martha Howard, and Martha Nussbaum, 7–26. Princeton: Princeton University Press.

Oldenburg, Veena. 2002. *Dowry Murder: The Imperial Origins of a Cultural Crime.* New York: Oxford University Press.

Olzak, Susan. 1992. *The Dynamics of Ethnic Competition and Conflict.* Stanford: Stanford University Press.

Olzak, Susan and Joanne Nagel (eds.). 1986. *Competitive Ethnic Relations.* Boston: Academic Press.

Omi, Michael and Howard Winant. 1994. *Racial Formation in the US: From the 1960s to the 1990s.* New York: Routledge.

Ong, Aihwa. 1996. Cultural Citizenship as Subject Making: Immigrants Negotiate Racial and Cultural Boundaries in the U.S. *Current Anthropology,* 37:737–751.

Padilla, Felix. 1985. *Latino Ethnic Consciousness: The Case of Mexican and Puerto Ricans in Chicago.* Notre Dame: University of Notre Dame Press.

Parekh, Bhikhu. 1994. Some Reflections on the Hindu Diaspora. *New Community,* 20:603–620.

Park, Robert. 1950 (1925). *Race and Culture.* Glencoe, Ill.: Free Press.

Peach, Ceri. 1994. Three Phases of South Asian Emigration. In *Migration: The Asian Experience,* edited by Judith M. Brown and Rosemary Foot, 38–55. London: St. Martins Press.

———. 1998. South Asian and Caribbean Ethnic Minority Housing Choice in Great Britain. *Urban Studies,* 35:16–57.

Portes, Alejandro (ed.). 1995a. *The New Second Generation.* New York: Russell Sage Foundation.

———. 1995b. Children of Immigrants: Segmented Assimilation and Its Determinants. In *The Economic Sociology of Immigration: Essays on Networks, Ethnicity and Entrepreneurship,* edited by Alejandro Portes, 248–280. New York: Russell Sage Foundation.

———. 1997. Globalization from Below: The Rise of Transnational Communities. Available at <http://www.transcomm.ox.ac.uk/working%20papers/>. Retrieved May 5, 2003.

Portes, Alejandro and Min Zhou. 1993. The New Second Generation: Segmented Assimilation and Its Variants. *Annals of the American Academy of Politics and Social Science,* 530:74–96.

Portes, Alejandro and Julie Sensenbrennar. 1993. Embeddedness and Immigration: Notes on the Social Determinants of Economic Action. *American Journal of Sociology,* 98:1320–1350.

Prashad, Vijay. 1996. Desh: The Contradictions of Homeland. In *Contours of the Heart,* edited by Sunaina Maira and Rajini Srikanth, 225–236. New York: Rutgers University Press.

———. 2000–2001. Genteel Racism. *Amerasia,* 26:21–33.

———. 2000a. *The Karma of Brown Folk.* Minneapolis: University of Minnesota Press.

———. 2000b. Beauty Queens and the Capitalist Beast. December 7, 2000. Available at <http://www. Zmag.org/sustainers/content/2000-12/07>. Retrieved January 20, 2001.

Purkayastha, B. 1999. *Asian Indians in Connecticut.* Storrs: Asian American Studies Institute.

———. 2000. Liminal Lives: South Asian Youth and Domestic Violence. *Journal of Social Distress and Homelessness,* 9:201–219.

———. 2002a. Rule, Roles and Realities: Asian Indian Families in the U.S. In *Minority Families in the U.S: A Multicultural Perspective,* edited by Ronald Taylor, 212–224. Upper Saddle Ridge, N.J.: Prentice Hall.

———. 2002b. Contesting Multiple Margins: Asian Indian Community Activism in the Early and Late 20th Century. In *Women's Activism and Globalization: Linking Local Struggles and Transnational Politics,* edited by Nancy Naples and Manisha Desai, 99–120. New York: Routledge.

Purushothaman, Sangeetha, Simone Purohit, and Bianca Ambrose-Oji. 2004. The Informal Collective as a Space for Participatory Planning. In *The Power of Women's Informal Networks,* edited by Bandana Purkayastha and Mangala Subramaniam. Lantham, Md.: Lexington Books.

Ratte, Lou. 1995. *The Uncolonized Heart.* Calcutta: Orient Longman.

Rayapol, Aparna. 1997. *Negotiating Identities: Women in the Indian Diaspora.* New Delhi, India: Oxford University Press.

Renteria, Tamis. 1992. The Culture of the Mexican American Professionals Today: Legacy of the Chicano Movement. Ph.D. dissertation. Department of Anthropology, Stanford University, Stanford, California.

Rex, John. 1995. Ethnic Identity and the Nation State: Political Sociology of Multicultural Societies. *Social Identities,* 1:6–20.

Robb, Peter (ed.). 1995. *The Concept of "Race" in South Asia.* New Delhi, India: Oxford University Press.

Roediger, David. 1991. *The Wages of Whiteness: Race and the Making of the American Working Class.* London: Verso.

Rose, Fred. 1997. Towards a Class-Cultural Theory of Social Movements: Reinterpreting New Social Movements. *Sociological Forum,* 12:461–494.

Rudrappa, Sharmila. 2002. Disciplining Desire in Making the Home: Engineering Ethnicity in Indian Immigrant Families. In *Second Generation: Ethnic Identity among Asian Americans,* edited by Pyong Gap Min, 85–112. Walnut Creek: Altamira Press.

Rumbaut, Rueben. 1995. The Crucible Within: Ethnic Identity, Self Esteem, and Segmented Assimilation Among Children of Immigrants. In *The New Second Generation,* edited by Alejandro Portes, 119–170. New York: Russell Sage Foundation.

Sacks, Karen. 1996 How did the Jews become White Folk? In *Race,* edited by S. Gregory and R. Sanjek, 78–102. New Brunswick, N.J.: Rutgers University Press.

Sanjek, Roger (ed.). 1990. *Caribbean Asians: Chinese, Indian and Japanese Experiences in Trinidad and the Dominican Republic.* New York: The Asian/American Center at Queens College, CUNY.

Sanneh, Kelefa. 2003. Jay-Z Sweet Talks a Punjabi Beat. *New York Times.* Arts and Leisure Section, April 27, 27.

Saran, Pradyumna. 1985. *The Asian Indian Experience in the United States.* Cambridge, Mass.: Schenkman Publishing.

Sarkar, Tanika. 1991. The Woman as Communal Subject: Rashtra Sevika Samiti and the Ram Janmabhoomi Movement. *Economic and Political Weekly,* August 31, 2057–2062.

Sarna, Jonathan and David Dalin. 1997. *Religion, and State in the American Jewish Experience.* Indiana: University of Notre Dame Press.

Sassen, Saskia. 2000. *Cities in a World Economy.* Thousand Oaks: Pine Forge Press.

Saxena, Nila Bhattacharya. 2004. *In the Beginning is Desire: Tracing Kali's Footprints in Indian Literature.* New Delhi: Indialog Publications.

Sen, Amartya. 1999. *Development As Freedom.* New York: Knopf.

————. 2001. A World Not So Neatly Divided. *The New York Times.* Op Ed Section, November 23, 39.

Sen, Aparna. 2003. Editorial. *Sananda.* May 1, 1.

Sengupta, Somini. 1999. Song of India Migrates as Table Hip-Hop. *The New York Times.* Section 9, April 18, 2.

Sengupta, Somini and Vivian Toy. 1998. United Ethnically and By An Assault: Two Groups of East Indians are Brought Closer, For Now. *New York Times.* Metropolitan Section, October 7, 1 and 3.

Shah, Sonia (ed.). 1997. *Dragon Ladies: Asian American Feminists Breathe Fire.* Boston: South End Press.

Shankar, Lavina and Rajini Srikanth (eds.). 1998. *A Part Yet Apart: South Asians in America.* Philadelphia: Temple University Press.

Sharma, Sanjay. 1996. Noisy Asians or "Asian Noise"? In *Disorienting Rhythms: The Politics of New Asian Dance Music,* edited by Sanjay Sharma, John Hutnyk, and Ashwani Sharma, 32–60. London: Zed Books.

Sharma, Sanjay, John Hutnyk, and Ashwani Sharma (eds.). 1996. *Disorienting Rhythms: The Politics of New Asian Dance Music.* London: Zed Books.

Sheth, D. L. 1999. The Nation State and Minority Rights. In *Minority Identities and the Nation-State,* edited by D. L. Sheth and Gurpreet Mahajan, 18–37. Delhi: Oxford University Press.

Sinha, Mrinalini. 2000. *Mother India/Katherine Mayo.* Edited and Introduced by Mrinalini Sinha. Ann Arbor: University of Michigan Press.

Soysal, Yasemin. 1998. Towards a Postnational Model of Membership. In *The Citizenship Debates,* edited by Gershon Shafir, 189–220. Minneapolis: University of Minnesota Press.

St. Louis Post-Dispatch. 2001. At A Glance. News Section, November 8, A10.

Statistical Abstract. 2002. Immigrants by Country, Table 7. Washington, D.C.: US Department of Census. Available at <http://www.census.gov/prod/2003pub/02statab/pop.pdf>. Retrieved June 25, 2003.

Sudbury, Julia. 2001. (Re)constructing Multiracial Blackness: Women's Activism, Difference and Collective Identity in Britain. *Ethnic and Racial Studies,* 24:29–49.

Suro, Roberto. 1998. *Strangers Among Us: How Latino Immigration is Transforming America.* New York: Knopf.

Swidler, Ann. 1986. Culture in Action: Symbols and Strategies. *American Sociological Review,* 51:273–286.

Takaki, Ronald (ed.). 1994. *From Different Shores: Perspectives on Race and Ethnicity in America.* New York: Oxford University Press.

Tatla, Darshan Singh. 1999. *The Sikh Diaspora: The Search for Statehood.* Seattle, Wash.: Washington University Press.

Taylor, Ronald (ed.). 2002. *Minority Families in the U.S.: A Multicultural Perspective.* Upper Saddle Ridge, N.J.: Prentice Hall.

Taylor, Verta and Nancy Whittier. 1992. Collective Identity Formation in Social Movement Communities: Lesbian Feminist Mobilization. In *Frontiers in Social Movement Theory,* edited by Aldon Morris and Carol McClurg Mueller, 104–130. New Haven: Yale University Press.

Torres, Rodolfo, Louis Miron, and Jonathan Inda. 1999. *Race Identity and Citizenship: A Reader.* Malden, Mass.: Blackwell.

Trivedi, Neheet. 2003. Am I a Native Anthropologist? Discovering Race, Class, Citizenship, and Power. *Catamaran,* 1:87–100.

Tuan, Mia. 1998. *Forever Foreigners or Honorary Whites? The Asian Ethnic Experience Today.* New Brunswick: Rutgers University Press.

Uberoi, Patricia. 1999. The Diaspora Comes Home: Disciplining Desire in DDLJ. In *Tradition, Pluralism and Identity,* edited by Veena Das, Dipankar Gupta, and Patricia Uberoi, 163–194. New Delhi: Sage.

U.S. Census Bureau. 2000. Region and Country of Birth. QT-P15. Statistical Summary File 3. Matrix PCT19. Available at <http//:www.factfinder.census.gov>. Retrieved July 15, 2004.

U. S. Civil Rights Commission. 1992. *Civil Rights Issues Facing Asians Americans in the 1990s.* Washington, D.C.: US Commission on Civil Rights.

Vertovec, Steven, 2001. Transnational Challenges to the "New" Multiculturalism. Paper presented to the ASA conference, University of Sussex, 30 March–2 April 2001. Available at <http://www.transcomm.ox.ac.uk/working%20papers/>. Retrieved May 5, 2003.

Vireswaran, Kamala and Ali Mir. 1999/2000. On the Politics of Community in South Asian-American Studies. *Amerasia,* 25:97–110.

Wartofsky, Alone. 2001. What's Shakin'? Bhangra, Big Time. *The Washington Post.* Sunday Arts, May 13, G01.

Waters, Mary. 1990. *Ethnic Options: Choosing Identities in America.* Berkeley: University of California Press.

———. 1995. Ethnic and Racial Identities of Second Generation Black Immigrants in New York City. In *The New Second Generation,* edited by Alejandro Portes, 171–196. New York: Russell Sage Foundation.

Wei, William. 1993. *The Asian American Movement.* Philadelphia: Temple University Press.

Wellman, Barry (ed.). 1999. *Networks in the Global Village: Life in Contemporary Communities.* Boulder, Colo.: Westview Press.

Williams, Monte. 1999. New Year Compromise for Chinatown and Mayor: Mock Fireworks. *New York Times.* Section B, February 13, 2.

Willis, Susan. 1990. I Want the Black One: Is There a Place for Afro-American Culture in Commodity Culture? *New Formations,* 10: 77–97.

Wollett, Anne, Harriett Marshall, Paula Nicolson, and Neelam Dosanjh. 1994. Asian Women's Ethnic Identity: The Impact of Gender and Context in Accounts of Women Bringing up Children in East London. *Feminism and Psychology,* 4:119–132.

Wong, Madeline. 2000. Ghanaian Women in Toronto's Labor Market: Negotiating Gendered Roles and Transnational Household Strategies. *Canadian Ethnic Studies,* 32:45–74.

Wu, Frank. 2002. *Yellow: Race in America Beyond Black and White.* New York: Basic Books.

Yang, Fenggang and Helen Ebaugh. 2001. Transformations in Immigrant Religions and their Global Implications. *American Sociological Review,* 66:269–288.

Yoshino, Kimi. 2001. Mistake Leads to Assault: Asian Indian Man, Celebrating His Birthday in Anaheim, is Beaten. *Los Angeles Times.* Tuesday Orange County Edition, Metro Desk, October 23, 3.

Yuval-Davis, Nira. 1994. Women, Ethnicity and Empowerment. *Feminism and Psychology,* 4:179–197.

———. 1997. *Women and Nation.* London: Sage.

Zhou, Min. 1997. Segmented Aassimilation: Issues, Controversies, and Recent Research on the New Second Generation. *International Migration Review,* 31: 975–1008.

Zhou, Min and Carl Bankston III. 1998. *Growing Up American: How Vietnamese Children Adjust to Life in the US.* New York: Russell Sage Foundation.

Zogby Polls 2001. *The American Muslim Poll.* November/December 2001. Available at <http://www.projectmaps.com/PMReport.htm>. Retrieved August 11, 2003.

Zukin, S. 1995. *The Cultures of Cities.* Cambridge: Blackwell.

Index

ABOUT THE AUTHOR

Bandana Purkayastha holds a joint appointment in sociology and Asian American studies at the University of Connecticut. She was educated at Presidency College (India), the University of Massachusetts, and the University of Connecticut. Her current research and publications focus on the intersection of race, gender, and class focusing on people of South Asian origin in the United States as well as India. Her book, coedited with Mangala Subramaniam, *The Power of Women's Informal Networks: Lessons in Social Change from South Asia and West Africa,* was published in 2004. She has won awards for her teaching, as well as a Woman of Color award for leadership, achievement, and service. She was recently honored for her research and activism relating to immigrant populations by the Connecticut State Legislature.